Capital Punishment in Canada

Capital Punishment in Canada

A Sociological Study of Repressive Law

David B. Chandler

The Carleton Library No. 94

*Published by McClelland and Stewart Limited
in association with The Institute of Canadian Studies,
Carleton University*

THE CARLETON LIBRARY
A series of original works, reprints, and new collections of source material relating to Canada, issued under the editorial supervision of the Institute of Canadian Studies of Carleton University, Ottawa.

0-7710-9794-8

The Canadian Publishers
McClelland and Stewart Limited
25 Hollinger Road, Toronto

Printed and bound in Canada

To Nan and Jerry Chandler

Table of Contents

Chapter 3 The Representative and The Constituency

List of Tables

List of Figures

Acknowledgements

This research began in 1966 at Carleton University in Ottawa and finished at the same university in 1974. Carleton and, particularly, the Department of Sociology and Anthropology, is a fine, informal, scholarly institution. I am indebted to it for generous support of this project.

Cornell University, the University of Hawaii, and the University of California at Berkeley have all generously provided resources necessary for this project.

The support of a great Canadian institution, The Canada Council, both for me at Cornell and later for the research costs of this project, is gratefully acknowledged.

Among the people who helped me, my friends and colleagues, Steve Fenton and Peter Pineo, were the most inspirational in the beginning of the research. At Hawaii, Jonathan Turner was most helpful in the interpretation of Durkheim and the organization of the project. Milton Bloomblaum rendered valuable methodological advice. Janice Shinshiro and Carol Muranaka were especially capable and dedicated research assistants. The patience and support of Douglas Yamamura was indispensable.

My Ph.D. Committee at Cornell, Gordon Streib, Edward Devereux and Donald Hayes, were dedicated scholars and patient advisors. I thank them for their constructive criticism and support in this project.

My debt to friends and colleagues at Carleton over the years is measureless. However, Frank Vallee has been a friend, teacher, helper and colleague for over a decade and my affection and gratitude is beyond expression. I would like to thank Dennis Forcese and Ken Hatt for their critical advice, Deborah Leach and Tony Falsetto for their dedicated assistance and Lynne Perley who is a marvellous typist. Susan Chandler has lived with this project for years and her help is measureless.

And finally, my old and respected friends who became my temporary family in the final writing of this book, Anne, Judy and Ken Mozersky deserve my special appreciation.

David B. Chandler
Ottawa, Canada
Spring 1974

Preface

This is a study in the sociology of law. It is relevant to the special curiosities of three areas of social and intellectual concern. In its attention to a particular codified law, capital punishment for murder, and the various social influences operating to preserve or change it, one of the basic questions of law is asked: Where does law come from? Attention to the legislative process and political institutions in Canada should interest those who are curious about Canadian government and political science. And finally, sociology has never shrunk from enfolding law and political science, their reluctance not withstanding, and this book is basically sociological. So the question concerns law, the institution under examination is political, and the theory and method are primarily sociological. This book marshalls empirical evidence on the public opinion and legislative behavior of the Canadian Capital Punishment debates of 1967 and 1973. It is intended, in addition, to foster discussion in the sociology of law in Canada by bringing forward empirical materials on the topic.

It must be added quickly that sociological theory and method place serious restrictions on the type of interpretation to which specialists in jurisprudence and political science are accustomed. The intentional attempt to maintain empirical rigour and theoretical generality beyond any one law, in any one society, require self-conscious restrictions in the richness of interpretation of the particular.

As sociologists, we are interested in repressive sanctions in society and how they originate. We, therefore, use the Canadian death penalty legislation as a case in this more general concern. The student of law is naturally and legitimately interested in laws as such and not as examples of more general social forces. The sociologist also carries a burden of explicit procedure and scientific method which makes some intuitive and plausible evidence used in legal studies inadmissable.

Political scientists generally share with sociologists a devotion to explicit replicable procedure in marshalling evidence in explanation. However, as specialists in the institutions of government, legislatures and politics, they are accustomed to a finer texture in explanations of legislative activity than that offered in this book.

And finally, some sociologists minimize the importance of formal official versions of law in explaining what happens to real people. The law which people experience is often only remotely related to the official version. This important problem is not central to this book but is discussed in the difference between *de facto* and *de jure* abolition of the death penalty, and also in Appendix II which presents data on those who were executed over a twenty year span of Canadian history.

So while this book may be less than fully satisfying and comprehensive to specialists in each area, it is intended to compensate by bridging the three traditions.

Vindictiveness, vengeance, punitiveness and retribution have all been used to describe laws which specify punishments for the guilty which seem to have no practical merit. In his sophisticated and scholarly work on this topic Svend Ranulf calls it the "disinterested demand to punish"[1]. By this he refers to the desire of individuals and groups, who have suffered no direct deprivation, to inflict punishment on deviants. This moral indignation is not generated by specific hatred nor by any reasonable expectation of eliminating crime.

Some have argued that hatred of the criminal is natural, proper and desirable. Thus, the legal punishments offer a "public provision of means for expressing and gratifying a healthy natural sentiment".[2] If we assume that there is an outrage to a strongly held public morality at the criminal act, then one function of law is to prevent the bloody orgy of mob vengeance. The history of criminal law is in part a history of the erosion of the right to inflict private punishment in society. Blood feuds, lynching, vendettas and duelling give way as specialized agents of the society progressively monopolize the right to punish.

Limitation and specification of criminal punishment did not necessarily make it more humane. The famous Hammurabi code (1750 B.C.) specified exact punishments for specific offenses. But severe as they were, one intention was to ensure that *no more* than an eye of the guilty was taken for the eye of his victim. The limitation and formalization of punishment also prevented rulers from exerting unqualified control over their subjects.

There are early examples of what is usually thought to be a modern trend to reducing the punitiveness of criminal punishment. King Ur-Nammu of Sumeria (2100 B.C.) replaced vengeance with restitution and fines in the law codes of that country.[3] But normally, earlier societies are described as having generally more repressive and punitive law codes than their modern, civilized offspring.

The evolutionary pattern of law is irregular and there is certainly no widely held theory of the history of criminal law. However, there is sufficient observable regularity in patterns of societal and legal types to tempt the theorist. There are roughly two types of theorizing on the cause of punitive legal sanctions. They turn out to be complementary in most instances.

One type emphasizes the properties of individual psychology, like the famous authoritarian personality notion. The other type emphasizes properties in the social structure such as Durkheim's concept of mechanical solidarity and repressive law.[4] Some scholars like Ranulf successfully bridge this distinction by showing that the individual's urge to punish is dependent, in part, on position in the social structure. He argues that the disinterested demand to punish arises most acutely in the envy and indignation generated by lower middle class existence.[5]

The task of creating plausible or even empirically verified explanations of repressive law is only one side of the matter. The practical side is taken up most eloquently by Karl Menninger who writes that resistance to penal reform lies in "The great secret, the deeply buried mystery . . . the persistent intrusive wish for vengeance".[6] He forcefully argues that what he calls our delicious satisfactions in opportunites for vengeful retaliation on scapegoats must be given up by each individual in order to preserve peace, public safety and mental health.

Those who see individual sentiment as the major obstacle to a humane and effective system of criminal law, as Menninger obviously does, must examine its psychological roots in order to eradicate it. Those who see retaliatory sentiment as rooted in social structure rather than personality look there for the key to eradicate it. This yields a generally more optimistic view. Harold Lasswell suggests that moral indignation will give way to calculated expediency as a basis of support for public order as diversity and disciplined calculation flourish in modern society.[7]

This sociological view of law is important and is emphasized in this book. The simplest rendition of this view is that the social structure of some societies and groups is more conducive to repressive sanctions than others. While this pattern is usually observed in the comparison of primitive and modern societies, or broad differences in social classes in the same society, variation in repressive sentiment and punitive sanctioning can be personally experienced by almost anyone. All of us have been subjected to the moral indignation of a parent or lover. Small cohesive groups like families or rural communities are settings where people take the symbolic significance of practically unimportant deviance very seriously. They are typically more repressive social settings than larger, less cohesive groupings. In these "secular" social situations, people are more likely to take a "relative" view of deviance and assess its significance only in its practical consequences. Sanctions are intended to restore and maintain a minimum level of orderliness in social coordination. The *same* people can be punitive in one social situation and "reasonable" in another. Social structure, therefore, is one important cause of repression.

In the particular case of the Canadian death penalty debates, examination of variations in Canadian social structure assist in explaining variations in public support for retaining the death penalty. The Canadian death penalty debate fits the latest phase of legal evolution in western democracies in which there is struggle to drop the symbolic punishment aspect of the law and make the "punishment" fit the criminal rather than the crime. This is the legal philosophic environment of the North American death penalty debates and is interpreted in this book as essentially a rhetorical and ideological dilemma between the instrumental and expressive views of law. This distinction also acts as an interpretive theme for the empirical materials used in this study.

One image of the criminal law system would be modelled on the laws and administrative procedures used to govern a system of roads and highways in a country. The apparent, although not explicit, goal of the system is to provide sufficient legal intervention so that people and goods can be moved from place to place with maximum efficiency and personal discretion. The minimal intervention prevents the chaotic disruption of the whole system which might occur if it were unregulated. It also holds the casualty rate, loss of life and property within the system at an *acceptable* level. In addition, and with a "no fault" insurance system, the risks of travelling are spread over the entire population, reducing the personal property loss if an accident occurs. Ideally, then, such a system is dispassionate and uses practicality, possibility and cost as policy decision criteria. It does not strive for zero loss of life and property because the cost to the system would be too high in enforcement and efficiency of the primary goal, the movement of people and goods.

This image of criminal justice, as a fully and exclusively rational control system, assumes that the purpose of criminal justice is to provide society with the maximum freedom to pursue a variety of personal and social goals with a minimal, but acceptable, level of disorder and personal loss as an understandable and tolerable cost.

Another image is that of a drama. This image emphasizes the opposite features of social life: the symbolic, emotional and nonrational. First, the law violator is depicted with enough sympathy to engage our empathy. Then, his motives are exposed as contemptible, his deceit in his own defense is exposed, and his weakness in receiving his punishment is displayed. Society's temptations have been displayed; the weak and the craven succumb, exposed and punished. Society has been fortified by strengthening the resistance of those who might fail, and reassuring the rest that the values are being observed and that symbolic order is intact.

This image assumes that the main function of criminal justice is to illustrate, if only by keeping a law on the books, that a society as a culture is unalterably opposed to the violation of certain values. It assumes that the symbolic needs of a people may be greater than their practical problems, and that if either should be mutually exclusive of the other, the expressive should be retained.

At least one pundit has suggested that the Canadian criminal justice system is like a bad play, in which there is *neither* a tangible nor an illusory effect. This could be rightly said about *any* criminal justice system, outside a totalitarian society. Statistical evaluation of these systems consistently show failure to deter. Reform occurs largely by accident, and excessive costs are expended pursuing prosecuting and and incarcerating those whose social damage is negligible.

In contrast, the instrumental image and its implications for law enforcement and correction prevent the delicious satisfaction of righteous indignation, but it also fosters reasonable, achievable expectations of criminal justice.

This instrumental/expressive dilemma is a theme of this book and is described in the opening section, which introduces and describes some concepts used by sociologists interested in deviance, social control and the sociology of law.

Chapter one follows with a description of the Canadian situation regarding the death penalty both in historical and comparative perspective.

Chapter two critically reviews the problems of public opinion polls on the death penalty in particular and punitiveness in general. In addition, original data on four national Canadian polls are analyzed and some determinants of the public attitude towards the death penalty are discussed.

Chapter three analyzes the legislative process on capital punishment. One of the central questions is the extent to which Members of Parliament represent the sentiment of their constituents on the capital punishment question. Data from parliamentary reports, biographical materials, opinion polls and interviews are used in this analysis.

Chapter four describes the classical structural explanation of repressive law advanced by Durkheim. This notion is subjected to empirical verification with data derived from the Canadian census, parliamentary reports and parliamentary biographies. Some implications of this structural view of repressive law are advanced.

Several appendices are included. One describes the technical details of the data used in this study and the methods of analysis. Another provides a statistical comparison of those convicted murderers who were executed, and those who were commuted, in the last twenty years the death penalty was actually used in Canada.

Footnotes

[1] Svend Ranulf, *Moral Indignation and Middle Class Psychology*, (New York: Schocken Books Inc., 1964).

[2] Sir James Stephen, *A History of the Criminal Law in England*, Vol. II (London: Macmillan, 1883), p. 81.

[3] Samuel Noah Kramer, *History Begins at Sumer* (New York: Doubleday, 1959).

[4] Both these concepts are taken up in more detail in later chapters.

[5] Svend Ranulf, *op. cit.*

[6] Karl Menninger, *The Crime of Punishment*, (New York: Viking Press, 1968).

[7] Harold D. Lasswell, "Preface", in Svend Ranulf, *op. cit.*

Introduction

This is a book about the penalty of death for the crime of murder. The situation under investigation is a decade of Canadian parliamentary and national debate about capital punishment. In this period several attempts to abolish the death penalty in Parliament failed, but a partial abolition succeeded.

Many societies have abolished or substantially reduced their reliance on severe criminal punishment and the death penalty, in particular, in the past fifty years. The arguments within societies undergoing these changes are remarkably similar, and are reflected in the Canadian debate. The social preconditions and processes of these changes also seem to be similar.

The Canadian experience will be investigated as a case which exposes important theoretical generalities about the evolution of criminal punishment. The evidence for such generalizations is difficult to obtain. The first task in an effort to clarify the theoretical contribution of a particular empirical case is to select from the welter of facts in the situation those which are relevant to the problem at hand. This requires that the problem be defined and the relevant questions sharpened.

An analysis of the intellectual context of the question is important. To ask a question often implies that other prior questions have been asked and answered, either with evidence or with assumptions. The intellectual context here is sociology, which uses a vocabulary intended to bring more precision to social concepts, some of which are seductively familiar. Some amplification and definition is therefore useful.

Our first task is twofold. It is to introduce some sociological concepts which will be useful in this research, and to come more precisely and self-consciously to the problem posed in the preface. Expressive and instrumental orientations to law sometimes lead to opposite positions on the merit of a particular law. In the case of repressive laws, what social forces are arrayed on each side of the instrumental/expressive dilemma?

The quality and importance of evidence that can be marshalled to this and related questions varies greatly. As a consequence, it is prudent to organize and assess these empirical materials in an explicit and systematic way. As a practical matter, laws bear only an indirect relation to the will of the people. They are most directly a result of legislative activity which is presumed to reflect popular sentiment. The first three sections of this book are devoted to this problem. The first is an outline of the Canadian legislative history of the death penalty. The second critically analyses what is known about Canadian public opinion on the death penalty. The third assesses the representativeness of Canadian Members of Parliament on the death penalty question. In the final chapter we come to the central theoretical question. Here we are aided by classic social theories of repression. Emile Durkheim's notions of the social sources and conditions of repressive laws are of particular utility in guiding our inquiry. His work helps us to focus more sharply on the issues and indicates which kinds of evidence are important. We are able to assess the contemporary validity of his classical ideas and explore some of the reasons for the instrumental/expressive stand-off in this legislative debate.

Some Conventional Sociological Wisdom

Sociologists have found the concept of social institution useful in building an understanding of society.[1] Like the concept of market in economics, social institutions are not concrete entities but rather are labels placed by social scientists on various activities in society. The institution of the family, for example, refers to social activity which is related to sex, procreation and kinship in any society. Included in this are cultural facets, beliefs and values about the family, and the organizational facets, structure and procedures of the family.

The extent to which family activity is recognized in a society as properly separated and different from other social institutions, such as religion, is conventionally referred to as the extent of the differentiation in society. It is widely held that the evolutionary process of society involves the process of increasing differentiation of social institutions. Thus, in a primitive society, the values and organization of the family may rationalize and control all economic, political and religious activity in that society. Later, in an evolutionary process, these activities may be differentiated with their own specialized organization having separate values and beliefs.

Modern industrial society is characterized by a great deal of institutional differentiation. We spend our lives, often each day, moving in and out of roles in various social institutions, often taking on radically different attitudes and social positions in each.

People in modern societies tend to conduct their discussions about their societies using some abstractions which are similar to those of the social scientists. Public discussions of the economy, for example, refer to the innumerable factors such as the exchanges of goods and services and borrowing or lending of money as the "economy" of a country. This concept summarizes for the man on the street and the social scientist approximately the same empirical phenomenon. The scientist is more likely to be awed by its complexity, more likely to have rules about what is to be included under the concept and is perhaps only a little less likely to reify it.

So the abstractions which refer to social institutions enter public and private discourse. The fortunes of religion, the fate of the family, and the future of politics, sometimes become topics in public policy efforts to improve society. Social scientists are being willingly swept into the debates about these matters to a greater extent than in the past.

One of the features of social science which distinguishes it from other forms of inquiry into the same topics is a greater self-consciousness about the way these problems are thought about. Most scientists are as concerned about which concepts are being used, their definition and relation to each other, in addition to concerns about the nature and quality of empirical evidence, as they are about the answer. The analysis of social institutions for both public policy and scientific understanding can be improved by the inclusion of additional conceptual distinctions.

Some Conventional Sociological Distinctions

So that analysis does not founder on the complexity of human society, it is necessary to circumscribe inquiries by making distinctions.

Intentions and Consequences

One distinction is between the intentions and consequences of human action. Usually what we intend by an act occurs. We are usually unaware, and properly unconcerned, that the intentional part of our behavior includes many factors such as culture, history and socialization. In addition, unintended consequences of our acts are far-reaching throughout the social systems we live in. Of course, consequences are connected back to the intentions of acts. People, both as individuals and in institutions, learn from their experiences. Sometimes patterns of consequences are an important ingredient in culture. Today's consequences become tomorrow's intentions.

Notwithstanding the empirical connections between intentions and consequences, the conceptual distinction has proven to be a useful one in cutting into the ongoing maelstrom of the social process to decompose and analyze it. Social institutions are closely connected to sets of major cultural values. We must distinguish what people and groups in institutional roles intend of their behavior in the short run, and the long run consequences of it.

Instrumental and Expressive

Another distinction which has analytic utility is the classification of the intentions of activity into two types. Instrumental acts are those which are intended to produce some effect. They are means to some end. Expressive acts, on the other hand, may be seen as ends in themselves. It is unlikely that there is ever, in reality, a pure type of either one. Most of us in everyday life exhibit carefully planned, goal directed behavior and unplanned, reactive behavior at others. The behavior associated with social institutions can be profitably interpreted with this distinction.

Economic activity is supposed to be characterized by the most rational, planned, pragmatic considerations. Quantitative measurement of output and efficiency checks are normal. There is relatively little that is sacred about it except the institution itself.

On the other hand, religion is largely an expressive activity. The activities involved in collective ritual observance or individual prayer are regulated by traditional rules or individual innovation. There is no tangible output from the institution and an aversion to any quantified interpretation of it. Religious activity is largely an expression by people of their feelings and a dramatization of their ideas. The point here is that economic and religious institutions differ widely with respect to the emphasis on the tradition, form and aesthetics of human conduct.

The distinction between instrumentally and expressively intended behavior reflects a longtime interest of sociologists. A wide variety of terms, for example, sacred and secular, have been used to try and contain the idea. The concept has been particularly important in attempts to capture the evolutionary process in society. It is widely held that, whatever the terms used, there is an increasing dominance of the rational and pragmatic over the aesthetic and impractical as societies evolve.

In addition to this use, this distinction points to common contradictions and tension in the norms of various institutions. The tendency for instrumental and expressive motivation to be mutually exclusive is seen dramatically in family relations. Children frequently leave home upon the righteous expression of traditional authority and parents are wracked with guilt when, for the sake of peace, they must wink at cherished family customs. Most secular family therapy seems to involve replacing the traditional moral blueprint of the family with practical, flexible norms. The evolutionary hypothesis is supported in the resolutions to the contradiction of the expressive and instrumental. More often "outworn" tradition gives way to "being practical" in such confrontations.

In sum then, any institution in society can be characterized relative to others in its proportion of instrumental to expressive activity. Particular points of contradiction in any institution between instrumental and expressive intentions can be located and the resolution of the contradiction can be analyzed.

The Formality of Sanction

Finally, we turn to one of the central notions in sociology. The regularities observable in human conduct, according to sociological vision, are a function, at least in part, of people following rules. These rules or norms are derived from, and articulated through, the culture. They are specified to particular social roles and incorporated into human behavior through socialization. A person's activity is continuously evaluated by members of society as to the extent of its compliance to rules. Responses to behavior are thought to be sanctions because they have the potential for altering compliance to rules.

Except for the unsocialized novice, most people most of the time are unaware of the presence of sanctions. They are a natural part of everyday life. For the sociologist however, it looms large as a concept which is essential to the understanding of society. Sanctions have been subjected to numerous classifications as to their formality, strength, origins and positive or negative effect on behavior.

The investigation of sanctions is central to the analysis of social institutions. In this respect people, sometimes unknowingly, adopt a sociological vision of society. Many "everyday life" theories of human conduct ascribe causality to genetic, physiological, intellectual, historical, or other immutable factors. Yet the attempts to bring such conduct into closer alignment with what is desired emphasizes social sanctions. The public concern about runaway children in families or runaway inflation in the economy turns to a discussion of the effectiveness of social sanctions in these institutions.

All social institutions are defined as having central beliefs and values which characterize desirable conduct within it. In addition, the desirability of types of sanctions and beliefs in their natural effectiveness for the institution are implied in the culture. Rational, self-interested conduct is desirable in economic matters and the application of monetary incentiveness as sanctions is supposed to largely control economic activity. Emotional, selfless conduct is desirable in families and the contingent use of love as a sanction is notorious. Both tragedy and comedy in our society depend to a great extent on cultural inconsistencies in these patterns. The impropriety of love on the job or the pursuit of financial gain through marriage are ubiquitous themes in the mass media. Sociological research on child rearing practices and productivity of workers is essentially the study of the intentions and effects of sanctions in various institutional settings.

While the concept of sanction is not restricting and does not help us to narrow and specify an area of inquiry, one of its subdivisions does. We can distinguish between formal sanctions and those that are more informal. Since formal sanctions are often written down and specified to particular activity, they are of particular interest. Their formality implies that they are considered socially important and reflect a social process specifying what the culture is. Whether this is a religious group attempting to interpret God's revealed truth or a set of work rules in industry, they distinguish important specified elements of institutionally desirable behavior and the means of achieving it.

The Specific Utility of these Distinctions

We now turn to the present study. The concepts and distinctions described above will help us to specify what is under scrutiny in the remainder of this book and what is not. Capital punishment is a *formally* designated *sanction*. It is a product of formal deliberations in legislatures which are part of the *political institution* of modern society. The point at issue in these deliberations seems to be whether criminal sanctions are *intended* to be *instrumental* or *expressive*, or whether they can be both. The resolution of this dilemma over the expressive/instrumental intentions of criminal punishment can be viewed, in part, as a derivative of the social processes operative in social evolution. It is within this context that we intend to locate the recent Canadian capital punishment debate.

The Law as an Instrument of Control[2]

Control over institutional behavior is largely located within institutional organizations. Both formal and informal sanctions are mobilized by persons acting in institutional roles, like fathers or employers. However, some formal sanctioning is delegated to the law to be employed on behalf of society.

In a modern society, the rule of law is very highly developed and pervasive. It might be argued that any social behavior is subject to the law. This occurs because any behavior can be placed before a legal agency for consideration of whether it falls under legal regulation or not. The rules of inclusion are present in the law and determined by agents of it.

The criminal code is a much more restrictive set of regulations over a narrow range of activities which are usually thought to be serious. One party to a criminal proceeding is usually the state, and the infractions and punishments specified in criminal codes reflect the values and beliefs of the whole society.

At the same time as it reflects the highest ideals and aspirations a culture sets forth about human conduct, the law is also charged with ensuring at least the minimal level of social control and order the society will tolerate.

Faith in the rule of law may have replaced faith in God or a King as a source of order in society. Therefore, the demand on legislators to produce efficient laws is heavy. Social problems are seen as solvable through the passage and enforcement of the right law. This faith may be, in part, unfounded.

Legitimacy and the Law

Sociological analysis of law and its sanctions often emphasizes the extent to which laws often criminalize behavior which is not productively controlled by subjecting it to legal sanction. Part of this problem is that people do not seem to voluntarily obey laws they do not believe in, and the extent to which they can be coerced in a free society is severely limited.

The legitimacy with which people view legal prohibitions seems to be largely a cultural matter. Compliance to laws will occur to the extent that laws codify the beliefs and values of the people. Then all the institutions, law, family, religion, etc. are integrated and provide a consistent set of expectations and sanctions all rationalized ultimately by the ideals of the society.

This imaginary state of legitimacy of the law is often conjured up when judges intimidate mumbling defendants into abandoning their desperate, self-serving explanations and admit to "doing wrong", and indicate a readiness to "take their medicine". The drama displays the assumptions of legitimacy of the prohibition and the sanction in the law.

Rarely in any society could such social integration and, consequently, such legal legitimacy occur. This is especially true in the case of large, modern, industrial, changing, stratified, ethnically plural societies such as Canada. It would be impossible to get nation-wide agreement on the importance of even a widely-held value in western civilization, such as the rights of individual freedom, when it is concretely specified in terms of social circumstances, as it must under the law. Rather, wide differences in the priority of the individual in different situations could occur between different class, ethnic, regional and age groups. The jury system and some local discretion in law enforcement mitigates the potential illegitimacy by putting the process in touch with the local standards of the time.

The regulation by law of private morality or personal conduct is praticularly subject to the problems of voluntary compliance. The legislation which produces these so-called crimes without victims, has been criticized as unnecessary and inefficient. The behavior it attempts to control is "naturally" controlled through socialization or community opprobrium, or not controlled at all. The application of legal sanctions seems to make little difference.

The apparent decline in the legitimacy of these laws shows another facet of the legitimacy problem. Even those whose personal conduct is exemplary, and who see the law as a accurate expression of their own personal standards of conduct, develop a kind of plural morality, and don't lust for strong controls on others. By viewing it as "their own business" or by seeing violators as sick rather than evil, the majority opinion reduces the total legitimacy of these laws.

One set of problems then, in understanding law as an instrument of social control, is to examine the extent of voluntary compliance which can be reasonably expected in the society at a given point in time. In short, how legitimate are the laws? This is largely determined by their fit with other aspects of the society, particularly the cultural standards.

Legitimacy and Law Enforcement

The explanation is not simple, of course, and laws sometimes gain legitimacy in proportion to their ability to be enforced. Thus if enforcement agencies are able to make arrests of some reasonable proportion of violators, and courts convict some reasonable proportion, there may be an opportunity for laws to increase their legitimacy over time. If the behaviour under control of the law is open to systematic scrutiny, then the potential for prompt and frequent apprehension of violators is increased. Under these conditions it appears that voluntary compliance with the law is high. Tax and traffic laws, for example, seem to be voluntarily obeyed in a population where the opportunities for violation are widespread. Whether this is a result of cultural values or fear of personal penalty is an important empirical question for deterrence research.

For law violation which is not open to systematic scrutiny, the possibility of increasing legitimation through law enforcement declines. Where policemen must engage in arduous or ignoble actions, as in vice or narcotic enforcement, the likelihood of systematic apprehension declines. Similarly, where the discovery of a law violation is a complex, costly or specialized process, such as in pollution, embezzlement and conspiracies, the potency of the law enforcement process is reduced.

The relationship between criminal law and behavior is complex. In a free society, law cannot venture too far away from the culture of the people; it can neither lead very strongly nor lag very far behind. In a complex, modern society, the capability of many laws to be enforced is very low, and the cost to the society of enforcing them is very high.

Faith in Law

In spite of these problems, the faith in law as a means of controlling society is widespread. Familiar statements, such as "this is a society of laws," "they ought to pass a law," "there ought to be more law and order," all reflect the theory that belief in, and the use of, law is basic to western thinking about social control.

Members of religious and political sects sometimes discard this assumption, but their limited members reflect, in part, the widespread endorsement of the rule of law. Most organized and successful religious groups, finding God's law and man's law in harmonious accommodation, do not seriously advocate a theocracy. Most socialist groups in North America find that, although the economy is as determinant of social relations as their theorists have argued, and the law reflects such economic arrangements, there are adequate legislative remedies to its most offensive inequities.

So everyone, it seems, accommodates to the rule of the law, no matter how much a pure form of their ideology would draw them into conflict with a faith in it.

There is, therefore, no fundamental disagreement in Canada about law both as a blueprint of the society and the mechanism to solve its problems. For historical reasons, western cultures have come to the point where law is generally regarded as the way in which control can and should be exercised in a state. To be sure, there is indirect control on income distribution and other economic features in western society through tinkering with the economy. The decline in family and religion are sometimes accused of being the source of unwanted behavior in society, but other than exhortation to be better, somehow, solution to the problem frequently comes to reside under the law.

The most general image of law is that it has evolved into a centralized, disinterested, legitimate, democratically responsive, effective sanctioning system. It has become a practical tool to be relied upon to solve problems, which can be changed if it doesn't work. The discussion of bad laws leads to sentiment to change laws, not to an abandonment of faith in the system of law.

Legislators and the Law

The political process of western democratic society involves the periodic election and continuous employment of legislators whose primary function is to make laws. In part because of this, many lawyers seek political office and are elected to legislatures.[3] Increasingly, the scale of modern problems inclines people to turn to government for a solution. Through the electoral process, there is a proper incentive for elected representatives to attempt a solution. Their solutions will be legislative. Election campaigns publicly raise the problems various people have, and often propose ideologically competing legislative solutions.

There is then a confluence of forces operating in western society which inclines the man on the street, the mass media, and politicians to see problems as solvable, if only the right law can be found, and if it can be enforced properly.[4]

Can Law Control?

Within this set of assumptions, the practical limits of the law as a means of social control are not exposed. Just as our society has faith that technology can control even its own bad consequences, it asserts that, while particular laws may be bad, law is good.

The effectiveness of a law is almost never put to rigorous empirical test,[5] and the public policy debates in and out of legislatures often rely on anecdotal evidence and competing assumptions about the nature of man and his behavior. Even if there were evidence which could not be discredited that the widest variety of conceivable laws, enforcements and punishments did not alter the incidence of some undesirable activity in society, such as suicide, the pressures for legislative remedy remain. The law, along with the economy, is the most rational and instrumental institutional arrangement yet evolved in society. At the same time, the law in every society expresses beliefs and values which are independent of rational efforts to control behavior.

Law and the Expressive/Instrumental Dilemma

Herein lies the contradiction if one views the law, as many legislators seem to, as an instrumental control mechanism in society. If we also view the law as an expressive drama which ritually displays the ideals of the culture, then what appear to be irrational efforts to control of the uncontrollable become understandable expressions of evaluation.

Sometimes, of course, instrumentally and expressively satisfactory law is produced. When the behavior to be controlled by law does decrease as a function of the severity of punishment, then there is no dilemma or incompatibility between the two orientations. There is some evidence that this will occur only in behavior which is highly rational, in which there is no criminal subculture, and in which chance of detection and apprehension are quite high. Since the severity of punishment appears to have no effect on the rates of murder, or many other personal and property crimes about which there is public alarm, for these crimes the potential dilemma remains.

It is with this theme that we interpret much of the empirical evidence on the public attitude and legislative behavior on the legal imposition of the death penalty in Canada.

Footnotes

1 The time has come for a number of cautions and disclaimers for the non-sociologist. There is some disagreement within sociology on the general utility of a social institution classification to the understanding of society. There is still more disagreement on the precise basis of the classification and how many and separate its divisions should be. There is some debate on the amount of difference that is or should be present in sociological and everyday life concepts.
This section intends to avoid these sometimes important questions. The description of the social institution approach is as simple a rendition of the framework as can be deduced from the way it is used in descriptive/interpretive research. It is being described only to locate the research which follows in a matrix of sociological questions and concepts.

2 It is beyond the scope of this review to raise the tangled and important definitional debate on law. For a review of this, see Jack P. Gibbs, "Definitions of Law and Empirical Questions," *Law and Society Review*, 2 (May 1968), pp. 429-446.

[3] There are approximately 67 lawyers, over 25 per cent of the total, in the Parliament (1973) of Canada.

[4] Interestingly, those who have the closest experience with law enforcement, the police and court personnel, often privately report a belief that in *principle*, laws cannot control some problems.

[5] A notable exception to this is the death penalty, the subject of this report.

Chapter 1: Capital Punishment

Capital punishment is a topic which has excited a great deal of debate and analysis both in Canada and elsewhere. In this section we briefly review the situation in Canada in comparison to several other societies. This material is well described and documented elsewhere. Therefore, this selective review emphasizes features which are important in this research.

Canadian Law

Unlike the United States, Canada's criminal code relating to murder is federal. Thus, there is a single definition of murder and specification of punishment for all of Canada. Section 91(27) of the British North American Act provides that criminal law and the procedures in criminal matters come under the jurisdiction of the Federal Parliament. Section 92(14), however, grants the provinces jurisdiction over the administrative activities within the province, such as maintenance and organization of its civil and criminal courts.[1] Prior to September 1, 1961, any person convicted of murder in Canada was automatically sentenced to death, and the sentence was carried into execution unless the Governor General, acting upon the advice of the Cabinet, commuted the sentence to life imprisonment. By amendments to the Criminal Code, made in 1961, murder was divided into capital and non-capital murder. Capital murder was defined as "murder that is planned and deliberate, murder committed in the course of certain crimes of violence by the direct intervention or upon the counselling of the accused; and murder of a police officer or prison warden, acting in the course of duty, resulting from such direct intervention or counselling".[2] Such a murder was still punishable by mandatory hanging except if the accused was under eighteen years of age. All other murder was punished by life imprisonment. The judge was required to ascertain whether the jury wanted to recommend clemency or not to the Cabinet. The Cabinet still reviewed each capital murder case and made a decision whether to act on the "prerogative of mercy" and commute the death sentence.

In addition, in 1961, an automatic review of all capital convictions by the provincial Court of Appeal was established as well as a full right of appeal to the Supreme Court of Canada. This was a review only of fact or law, in the conviction, since the sentence was mandatory and could be reduced only by the Cabinet.

Executive review of the death sentence occurred after all legal remedies to the conviction were exhausted. The staff work for this review was carried out by the remissions office in the Ministry of Justice. This was a comprehensive compilation of information on virtually every facet of the whole process. As Sheehan reports, "the basic purpose of this system of executive review is an attempt to clarify not only the degree of guilt as it rests within a social context, but also to review the whole judicial process including that of police".[3]

Mitigating and extenuating circumstances could be brought forward at this time as there was no restrictive procedure, such as the admissability of evidence. The remissions office was able to seek information from official sources, such as police, prisons and attorneys. Other materials generally depended on the initiative of advocates of the convicted.[4]

On November 30, 1967, the Criminal Code was further amended by the Canadian Parliament confining the imposition of the death penalty to the murder of police officers and prison guards for a five-year, experimental trial period. Any person whose sentence of death had been commuted to life imprisonment, or any person upon whom the sentence of life as a minimum punishment had been imposed, would not be released without prior approval of the Governor in Council. On January 26, 1973, after the expiration of the five-year experiment, the Solicitor General of Canada introduced legislation to the Parliament for a continuation of the partial ban on capital punishment. This legislation became law.

Since there have been no executions in Canada since 1962 (see Table 1), Canada finds itself at the end of a decade of *de facto* abolition of the death penalty. Unless Parliament acts otherwise, Canada will be in a decade, 1967 to 1978, of very restricted *de jure* application of the death penalty.[5]

A Brief Legislative History of the Death Penalty

For many years the issue of capital punishment seemed of relatively little concern to lawmakers' throughout the world. It became controversial in the period between World War I and II, with the emergence of authoritarian systems of penal law. Abolition movements began developing in many countries. In England, the Royal Commission of Capital Punishment carried out an intensive study in the years 1949-1953. The great Penal Law Commission was established in 1959 by the Federal Republic of Germany. Several states of the United States of America set up commissions or conducted studies on the issues of capital punishment. In Russia, between 1954 and 1960, penal legislation was reviewed and reformed. Seminars were organized in Athens, France and among the European Committee on Crime to investigate capital punishment in 1953. While an overall trend can be seen throughout history toward the limitation and confinement of offenses punishable by death, revision and reform on a major scale is fairly recent.[6] France, the United States and England offer interesting comparisons for the analysis of the Canadian case.

The French Situation

France is one of the few western European nations to have retained the death penalty. To date, the method of execution is still the guillotine. The French Penal Code of 1810 provided for 36 crimes punishable by death. In 1949 the number had dropped to 12.[7] It is important to note that, while the overall trend has been to limit the number of offenses punishable by death, it is common for legislators to attempt to control a recent crime wave or react to a particularly heinous crime with legislation which makes that specific crime a capital offense. In 1971, for example, an attempt was made to extend capital punishment to drug traffickers in France. In the recent past, there have been very few actual executions so France is moving toward *de facto* abolition, but with no evidence of judicial or legislative abolition.

The United States Situation

In June, 1972, the United States Supreme Court held in the *Furman v. Georgia* decision that the death penalty as currently administered, with judges and juries having discretion over the sentence rendered, was unconstitutional because it violated the eighth and fourteenth amendments of the Constitution as cruel and unusual punishment. The majority opinions of the judges outlined the arbitrary and discriminatory nature of the administration of the death penalty as major concerns. That Supreme Court ruling was very narrow and within two years, the legislatures of several states enacted death penalty legislation which might be constitutional. This legislation may meet the standards of the court on the fairness and normalcy of administration of the penalty. To do so, it would have to make the death penalty mandatory or provide very clear rules for its discretionary imposition. Another narrow Supreme Court decision in *Witherspoon versus Illinois* addressed the issue of whether a jury which is selected with all members in favour of the use of the death penalty, in principle, was unbiased on the guilt of the accused. Both these decisions resulted in a reduction in the number of condemned wainting in U.S. prisons. From 1967 to 1974, none have been executed.

Unlike most other countries, the recent evolution toward the abolition of capital punishment in the United States is occurring, for the most part, in the judiciary rather than in the legislature. Significantly, social science findings on matters relating to these Supreme Court decisions seem to be invited, and have been more important[8] in the evolution of the death penalty than in the legislatures of other countries.

Summary

While France is characterized by relative inactivity on the legislative abolition of the death penalty, and the United States by judicial abolition but legislative retention, the recent history in England bears the closest resemblance to the emerging Canadian situation. This occurs, in part, because of the impact of its early colonial status on Canadian law and because the form of government is quite similar in the two countries.

The English and Canadian Situation

The Royal Proclamation of 1763 replaced the prevailing Canadian system of justice with the laws of England. The British Criminal Code listed between 220 and 230 offenses which were punishable by death "from stealing turnips to being found disguised in a forest".[9]

Attempts to more realistically align punishments with more generally acceptable societal values began in England around 1800. In 1808, Samuel Romily introduced legislation into the House of Commons to abolish capital punishment for shoplifting, if the value of the shoplifted item was under five shillings. Between 1810 and 1820, this was passed by the Commons six times and defeated by the House of Lords each time. Not until 1832 did this bill finally pass both Houses.

Public opinion in England apparently opposed the provision of the death penalty on such a broad scale because juries, reluctant to convict capital cases, began acquitting those defendants for whom the penalty outweighed the crime. Koestler argues that, whenever social progress outpaces the law and penalties appear to be disproportionately severe to the public conscience, juries will not convict and reprieves, instead of being an exception, become virtually the rule.[10]

In Canada, the number of offenses punishable by death was reduced in 1859. The Constituted Statutes of Canada maintained the death penalty for "murder, rape, treason, administering poison or wounding with the intent to commit murder, unlawfully abusing a girl under ten, buggery with man or beast, robbery with wounding, burglary with assault, arson, casting away a ship and exhibiting a false signal endagering a ship". By 1865, the death penalty had been abolished in all cases except murder, treason and rape.

Reforms in the administration of the law also occurred. In 1836 a prisoner charged with a capital crime was allowed to secure legal counsel. Later, in 1898 a prisoner was allowed to give evidence on his own behalf and in 1907, he was permitted to appeal his case.

A vigorous attempt to abolish capital punishment began in 1914 with abolitionist, Robert Bickerdike. Bickerdike passionately argued that capital punishment was essentially murder committed by the state, a blot on Christianity, a brutal and unnecessary form of punishment, ineffective as a deterrent and that the possibility of judicial error made it an unconscionable form of punishment.[11]

In early 1914, Mr. Bickerdike introduced an abolition bill in the form of a Private Members Bill. It was discussed briefly and defeated by a motion for adjournment. Again in 1915 and in 1916, Mr. Bickerdike introduced legislation to amend the criminal code and abolish the penalty of death but to no avail.

On January 31, 1917, Mr. Bickerdike once again introduced his abolition bill. During this brief debate, he attempted to introduce an amendment which abolished capital punishment for women and children. This amendment was ruled out of order by the Speaker of the House. Mr. Bickerdike then introduced an amendment prohibiting the capital punishment of an 18 year old youth who had been sentenced to death. This was ruled out of order as it dealt with the issue of Royal Prerogative. Not until April 1924 was the issue debated again in Parliament. A free vote was permitted and the abolitionist bill was defeated.

In 1949 a Royal Commission on Capital Punishment was established in England. The purpose of this commission was to study the advisability of *limiting* or *modifying* the capital punishment legislation and inquire into what consequences would occur by such alterations. In 1953, the Commission reported its findings. It stated that it was impossible to frame a definition of murder, or to create classes or degrees of murder that would effectively limit the scope of capital punishment.[12] It agreed that, while there were obvious disadvantages, the best solution was to adopt the system whereby the jury has the power to decide in each case whether life imprisonment can properly be substituted for capital punishment.

In 1957 the British Parliament adopted the Homicide Act which redefined murder and created a distinction between capital and non-capital crime. After several unsuccessful attempts, a bill abolishing capital punishment for a five year trial period was passed by the House of Commons in July, 1965 and became law in November. Of interest, when comparing the English situation to the Canadian one, is that the English Parliament passed the abolition bill by a free vote, with each Member expressing his opinion and making his decision according to his own personal preference. In addition, while the abolition bill was adopted by a vote of 200 votes to 98, a public opinion poll of the time had shown that 79% of the English people favoured the retention of capital punishment.[13] On December 16, 1969, the British Parliament, again in a free vote, made the abolition of the death penalty a permanent feature of British law.

In the Canadian Parliament, a private members bill was introduced in 1950 to amend the Criminal Code to abolish the penalty of death. Again in 1953, the same bill was introduced. This bill was withdrawn but subsequently, a Joint Committee of the Senate and the House was established. This committee was to investigate capital punishment, corporal punishment and lotteries. The mandate of this committee permitted it to study the feasibility of the abolition of capital punishment and make recommendations accordingly. In 1956, the committee's report recommended the retention of capital punishment. It suggested no reform in the definition of murder. It did recommend abolition of capital punishment for children under 18. Many administrative reforms were delineated. The committee suggested full disclosures of the Government's case to the accused, the provision of legal counsel, a mandatory plea of not guilty for capital charges, and automatic appeal, among others.[14]

Pursuant to the Joint Committee's findings, bills to amend the-Criminal Code were introduced in 1957, 1958, 1959 and 1960.

In November 1960, the Government introduced legislation which reclassified murder into capital and non-capital offenses in spite of the earlier committee recommendation. Capital murder, that which was planned and premeditated, was punishable by death. Non-capital murder, that which was unplanned, was punishable by life imprisonment. This bill was not intended to be considered as a first step towards abolition, but rather an updating of the Criminal Code. It was adopted by a vote of 139 to 21.

In 1962 a bill was introduced to amend the Criminal Code to abolish capital punishment except for treason. This and other attempts to review the question were proposed and defeated.

In November 1963, a general election was held in which the Liberals gained power from the Progressive Conservatives. A private members' bill was again introduced to abolish capital punishment and debated in 1964. The Parliament adjourned, however, without voting on this issue. The new Liberal government had no publicly defined position on capital punishment and indicated no apparent interest in bringing the issue up for a vote. Of importance, however, is the fact that no person had been executed since the Liberals came into power, and the Progressive Conservative government before them had commuted almost 80 per cent of the death penalties during their tenure from 1957 to 1962.

In the opening speech of Parliament in 1965, the Liberal government declared its intention of affording the House of Commons the opportunity to discuss the issue of capital punishment. The Minister of Justice authorized the Department of Justice to prepare a "white paper" on capital punishment. Because of the non-partisan nature of the debate and its emotional potential, the Government called for a free vote, releasing all Members of Parliament from party discipline. A major debate and several votes on the death penalty took place in 1966 and 1967. The experimental partial abolition bill which finally passed in 1967 was renewed (119 in favor, 106 against) in 1973, again in a major and contentious Parliamentary debate.

In summary, we find that Great Britain moved early to full abolition; whereas across the channel in France, the death penalty appears to be still legally entrenched. In North America, the United States finds itself in *de facto* abolition with the Supreme Court showing a tendency towards abolition on various constitutional grounds and some State legislature moving in the opposite direction to restore the penalty.

Canada is presently in the middle of these socio-legal trends. *De facto* abolition is established, but still on a case-by-case basis. The Parliament appears able to muster only enough support for partial and temporary *de jure* abolition.

Against this more general backdrop, we turn to the detailed analysis of two recent periods of Canadian Parliamentary debate on the death penalty.

Research Case One: The 1966/67 Debate

It appears that the extensive debate on capital punishment which occurred in 1966 over a multi-party Private Members' Bill exhausted the debate and set out the various positions of the Members of Parliament. Eight months after the 1966 full abolition bill was defeated 143 to 112, the government introduced a bill which incorporated the two principal amendments which gained wide, but insufficient, support in the previous debate. Capital punishment was to be abolished, except for the murders of police and prison guards, for a five year trial period. This bill passed 105-70.[15]

The first portion of the Parliamentary debate on the abolition of the death penalty took place in the spring of 1966. On March 21, 1966, the House leader moved that three days be devoted to the capital punishment debate but there were many Members who wished to speak at length and the debate was extended. At issue was a Private Members' resolution calling for the abolition of the death penalty in respect of all offenses under the Criminal Code, and for the substitution of a mandatory sentence of life imprisonment in those cases where the death penalty was mandatory. In addition, this resolution stipulated that a person on whom a mandatory sentence of life imprisonment was imposed could not be released without prior approval of the Governor in Council. The debate was extended and the motion finally defeated on April 5, 1966.

Several amendments were introduced and defeated. An amendment whereby the death penalty would be retained for capital murders, as then defined, committed while a sentence of life imprisonment was being served, was defeated by a vote of 199 to 23. A second amendment, intended to abolish the death penalty only on a trial basis of five years, was rejected by a 138 to 113 vote. A third amendment abolishing capital punishment except in the case of the murder of a police officer, prison guard or any member of a prison staff was defeated 179 to 74. The entire motion was defeated by a vote of 143 to 112.

A bill proposing to abolish the death penalty for five years, except for the murderers of policemen and prison guards, was sponsored by the Liberal government in 1967. This debate continued sporadically from November 9, 1967 to its final approval by 195 to 70 on November 30. This was also a free vote. Several amendments, including a full abolition amendment, were defeated. The number of Members present in this debate was relatively low as the final vote indicates.

Major Themes

The content of debates in various legislatures provide one source of information and insight into legislative decision making on the death penalty. For Canada, verbatim accounts of these debates are published in the official report of the House of Commons. In addition, the two volumes on capital punishment prepared by the government[16] include extensive description of the 1966 and 1967 debates as well as the 1965 debate in England. The Report from the United Nations also describes the arguments. Literally hundreds of speeches contain wide variety of arguments on various sides of the question. The clarity of the choices on this legislative question, which transcends particular points in history and even countries with a variety of legal systems, is remarkable. It makes this public policy issue one of great interest to the student of comparative law and society.

Several major themes can be imposed on the arguments in this wide-ranging debate. These themes have been selected for this research and do not purport to exhaust the analysis of the content of these debates.

Deterrence

The pivotal significance of the deterrent effect in speeches was most noticeable in the early debate (1966/67). Here there was a dispute in both fact and ideology on *general* deterrence of the death penalty. *Specific* deterrence, which means that at least the convicted murderer cannot kill again if he is hanged, seemed to be less important. Most recognized that the execution of known murderers, even in relatively large proportions, would not provide any tangible increase in public protection. Abolitionists went on to cite statistics about the relatively favourable parole and prison behaviour of convicted murderers. Retentionists sometimes cited a few cases of murderers who had killed again.

The main point of contention was *general* deterrence, that is, the inhibiting effect of the death penalty on *potential* murderers. Most reliable statistical evidence in 1966-67 showed that the death penalty had no *general* deterrent effect, and these were frequently cited by abolitionists. However, these studies had two disadvantages in the early debate. There were no comprehensive studies done of deterrence in Canada. Thus, the retentionists could successfully argue that one cannot tell, for certain, whether the death penalty in Canada has a general deterrent effect or not. To meet this objection, a special study of the general deterrent effect in Canada was commissioned to be done in the five year trial period, to be available when the trial period was at an end in 1972.[17] This study summarizes deterrence research, its theory, methods and findings to the present. It details a multifaceted analysis of rates of crimes of violence in Canada, focussing on the eight years from 1962 to 1970. Data from a variety of official sources are assembled to contrast rates of criminal homocide against other crimes of violence, through time and by region. It concludes that changes in rates of criminal homicide cannot be attributed to changes in the death penalty. Other crimes of violence have increased more than murder since the partial suspension of the death penalty. Other variations in rates of violent crime through time and across regions are inconsistent with any deterrent effect of the death penalty. Rather, the evidence shows that rates of criminal homocide are totally a function of the same social forces which produce other crimes of violence, and thus reinstating the death penalty cannot be justified through its alleged unique deterrent effect.

Another problem was the counter-intuitive findings of deterrence research. Firstly, it derives from statistical data on rates of murder and there is no way of personifying the explanation. Thus, unless a person is accustomed to trusting and making conclusions from quantitative, aggregate information, it is an unfamiliar experience. When the conclusion is opposite to what one intuits on the basis of personal experience, for instance, that rewards and costs are the important determinants of a rational person's behavior, then there is great skepticism. Retentionists also found persons with authority, such as policemen, who because of their special experience, testified that criminals were inhibited by the death penalty.

Thus, the conclusions to be drawn from evidence of deterrence research outside of Canada were argued. Not only did the abolitionists want to believe it and the retentionists not, but the two groups seemed disposed to be different in the acceptance of statistical, as opposed to case study, evidentiary bases for public policy.[18] However, many retentionists in that debate stated that, if they were satisfied there was no deterrent effect, they would become abolitionist. So much of the 1966-67 debate apparently turned on the empirical debate about the instrumental merit, deterrent effect of capital punishment.

Free Will Versus Determinism

This philosophic difference appeared to distinguish the abolitionist from the retentionist. Abolitionist speakers tended to emphasize their belief in the determination of people's behavior in heredity and environment. These speakers adduced evidence and authoritative opinion that unusual circumstances and predispositions caused murder. Not only is it not deterrable with severe punishment, but it is neither just nor fair to punish in such a circumstance.

The retentionists tended to endorse a "free will" view of man and argue that the personal accountability implied by this position justified, indeed necessitated, punishment. They further argued that the law courts have the precedent and experience to adequately assess degrees of diminished responsibility. They worried that one philosophical underpinning of society, free will and accountability, would be weakened by the abolition of the death penalty.

Abolitionist and retentionist positions tend to differ in their emphasis on certain values. Retentionists find the abolitionist's direct or implied determinism a threat to the value of free will and accountability.

Sanctity of Life
Another value which both sides claim to endorse is the sanctity of life. Retentionists assert that the life of the victim is trivialized by not exacting the strongest penalty. Abolitionists claim the dispassionate execution of the murderer cheapens all life. Both sides legitimize their positions in the authoritative, cultural literature of western civilization and the judeo christian tradition. In this case, the same value is being emphasized and expressed but through completely different legal positions.

Protection of Society
Both sides argue that their position protects society. The retentionist argues it through the possibility of specific and general deterrence. The abolitionist argues that a long prison sentence is protective and that a changing philosophy on correction and prevention of crime will ultimately lead to greater societal protection. Progressive crime prevention and practical control is frustrated by the vindictive attitude to criminal behavior.

Both sides share a utilitarian, instrumental orientation but differ on the means to achieve societal security.

Administration of the Law
Abolitionists point to several aspects of law enforcement which can be jeopardized by the death penalty. The first is the irreversibility of the penalty. With a fallible system of justice, the possibility of error exists and, therefore, the death penalty should be abolished. Unlike England, in which a case of erroneous execution seemed to strengthen the abolitionist case, no Canadian case of executing the wrong person has been demonstrated. Retentionists point to this and to the provision of safeguards in 1961 to argue that the risk is negligible. Abolitionists argue that there is unavoidable and unacceptable bias in the tendency to convict and finally execute more of the underprivileged and weak in the society. Analysis of data on executions in the United States supports this view. There were, however, no reliable studies of this for Canada at the time of this debate. (See Appendix II.)

Abolitionists assert that mandatory death penalties, or any penalty which is excessively severe in the view of a jury, will tend to result in a bias towards acquitting the guilty. The law as a practical instrument of social control, with its dependence on legitimacy and scrupulous fairness, is frustrated by excessive severity of punishment. According to the abolitionist, the death penalty frustrates the law as an instrument.

Retentionists counter that evidence of such frustration of the law in Canada is absent and that there are other remedies for these problems than the removal of the death penalty. Their primary argument is that the legitimacy and respect for law depends on the grading of punishment to fit the crime. The law as an instrument of control needs the maximum punishment for the atrocious crime.

Retribution

This last point reveals the major difference between the retentionist and the abolitionist. Some retentionists will argue that, even with no general deterrent effect and with the risks of judicial error, the death penalty is simply justified as righteous retribution. It is morally justified as such and accords with the sentiment of Canadians that a murderer must forfeit his life. To do otherwise is to weaken the value on the sanctity of life. This sentiment seemed to be particularly strong for the murderers of policemen and prison guards who were often depicted as on the front line of defense against violent crime.

All abolitionists found the retributive motive unacceptable, though some claimed to find it understandable. As a motive, it was described as brutal and uncivilized.

In addition to a moral claim on the brutality of the death penalty, the counter arguments of the abolitionists were based on rational, instrumental criterion. Their sources tended to be modern, scientific criminology and jurisprudence. The absence of deterrence, the fact that the law didn't do what it was supposed to, was their main theme. The retentionists, on the other hand, seemed to put a strong burden of proof on the instrumental deterrence argument, while the theme of expressing a strong value on the victim's life was uppermost.

So one general theme of these debates both in Canada in 1966 and 1967 and elsewhere was the fundamental disagreement over whether the emphasis in law should be the expression of values or the practicality of instrumental control. Abolitionists, both in Parliament and in the country (as seen in editorials and "letters to the editor") tended to show an instrumental orientation to law Retentionists' arguments seemed to betray a more expressive assumption about the function of law.[19]

Research Case Two: The 1973 Debate

The five year moratorium on the death penalty in Canada expired on December 29, 1972. On January 26, 1973, the Honorable Warren Allmand, Solicitor General of Canada, moved to amend the Criminal Code in order to repeat the five year partial ban on capital punishment. A poll of the Members of Parliament conducted by *The Globe and Mail* newspaper, reported on February 3, 1973, showed that 192 of the 264 MP's were already decided on their position regarding the death penalty. However, it was only after 13 days of debate and over 100 speakers later that the Parliament adjourned for the summer without taking final action on the capital punishment bill.

The environment for the death penalty debate had changed substantially since the earlier period. Public opinion had apparently become more supportive of retaining the death penalty (see Chapter 2) with Canadians reportedly increasingly concerned about crime. The Progressive Conservative gains in the general election of 1972 had reduced the Liberal government to minority status in Parliament.[20]

Some reforms in the penetentiary system of recent years had resulted in some spectacular and audacious escapes which received wide press coverage which was unflattering to the Trudeau government. In addition, there had been several serious difficulties in some of the changes attempted in the penetentiaries and parole systems.

In addition, inflation was a problem of great concern and the government's approach to it in Canada was being vigorously criticized. The Progressive Conservatives, who were preparing for another election, saw the Liberals as vulnerable on the issue. The socialist New Democratic Party effectively held the balance of power and was pressing its approach on a dependent Liberal minority.

Retentionist MP's thought the adjournment for the summer would increase their numbers by bringing wavering abolitionists into contact with retentionist sentiment in their constituencies. Some abolitionists thought the "cooling off period" from a rancorous parliamentary debate might bring wavering retentionists to a more "rational" position.

The debate continued after the summer recess and the compromise legislation of 1967 was renewed for another five years on October 24, 1973 by a free vote of 119 to 106 in Parliament.

The proposal to renew the 1967 bill was felt by abolitionists to be the most they could get given the mood of the country and the

Parliament. In introducing the government bill, the Solicitor General, an abolitionist, presented the case for abolition.

In his summary of the general moral position of the abolitionist, he contended that it is wrong to kill and that execution by the state does not erase the crime of murder, as is sometimes argued, but rather repeats it. Hanging is contrary to the Judeao-Christian moral principle, "Thou Shalt Not Kill" and capital punishment weakens the moral fabric of the society and brutalizes it. The state must set an example of respect for human life. He listed as opponents of the death penalty the United Church of Canada, the Anglican Church and the Unitarian Church, all concurring that capital punishment is unchristian and immoral.

On deterrence, he argued that capital punishment does not, in fact, protect the public and that the best deterrent to crime is the certainty of detection and conviction.

The Solicitor General charged that the onus of proof lies with the retentionists to prove that any increase in the murder rate is related to the lack of the death penalty. He cited the possibility of judicial errors resulting in the suffering of the innocent. The potential for discrimination and unequal application of the death penalty was an abolitionist concern.

The Deterrent Effect Report

Of special interest to the 1973 debate is the discussion of statistical evidence to support the opposing positions. The initial five year trial period legislation passed in 1967 was to allow a time of intense study and analysis so the question of the deterrent effect of capital punishment in Canada could be answered with facts. The Department of the Solicitor General of Canada authorized and subsidized a research project to do this. Dr. Ezzat Abdel Fattah, a criminology professor at the University of Montreal, conducted the research. The report was distributed to the Members of Parliament and drawn upon heavily throughout the 1973 debate. It is particularly interesting to note that, even with a research project conducted especially for the Canadian Parliament specifically on the issue at hand, the question of the deterrent effect of capital punishment was hotly contested. The concluding section of Dr. Fattah's research states that homicide rates are conditioned by factors other than the death penalty. "The increase in criminal homicide . . . cannot be attributed to one factor or one variable such as the suspension of the death penalty."[21] The Solicitor General concluded that nothing emerges from the research that would support, or even suggest, that the suspension of the death penalty has caused an increase in the criminal homicide rate. While this cautious, rational, documented statement could be expected to lay the issue to rest, even Mr. Allmand, the Solicitor General, equivocates and argues that, since the study only has analyzed the data through the 1971 statistics, Parliament should make no change in the law until the complete research project of five years is analyzed. Aware of the tenuous reputation researchers, statisticians, sociologists and criminologists seem to have among some of the MP's, Mr. Allmand feels obliged to debate past the point of empirical research.

A theme of this research which was found in the 1966-67 debates is that there will be a contradiction between the rational, pragmatic orientation to law and the moral, expressive aspect. It appears that retentionists tended to express retributive morality in the death penalty debate and the abolitionists took the more pragmatic argument. Both sides include as many pragmatic and moral arguments as can be mustered.

Deterrence Arguments in 1973

The opening retentionist speech addressed the instrumental issue of deterrence by arguing that no accurate information can be gathered on the true number of people deterred by capital punishment. People who are in fact deterred do not commit a crime so are not in the statistics. Based on common sense or intuition, the statement that the death penalty is not a deterrent is to say that man does not fear death. "That is an incredible assertion."[22]

The Honorable Erik Nielsen countered the Solicitor General's comments by the general assertion that the use of statistics does not prove anything. He reasoned that since every capital case has been commuted, the data of the trial period is invalid. Furthermore, the hundreds of cases that are reduced from charges of murder to manslaughter "dilute" the statistics. Many retentionist speakers echoed these sentiments. The discrediting of statistics and statisticians, as obscuring rather than revealing the truth, was common.

Abolitionists cited statistics to demonstrate that the states in the United States without the death penalty actually have a lower murder rate than do retentionist states.

It was proposed that the absence of the death penalty actually reduces the risk to law enforcement officers of apprehending a murderer since the criminal would be less desperate. This argument is usually phrased in the opposite manner by retentionists who argue that without capital punishment a murderer has an incentive to kill witnesses. Some suicidal criminals, it was reasoned, may, in fact, kill in order to be executed by the state; thus, the existence of capital punishment could be a cause of murder. It was also argued that juries, reluctant to sentence a criminal to death, in fact err on the side of acquittal when capital punishment exists in the law books. Thus, the death penalty produced unwanted discrimination and the possibility of irreversible judicial error.

Summary

It can be fairly said that the deterrence report, spawned in the concern in 1967 for current research on the Canadian death penalty, probably had almost no effect in the 1973 legislation. In the first place, the modern statistical procedures which are necessary to marshall evidence to such a complex phenomenon are not readily understandable by those not specifically trained in their use. The Fattah Report is a very sophisticated rendition of this kind of research. Secondly, the report is cautious in its conclusions that the incidence of murder in Canada is apparently not dependent on the death penalty. While this corresponds to the evidence from studies accumulated and analyzed over several decades and countries and should be persuasive on the question of the general deterrent effect, it is not dramatic. It is not affirmative for abolition unless the assumption of the burden of proof on the retentionist is made. Many in Parliament did not make this assumption in 1973 and thus the report appeared to change very few retentionists of 1967 to abolitionists in 1973. Many retentionists did speak to the point of discrediting the report and since the government decided on a renewal of the five year partial abolition, rather than full abolition, the importance of the issue was diminished.

Parliamentary rhetoric on the deterrent effect, the Fattah report and social science in general are of some interest. Statistical rates and social scientific assumptions do not seem to lend themselves easily to dramatic and persuasive appeals. The counter-intuitive conclusion on a general deterrent effect of the death penalty seems almost unbelievable to some Parliamentarians. Some abolitionists were not content with responsible and conservative statistical analysis. They extended by speculation and logic some selected empirical findings to try to show that the death penalty actually encouraged certain kinds of murder.

One interesting theme emerges in a cursory analysis of these speeches. The retentionist, who generally emphasizes the symbolic and expressive functions of the law, assumes man to be a fully rational, self-interested person who calculates the potential risk to himself of committing murder and is deterred. The abolitionist, who tends to be more practical and instrumental in his view of law, argues for the irrationality of man from which murder is usually an underterrable crime of passion and even some proportion of murders are committed by persons in order to be executed by the state.

Like the abolitionists, the retentionists of 1973 took the positions of their 1967 counterparts. Apart from discrediting the deterrence research report, the retentionists took a similar moral stance regarding law as they had in 1967.

The Honorable C. A. Gauthier represents this approach. Mr. Gauthier commenced his debate with the reasoning that as man must safeguard his own life, so it is his duty to respect the life of others. Murder is prohibited by moral law as well as civil law. It is the duty of civil authority to uphold order, to impose penalties and seek redress from those who violate order and the law.[23] Capital punishment is necessary to ensure justice and the security of Canadian citizens. Punitive or vindictive justice requires that the punishment of a crime be as equal as possible to the crime committed. To ensure the security of Canadian citizens, the strongest restriction available against the violent acts of a murderer must be applied. Life imprisonment is not strong enough. These expressions demonstrate the personal convictions, values and belief of many of the retentionist speakers.

Mr. Gauthier does address the abolitionist concern of judicial errors and contends that such a rare possibility does not constitute reason to depart from the general principle.

Public Opinion and the Death Penalty[24]

The 1973 debate was characterized by more references to public opinion than in 1967. Not only were the national polls indicating an increase in public support for hanging over the years, but many Members were becoming more accustomed to polling as electoral and policy tools. Thus, several MP's took polls of their own constituencies on this question.

Frequently throughout the retentionists' speeches, the issue of public opinion polls, constituency surveys, and the Members' obligation to "represent" the wishes of his riding was asserted. However, many abolitionists countered with the position that a Member of Parliament is much more than a mere representative of his riding, much more than a rubber stamp of his constituency's wishes. The Rt. Honorable J. G. Diefenbaker eloquently argued the position that Members of Parliament must vote in consonnance with their conscience and use their responsible, mature decision-making processes for which the constituents elected each member. The abolitionists reiterated the famous speech by Edmund Burke in 1774 and quoted from it:

> Certainly, gentlemen, it ought to be the happiness and glory of a representative to live in the strictest union, the closest correspondence, and the more unreserved communication with his constituents. Their wishes ought to have great weight with him; their opinion high respect; their business unremitted attention. . . . But his unbiased opinion, his mature judgment, his enlightened conscience, he ought not to sacrifice to you – to any man, or to any set of men living.

Since the vast weight of public opinion seemed to support the retentionists' opinion, they continually put into evidence statistics of this sort and these were politically difficult to counter. At times, the abolitionists were reduced to disdaining the "mere" representative role of an elected official in the United States House of Representatives. Of course, this position can be easily reversed depending on the current public opinion poll. In 1966, some abolitionists fervently argued that the MP's should follow the dictates of their constituents. At that time, public sentiment in some areas seemed to favour abolition.

A closely aligned issue was the question of holding a national referendum. Retentionists frequently suggested that a national referendum would answer the death penalty question once and for all. On the other hand, some abolitionists protested that if the House of Commons merely let public opinion legislate, there would be no need for a House of Commons. With most, if not all, abolitionists against it, and many retentionists concerned about the precedent of a referendum, even if confident that the people would vote for it, the suggestion died.

Statistical Versus Case Studies

There are roughly two forms in which social scientific knowledge is packaged for consumption by those responsible for public policy. Leaving aside the authoritative, expert witness who might use either or both in coming to his opinion, there is a case study form and a statistical form. Some observations, which may be more general than the two legislative debates under consideration here, can be made.

Public opinion polling, a statistical form of information, seemed to be widely accepted by both retentionist and abolitionist as a true reflection of the public mood. Many of the polls and surveys reported in Parliament were so seriously deficient in design and execution that almost no conclusion about public opinion could be responsibly drawn from them.[25]

However, the political parties are now using public opinion polling extensively in conducting their election campaigns, so many MP's seem to be accustomed to, if uncritical about, their use. The statistical format of the report on the deterrent effect of the death penalty, on the other hand, seemed to generate confusion and some hostility among the Members. Some seemed to disbelieve it, although it was carefully done by independent, professional researchers.

The case study, on the other hand, looms large in debate on the death penalty. The well-known English case of Timothy Evans, who was hanged in 1954 and later vindicated when a person named Christie was found guilty of the crime, is a widely quoted abolitionist case study which shows the possibility of irreversible error. The use of case studies is popular in the Canadian House of Commons Debates. In 1966, the famous Steven Truscott case was recounted avidly by the abolitionists. Steven Truscott was a boy of 14 who, in 1959, was convicted of raping and murdering a 12-year old girl. Controversy raged over the case since no direct evidence connected the boy with the murder. The boy was admittedly in the company of the girl prior to the crime and the jury found enough evidence to convict. A popular book written on the Truscott case by Mrs. LeBourdias concluded that a judicial error was indeed made. Steven Truscott's sentence was commuted to life imprisonment, and in 1961, legislation was passed which prohibited the death penalty for youths under 18 years. The sustaining issue, however, was the fallibility of the administration of justice. A judicial error could have occurred and would have been irreversible if the death penalty had been carried out. Abolitionists repeatedly pointed to the Truscott case as a near miss.

The Truscott story demonstrates that case studies have the capacity to carry a poignancy and empathy into legislative debate that statistical studies cannot. The vision of a fourteen year old boy huddled in a cell for the condemned generated great sympathy.

The retentionists have many more varied case studies to choose from. Almost any recent, horrible murder can be described by retentionists. Many debators use crimes which occurred in their own jurisdiction or area in an attempt to "bring the issue home". A notorious case commonly discussed in the 1966 debate was the "Santa Claus" murder. A man named Marcotte, dressed in a Santa Claus suit while attempting to rob a bank, shot and killed two policemen. He was convicted of the crime and was granted two appeals. No court recommended clemency, yet his sentence was commuted to life imprisonment and he will be eligible for parole. In 1973, the notorious Head case was most popular in the debates. In

Vancouver, Charles Head was convicted four different times of sexual assaults on children. He was declared insane and sentenced to life imprisonment. He was subsequently released on a weekend pass and later convicted of killing a six-year old girl, the daughter of his prison guard.

These case studies illustrated the retentionists' conviction that the protection of society must remain paramount over rehabilitation of criminals. They also carried the same emotional appeal as the Truscott case. It is a fair guess that if the abolitionists could find a persuasive case of erroneous execution a full abolition bill could be passed in the Canadian Parliament.

In social scientific explanation, the case study has an important place. It shows the dynamics of a social event and is persuasive on how it is possible for something like a murder to occur.

Statistical studies often do not expose these sequential dynamics. However, social scientists generally recognize the serious limitations of case studies. The most important is that they give no information about the distribution of a phenomenon. How many Truscott, Marcotte or Head cases occur? Under what conditions do they occur? All these important legislative questions are unanswered by the case study. Each case may be very common or unique. Statistical studies, on the other hand, display distributions and, if carefully done with modern techniques, specify the degree of importance to be assigned to various facets of a problem. They are more effective at eliminating incorrect and partially correct, but widely believed, theories of human behavior than the case studies.

The study of the critical use of social scientific information in legislative and judicial matters is not yet well developed. In legislative committees, legislators have an opportunity to familiarize themselves with a variety of information, and its format, on the problem at hand. They also have trusted technical experts to translate the more esoteric information and evaluate its quality. The acceptance of this information is, of course, much easier if it does not contradict cherished beliefs or common sense. However, legislative innovation sometimes requires disputing with evidence and rhetoric the assumptions of yesterday. When "moral" issues loom large in a legislative decision, such as the death penalty, there seems to be a tendency to reduce reliance on special committees and debate matters in "committees-of-the-whole".

In these sessions, the productive and soundly critical use of social science statistical reports, for example, deterrence and public opinion reports, is quite low. At this point in the history of the death penalty in Canada, one is inclined to see Sellin as more right than wrong when he says:

> The question of whether the death penalty is to be dropped, retained or instituted is not dependent on the evidence as to its utilitarian effects, but on the strength of popular beliefs and sentiments not easily influenced by such evidence. These beliefs and sentiments have their roots in a people's culture. They are conditioned by a multitude of factors, such as the character of social institutions, social, economic and political ideas, etc. If at a given time such beliefs and sentiments become so oriented that they favor the abolition of the death penalty, facts like those presented in (research) paper(s) will be acceptable as evidence, but are likely to be as quickly ignored if social changes provoke resurgence of the old sentiments. When a people no longer *likes* the death penalty for murderers it will be removed no matter what may happen to the homicide rate. This is what happened in the past in connection with crimes against property.[26]

Summary of Debates

The Parliamentary debates of both periods are notable for the similarity of argument. The themes of these arguments are world-wide.

The early debate was not as politicized and party loyalty was not as evident as in the 1973 debates. The atmosphere of a politically insecure, minority government and some badly received efforts by the Solicitor General to modify the legislation in committee tended to focus some of the debate on the Parliament itself which was not evident in the early debate.

Both debates fused abolitionism with being soft on crime and retentionists exhibited righteous indignation at the coddling of criminals. The government's attempts at progressive penology, such as the temporary absence program, was criticized as jeopardizing the safety of citizens as well as allowing criminals to escape meaningful punishment.

On the other hand, abolitionists were unwilling to move to "tougher" sentencing such as a mandatory 25 year, no release sentence for capital murderers which might have produced full abolition, because it would be retrograde and inconsistent with modern penology. The House of Commons seems balanced on the sentiment for and against repressive legislation.

Both abolitionists and retentionists seemed to be depending on moral sources in the early debates, although the retentionists in both debates were more morally outraged. Thunderous and complex interpretations of biblical justifications for and against the death penalty were more common in the early debate. Fear of organized, gangland murderers was more apparent in the early debate, and kidnappers and hijackers were more salient in the later one.[27]

All death penalty debates act as a lightening rod for other issues. One theme in the Canadian death penalty debates on both the central and peripheral issues is that a fundamental difference in orientation to deviance is exposed. On the one hand is a practical, instrumental response. On the other, is a response which emphasizes expressions of evaluation.

Footnotes

[1] Hon. Jean-Pierre Goyer, *Capital Punishment New Material*: 1965-1972 Ottawa: Crown Printers, 1972), p. 0.

[2] Hon. Guy Favreau, *Capital Punishment: Material Relating to Its Purposes and Values* (Ottawa, 1965), Foreword.

[3] Thomas M. Sheehan, "Administrative Review and Capital Punishment: The Canadian Concept," *American Journal of Correction*, Vol. 27, No. 1 (Jan. Feb., 1965), pp. 24-25.

[4] There were wide differences in the volume of testimonials, the enthusiasm of relatives and community leaders and lawyers in bringing forward materials for use in the report and recommendation the remissions office would make to the Cabinet. The ex-director of this office reported that this was a known and largely unavoidable bias which might tend to favour the capital offender who was well placed in financial and community matters. (Personal interview, February, 1974) See Appendix II for a statistical comparison of those executed and commuted.

[5] *De jure* and *de facto* abolitionist countries are listed in "Capital Punishment" (United Nations Report, 1968).

[6] For an excellent discussion of the world-wide historical situation, see *Capital Punishment* (New York: Department of Economic and Social Affairs, United Nations Report, 1968).

[7] Jean-Pierre Goyer, *Capital Punishment, New Material: 1965-1972* (Ottawa: Crown Printers, 1972), pp. 19-23.

[8] Leading the legal attack on the death penalty in the courts have been the attorneys of the Legal Defense Fund of the National Association of the Advancement of Coloured People. These attorneys have come to rely on and become experienced with the use of social science materials since the 1954 school desegregation decision of the Supreme Court. Both the Witherspoon and Furman decisions were influenced by the use of social science evidence. There appear to be two broad areas of social science research related to the death penalty upcoming in the United States. One is on the effectiveness of mandatory sentencing at eliminating constitutionally impermissable biases, such as race, in the imposition of the death sentence. The other is the possibility that sophisticated attitude and public opinion research will be relevant to a direct Supreme Court decision on whether the death penalty is cruel under the eighth amendment. The court has indicated that "the evolving standards of decency that mark the progress of

a maturing society" can be the basis for a decision on whether a punishment is cruel, and that social scientific evidence is one way of assessing these standards. For a current review of public opinion on the death penalty as well as its potential relation to Supreme Court deliberations on the death penalty, see Neil Vidmar and Phoebe Ellsworth, "Public Opinion and the Death Penalty" in *The Standford Law Review* (1974). Also, Hugo Bedau, "The Future of Capital Punishment – A Problem for Law and the Social Science," Project Statement, Russell Sage Foundation, 1973 Mimeo.

[9] Arthur Koestler, *Reflections on Hanging* (London: Victor Gollancz, Ltd., 1956), p. 13.

[10] Arthur Koestler, *op. cit.*, p. 42

[11] C. H. S. Jayewardene, "The Canadian Experiment with the Penalty of Death" unpublished manuscript, Department of Criminology, The University of Ottawa, 1973, p. 173.

[12] Hon. Jean-Pierre Goyer, *op. cit.*, p. 1.

[13] Hon. Jean-Pierre Goyer, *op. cit.*, p. 3.

[14] Hon. Guy Favreau, *Capital Punishment, Material Relating to its Purpose and Value* (Ottawa: Crown Printers, 1965), pp. 4-5.

[15] There were 16 MP's who switched to support the modified proposal but 6 who switched to oppose it. The success of the 1967 bill depended on the absence of 64 of those MP's who had opposed the earlier abolition attempt, whereas only 25 of the supporters were absent. There are a total of 264 MP's in the Canadian House of Commons.

[16] Favreau, *op. cit.*, 1965; Goyer, *op. cit.*, 1972; UN Report.

[17] Ezzat A. Fattah, *A Study of the Deterrent Effect of Capital Punishment with Special reference to the Canadian Situation* (Ottawa: Queen's Printer, 1973).

[18] This point is explained in more detail later in this chapter, under the sub-heading "Public Opinion and the Death Penalty."

[19] These may not be permanent differences. If the deterrence research was supportive of the effectiveness of the death penalty in reducing murder, abolitionists might remain abolitionists but emphasize the humanitarian values theme of abolition. Likewise, if the detèrrence research showed that the death penalty increased the murder rate, as some have argued through encouraging some psychotics to kill in order to be killed, then some retentionists may change. If not, they could argue that the expressive function is worth some casualties.

[20] Several Progressive Conservative MP's reported in personal interviews, February 1974, that they felt their electoral gains in 1972 were a mandate for a strong stand on crime including the retention of capital punishment.

[21] Ezzat Abdel Fattah, *A Study of the Deterrent Effect of Capital Punishment with Special Reference to the Canadian Situation* (Ottawa. Queen's Printer, 1973), pp. 191-194.

[22] The House of Commons Debates. Vol. 117 (17) 1st Session, 29th Parliament, Jan. 26, 1973 (Ottawa: Queen's Printers), p. 694.

[23] House of Commons Debates, *op cit.*, p. 700.

[24] See Chapter 2 for an extensive discussion of public opinion polling on the death penalty.

[25] See Chapter 2 for a detailed discussion of this problem.

[26] Fattah, *op. cit.*, p. 194.

[27] As new crimes emerged and became widely known, the legislator is faced with the necessity of adapting present legislation or creating new legislation for it. This process of making explicit what it is about a "crime" which renders it serious or frightening exposes important assumptions and values about crime and society. See David B. Chandler, "Towards a Classification of Violence," *Sociological Symposium*, No. 9 (Spring 1973), pp. 69-83.

Chapter 2: Public Opinion and the Death Penalty in Canada

Public Opinion and Legislation

Any social science model is designed to simplify and highlight important features of the real life phenomenon about which there is curiosity. Models of the legislative process, or more general models of the relation between law and society, are, therefore, intentional over-simplifications.

One model which corresponds to democratic ideology depicts law as reflecting the beliefs and values of people. The assumption here is that legislative institutions create law that mirrors public opinion.

This over-simplification is not always even the goal of democratic legislatures, let alone a description of the reality of legislative activity. Often, a qualifier such as "enlightened" is added to public opinion. This means that a legislator, even after assessing what the public sentiment is (in itself a prohibitively difficult task), reserves the right to discount some of it as unenlightened. Thus, if a public attitude is based solely on a demonstrably false belief, or on an unacceptably, out-of-date value, even legislators who advocate the representative role for legislators feel released from this responsibility.[1]

However, as a general model of the relation between law and culture in western democracies, the correspondence between law and public opinion is probably the best, simplest description. This correspondence will obviously vary in strength depending on many other features of the society and legislature.[2] Capital punishment is a legislative issue for which public opinion is particularly important. Compared to most legislative topics, it is widely discussed in the press and legislators report heavy mail on the topic.

In this chapter, we describe and analyze public opinion in Canada on the death penalty at the time of the two Parliamentary debates. In Chapter three, the extent to which elected representatives reflect the public view is examined.

The Death Penalty: Public Opinion and Legislation

In his famous reader on the death penalty, Hugo Bedau expresses the opinion that the death penalty will stand or fall on the attitudes of people to it.[3] He feels that these attitudes will be independent of the crime rate, and further, that what people feel on such an issue is not entirely a function of what they know or consciously think. Although the first part of this formulation is probably more right than wrong, the degree of correspondence between legislative activity such as the repeal of the death penalty and people's attitudes is extremely complex. The political scientists in democratic societies spend much time and treasure attempting to lay bare the conditions under which elected representatives represent, when and how they respond to other pressures. Of course, the commitment of observers of democratic legislatures to an ideal of representativeness may vary with their personal position on the issue at hand. Those who favour the abolition of the death penalty but who believe that the citizens are mindlessly repressive see as admirable the elected representative who takes a "moral leader" orientation to his responsibilities and votes to abolish it.

On the other hand, a representative who is more responsive to powerful interest groups, wealthy supporters or party friends and influentials at the expense of the constituent, may be despised by the same observer. Whether one takes the Burkean[4] position on the representative role seems to depend largely on the issues at stake.

Before one can describe the extent to which Members of Parliament do or do not reflect public opinion, it is necessary to describe that opinion. This is very difficult. Those who claim to describe the public attitude on this issue have either not muddied the water with evidence or do not critically assess the evidence available. As will be seen in the following, the evidence of public opinion on the death penalty does not lend itself to simple interpretation.

The allegation that the public attitude to the death penalty is more a matter of feeling than rational assessment also points the way to a forest of complexity. In 1967, Bedau reported on an era in which there was relatively little opinion polling done on this matter. Approximately a decade later, there has been much more research done, but the capacity to be conclusive on the public view and its determinants is, if anything, further away.

Some Criteria in Evaluation of Public Opinion Evidence

There are several considerations in the evaluation of evidence which allow conclusions on the "public mind" to be drawn. In the first place, there is no such thing as the Public Opinion. The term, and nouns like it, are convenient concepts, conventional ways of referring to statistically aggregated individual acts (reports to an interviewer or checks on a questionnaire). As every student of social science knows, there is a large body of specialized knowledge and technique which is entirely occupied with the various ways of making sense of these statistics.

Sampling

Since limitations of time and money make it impossible to find out what each member of the public thinks about an issue, selecting a small number of people to study as a reflection of the whole population becomes a substitute. One of the most basic considerations in this field is, therefore, the problem of generalization from a sample to a population. It is the inference that can be drawn about a population from the empirical evidence of a sample drawn from that population which is important. It has been shown that, whenever a small number of people are drawn randomly from a large population, their behavior will provide a reliable basis for estimating the behavior of the population. Even more important is the development of reliable techniques of calculating the amount of error to be expected in such estimates. So the opinion of a random sample of people can be used to make estimates of the opinion of the population about the death penalty.

None of the evidence on public opinion on the death penalty meets the most rigorous standards of random sampling. Some is much better than others. The Gallup polls use a form of quota and area sampling which is reliable. They also provide information on the range of error to be used when making population estimates from their sample data. We can be confident that these estimates are useful in gauging the public mood.[5] They are certainly the best evidence available for this period of Canadian opinion.

The weakest sampling technique is where the phenomenon under diagnosis affects the characteristics of the sample. Almost no reliable generalizations about the population can be made under these circumstances. Unfortunately, many Members of Parliament fell unwittingly into using precisely this kind of sample to generalize about public opinion in their own constituencies. A typical example of this is as follows. An MP mails out to every household in his riding a questionnaire asking some question designed to indicate opinion on hanging. After some period of time, 10 per cent of the questionnaires have been returned, and it appears that very few additional completed questionnaires will be returned. When he tallies the responses, he finds that 85 per cent of the respondents are in favour of the death penalty. The Member is usually sobered, if he is an abolitionist, by the unexpected brutality of his people and worries about his plan to vote abolitionist when the flow of public opinion is a tiderace against him. The retentionist may as well be sobered by the brutality of the comments written in the margin but is encouraged that he has the will of the people on his side.

Such a "poll" of people's sentiment leaves more questions unanswered than answered and may, in fact, be very misleading. A trained social scientist immediately attends to the small proportion of questionnaires returned and their probable bias. For a host of unknown reasons almost all of the questionnaires are not returned. Included in these reasons may be a large number of people who do not have any strong view on capital punishment. That is, there may be no "public opinion" of any intensity on the question. Those who have a strong opinion in favour of the death penalty may, for a host of unknown reasons, be more likely to return the questionnaire than those who have a strong opinion against it. Because of the large number of unknowns in this situation and because there is little or no basis for estimating the reasons for these unknowns, the Member of Parliament knows only that 8.5 per cent of his constituents favoured the death penalty at the time they returned the questionnaire. He has no basis for making any wider generalizations. He may, of course, choose to infer that those returning the questionnaire had strong opinions and, therefore, the texture as well as the pattern in the material of public opinion should be attended to. MP's typically and naturally respond to the salience of political issues as measured by those who take the trouble to write or vote.

Stability of Opinion

Another problem in generalization from the evidence of a sample to a population is even more difficult. It is to estimate the extent of stability over time of an element of public opinion. Obviously, if people's responses to a question on a questionnaire are changeable from moment to moment, there is very little point in attempting to gauge these responses for public policy or any other purpose. By definition, attitudes, values, opinions and all the other concepts which are used to summarize people's responses to questions are stable attributes of personality, culture or some combination of these with social situations. Because they are stable over time, it is possible to predict the opinions of authoritarian personalities, English Canadians, and men in war, for example.

The practical issue, here, is the extent of stability of an opinion irrespective of changing circumstances. When a person's opinion is relatively unchanging under differing circumstances, it is probably anchored to some relatively unchanging attribute of his personality. When a group of people differ consistently from another group, their opinions are probably anchored in some shared cultural value. When people insist that "it depends on the situation" or when their opinion changes as the immediate social situation changes, their opinions are anchored more in social situations than in personality or morality.

The opinions in the latter case are more subject to natural and induced change than those connected to psychology and culture. Part of the social situation can be information and, as a result, opinions may depend at least, in part, on education or propaganda. Naturally, those who have a practical interest in the death penalty legislation and who are attempting to persuade others, are interested primarily in these potentially changeable opinions.[6]

In addition to an interest in the situational determinants, those whose inclination is towards more basic research are curious about the extent and circumstances of psychological and cultural determinants of public opinion. For these scholars, capital punishment can be but one indicator of a more general condition of repressive law,

Table 1:
Public Opinion on the Death Penalty in Canada in Selected Years*

Years Selected by National Opinion Polls	Opinion on the Death Penalty (Percentages)	
	For	Against
1943	73	20
1953	71	22
1958	52	33
1960	51	41
1965	54	35
1966	53	37
1970**	70	20
1971	63	30

* Solicitor General of Canada, *Capital Punishment: New material 1965-1972*, p. 69; also Ronald Manzer, *Canada: A Socio-Political Report* (Toronto: McGraw Hill, 1974), p. 287.

** Question specified opinion on death penalty for kidnappers of political figures.

punitive sanctioning, revenge or moral indignation. When cast in such general terms, the quest to describe and understand the opinion of Canadians on the death penalty is linked to major traditions of work in psychology, sociology and anthropology.

Finally, to reiterate one theme of this book. Opinions on public policy that are primarily anchored in cultural values could be seen as expressive. On the other hand, opinions which depend more on the practical assessment of the situation, could be interpreted as instrumental in origin.

The Canadian Opinion

From the time of the first opinion polls, the majority of Canadians have supported the retention of the death penalty. There appears to have been a steady erosion in this support until 1971 when the trend reversed and support increased. (See Table 1) There is no way of knowing at this point whether this is a stable shift or whether it is only an anomaly in the international, historical trend towards abolition. The pattern in Canadian sentiment, as tapped by the Gallup poll, corresponds to a similar pattern of decline in the United States over the same period. (See Table 2)

Table 2:
Public Opinion on the Death Penalty in the U.S.A. in Selected Years

Years Selected by National Opinion Polls	Opinion on the Death Penalty (Percentages) For	Against
1936	62	33
1953	68	25
1960	51	36
1965	45	43
1966	42	47
1969	51	40
1971	49	40
1973	59	31

All Polls are reported in the *Gallup Opinion Index* Dec. 1971, Report #78. 1973 is found in *Roper Public Opinion Research Center*, Vol. 1, Issue 8 (August 1973).

The Canadian public appears to be somewhat more inclined towards the use of the death penalty than are citizens in the United States. It is not unexpected that there would be broad correspondence between the two public attitudes on many questions. Not only do the two societies share roughly similar economies, populations, histories and cultures, but United States mass media is widely exposed to Canadians.

United States' politicians found the fear of crime widespread and a law and order program to be politically popular in the late 60's and early 70's. The Canadian elections of the same period did not dramatize these issues to the same extent. Moreover, the opinion of observers seems to be that North America was in the throes of some vague cultural shift which was expressing itself in increased punitiveness to the wrongdoer. Canada did not have, in the same period, protesting minority groups, campus violence and a polarizing war policy. It did, however, experience some terrorism in Quebec and an increase in political emphasis on the average Canadian. Possibly this evidenced the rising of the lower middle class paralleling the United States preoccupation in that period with the so-called "middle American".[7]

Although all of these poll results are produced by reputable professional polling organizations using properly administered sampling techniques, the reported marginal distribution tells us very little about the stability, strength, or reasons for the opinion and what sub-groups hold variations on it. We now turn to the task of decomposing the recent Canadian poll results on the death penalty. Evidence from several sources[8] will be marshalled to put into a more detailed and analytic picture of Canadian public opinion.

The Measurement of Capital Punishment Opinion

The simplest and most direct question about capital punishment is to ask the subject whether he or she approves of it, disapproves of it, or has no opinion. With minor variations, that is the question typically asked in national opinion polls. This technique is satisfactory for some purposes but does not allow inferences to be made about the strength or salience of the opinion to the subject or the details of any conditional use of the death penalty. To measure the salience of an opinion, many techniques can be used. One, which was developed specifically for assessing the intensity of opinion on capital punishment, secures the subject's approval or disapproval with fifteen statements of varying strength (as developed by independent judges) and, thus, can generate substantial measureable variation in intensity with which to compare groups.[9] Unfortunately, no national polls assess the intensity of opinion in North America.[10]

An interesting research project, which was designed to explore the psychological attributes behind capital punishment attitudes, reports on a wide range of responses which allow an inference of intensity to be made. A randomly selected group of 144 adults were interviewed in London, Ontario, in January, 1973. To the question "Which of the following four alternatives best describes your attitude toward the death penalty?", the following results were found. (See figure 1). The distribution of responses to this form of question generates a somewhat more interesting pattern than does a dichotomous choice. In Figure 1, we see that about 40 per cent of the sample takes an extreme and unconditional position on this question on each side. Sixty per cent of the respondents wish to equivocate and qualify to some extent. Of these, it is fair to say that 30 per cent are leaning heavily toward abolition, leaving the choice of executing or not in a *few* cases where it *may* be appropriate to some expert. One interpretation of these answers is that 53 per cent of the sample would not strenuously resist the removal of the death penalty. The significance of this lies in the fact that many polls of this period in Canada were reporting 70 to 90 per cent retentionist sentiment in the country. It appears that the dichotomous question can yield a false impression of unanimity and, perhaps, when it is corroborated enough by the widespread reporting of polls of very dubious design, an impression of enthusiastic support for the noose. Figure 1 can also show that 78 per cent of the respondents favored the use of the death penalty to some degree. But a reasonable inference is that the saliency of retentionist opinion is very low for 31 per cent and only moderate for another 29 per cent.

Figure 1: Attitudes Towards the Death Penalty*	Percentage of Sample
I am *opposed* to the death penalty *under any circumstances*	22%
I am *opposed* to the death penalty *except in a few cases* where it may be appropriate	31%
I am generally *in favour* of the death penalty except in a few cases where it *may not be* appropriate	29%
I am *strongly in favour* of the death penalty as an appropriate measure	18%

* From Neil Vidmar, "Retributive and Utilitarian Motives and Other Correlates of Canadian Attitudes Toward the Death Penalty," the *Canadian Psychologist*, Vol. 15, 4 (October, 1974), pp. 344-345.

Another variation on the way the death penalty opinion can be measured is to locate it in a social context. In the research reported above, the opinion was assumed to be a property, to some important extent, of the personality of the respondent.

Another assumption is that it will depend on the social circumstances and their meaning to the respondent. If a capital punishment questionnaire conjures an image of an inconsolable husband facing the noose after fatally injuring his wife, the response may be more abolitionist. If, on the other hand, the image is of the sneering, sadistic, child murderer, then hanging might be too good for him. Important variation may be preserved if questions are designed to put the respondent into a social context, and ask questions about a variety of responses he might have to the situation.

There is an interesting report in which a range of responses to a contextual question are reported for a Canadian sample.[11] In London, Ontario a randomly selected group of 1000 household heads received a mailed questionnaire in the summer of 1970. Of these, 45% were returned. The sample matched the population closely on certain known demographic features such as age, sex and religion, and so the researchers concluded that there was no apparent bias in the responding group.

Questions were asked about the person's opinion on the maximum, minimum and most frequent penalties for 30 crimes. The crimes were described in detailed legal language. For example, to measure the opinion on capital murder, the sample was asked what the maximum, minimum and usual penalty should be for a person who "intentionally causes or assists in causing the death of a law enforcement officer". These data are shown along with the responses to several other personal crimes in Table 3.

Capital murder receives the most punitive sentences from the sample: 70 per cent suggest the death penalty as the maximum sentence. However, only 36 per cent think it should be the usual punishment. Again, we find that when people are allowed to express a variety of responses to capital punishment, we find a very small proportion who wish that it is always used, even for the most serious crime (21 per cent) and only one-third (36 per cent) see it as appropriate in most cases. The majority (70 per cent) are in favor of it, but apparently have no strong wish to see it widely used.

Support for mandatory execution falls off rapidly as the seriousness of the murder diminishes under law. Only 13 per cent want mandatory execution when a citizen is intentionally killed (non-capital murder) and only four per cent see a passionate killing (2nd degree murder) as deserving the death sentence. All these data point to wide areas of discretion, contingency and low saliency in the public opinion on crime and, in particular, the opinion on the punishment for murder.

Table 3:
Percentage Distribution of Penalties Assigned to Personal Crimes*
(1970, 450 Responses from 1000 Randomly Selected Households in London, Ontario)

	No Penalty	A Fine	Probation	30 days or less	31 days to 6 months	6 months to 2 years	2 years to 5 years	5 years to 15 years	15 years or more	Execution	No Response
1. Capital Murder											
Most Frequent	–	–	–	–	–	4	8	14	31	36	7
Minimum	–	–	–	–	1	5	11	19	34	21	9
Maximum	–	–	–	–	–	–	2	5	19	70	4
2. Noncapital Murder											
Most Frequent	–	–	–	–	1	4	9	26	35	19	6
Minimum	–	–	1	1	1	6	14	29	29	13	6
Maximum	–	–	–	–	–	–	4	6	35	51	5
3. 2nd Degree Murder											
Most Frequent	1	–	2	1	1	9	24	30	19	6	7
Minimum	2	–	6	1	3	18	26	23	13	4	4
Maximum	–	–	–	–	1	3	8	21	39	22	6
4. Rape											
Most Frequent	1	1	2	4	8	21	27	20	8	1	7
Minimum	1	1	7	6	13	26	20	16	4	–	6
Maximum	1	–	1	1	3	28	20	27	29	5	5

5. Attempted Rape											
Most Frequent	1	2	4	4	12	24	26	16	6	1	4
Minimum	3	2	11	6	16	24	20	8	4	–	6
Maximum	–	–	1	1	4	12	25	25	29	3	5
6. Kidnapping											
Most Frequent	–	1	–	1	2	10	25	35	19	2	5
Minimum	1	1	2	1	8	19	27	22	13	1	5
Maximum	–	–	–	–	–	3	8	24	53	9	3
7. Robbery											
Most Frequent	–	2	1	3	12	28	32	15	2	–	5
Minimum	1	2	4	10	18	32	22	5	2	–	4
Maximum	-	1	-	-	2	10	24	37	21	1	4
8. Assault											
Most Frequent	1	15	6	17	19	21	11	4	2	–	4
Minimum	4	15	19	17	16	14	7	2	1	–	5
Maximum	–	2	2	7	12	25	25	13	9	1	4

* Craig L. Boydell and Carl F. Grindstaff, "Public Opinion and the Criminal Law: An Empirical Test of Public Attitudes toward Legal Sanctions," in *Deviant Behavior and Societal Reaction* (edited by C. L. Boydell, C. F. Grindstaff and P. C. Whitehead (Toronto: Holt Rinehart and Winston of Canada Ltd., 1972).

While the two studies cited above have sharply limited generalization, they do provide us with a glimpse of the complexity in attitude which stands behind the simple yes or no answer to the death penalty. It is apparent that this complexity is not chaotic but does take some form. We can now make some guesses about the attitude structure which might lie behind various responses on capital punishment.

A small number of people on each side of the question appear to have made up their minds. An estimate of 10 per cent to 30 per cent seems like a reasonable guess on the proportion who want to retain the death penalty without qualification and the same proportion want it abolished. Most dichotomous polls compare, in effect, the proportion of committed abolitionists to all others. The attitudes of this group of people with strong opinions on each side of the question, which could range from 20 per cent to 60 per cent in any time period or subgroup of the population, should be anchored in either relatively unchanging personality characteristics or in a relatively unchanging cultural milieu.

The remaining proportion, of between 40 per cent to 80 per cent of the population, has an opinion which is not anchored as much in relatively fixed attributes such as culture and personality but in the changeable social situation. The death penalty to these people has relatively low saliency, does not call forth strong moral or personal feelings, but rather a cooler, more pragmatic response.

This simplification of the material of public opinion, to highlight its design *and* texture, allows us to make some reasonable assumptions which are necessary if we are to proceed.

The most comprehensive and reliable information we have about the public's opinion on the death penalty is from the national polls. But we are now cognizant of the limitations in making inferences about the intensity and distribution of public sentiment from dichotomized responses on capital punishment. However, if we assume that the texture or saliency of the public opinion takes the shape of the hypothetical curve shown in Figure 2, we can make inferences about texture from information about the pattern.

On dichotomous questions, those whose endorsement of abolition is unqualified are compared to all others (those over the 70th percentile in Figure 2 to those under). Thus, an extreme position on the distribution of opinion, and very likely, saliency, is compared with the remainder of the distribution, which is broad both in content and intensity. It includes those who say they oppose the death penalty, except in a very few cases, and those who want to use it frequently. In addition, it includes those who are relatively unconcerned about the issue and those who feel strongly about it.

In most polls, there is a third choice of no opinion. But the issue

Figure 2
Hypothetical population distribution showing the relation between position on the death penalty question and its intensity.

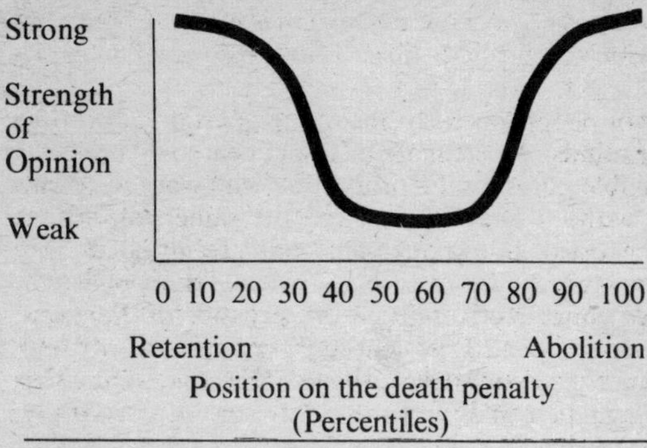

*It is conventional in social science to assume that the phenomenon under investigation can be usefully represented on one or more dimensions. It is well to remember that these are imposed on the phenomenon and are, sometimes, as in this study, not tested empirically for their fit with reality. Alternative mappings of the phenomena can be equally useful.

of capital punishment is so widely discussed and appears to be straightforward and simple. Relatively few people should report "no opinion". The no opinion category is more likely to contain those who have a wide range of contradicting opinions than those who are devoid of opinion. Saliency of "no opinion" holders should be low so they should appear in the middle and lowest portions of the curve in Figure 2.

Remembering that the dichotomous responses of polls represent at least a two-dimensional conception (saliency and content) of opinion on capital punishment and that percentages in Gallup polls have about a ±3 per cent variation because of normal variations in samples, we turn to the analysis of Canadian opinion.

From 1965 to 1972

This is the period upon which this book focuses. Because of the Parliamentary votes on the death penalty in 1966, 1967 and 1973, the opinion climate during this period becomes significant for both

Table 4;
Public Opinion on the Death Penalty in Canada from 1965 to 1972 Showing Ranges in Population Estimates

Year* Poll Taken	Sample Size	% of Sample in favour of Death Penalty	Lower Population Estimate −3%	Upper Population Estimate +3%	% of Sample against Death Penalty	Lower Population Estimate −3%	Upper Population Estimate +3%	% of Sample who had No Opinion	Lower Population Estimate −3%	Upper Population Estimate +3%
1965	(732)	54.8	51.8	57.8	35.8	32.8	38.8	9.4	6.4	11.4
1966	(658)	53.0	50.0	56.0	37.7	34.7	40.7	9.3	6.3	11.3
1970	(692)	70.1	67.1	73.1	20.2	17.2	23.2	9.7	6.7	11.7
1971	(720)	63.1	60.1	66.1	30.1	27.1	33.1	6.8	3.8	9.8

*Some variation occurs in the wording of the question measuring attitudes toward the death penalty in different years. 1965: "Some people say we should do away with capital punishment, that is, executing people for murder. Do you think we should or should not abolish capital punishment?" *CIPO Poll* #310; 1966; "If a national referendum were held today on the question of capital punishment, that is, executing people for murder, would you vote for retaining the death penalty in Canada or abolishing it?" *CIPO Poll* #317; 1970: "The criminal code was recently changed to abolish the death penalty except for certain crimes such as killing a policeman or prison guard on duty, on a five year trial basis. Do you or do you not think that the death penalty should be reinstated for the kidnapping of people in public or political life?" *CIPO Poll* 344; 1971: "As you may know, some years ago Canada suspended the death penalty except for the killing of prison guards or policemen on duty on a 5 year trial basis which comes to an end shortly. In your opinion, should the death penalty be brought back or not?" *CIPO Poll* #350.

social policy and social research. National Gallup Polls were taken on this question in 1965, 1966, 1970 and 1971. In the early period (1965 and 1966), the opinion was quite stable over time. (See Table 4.) Holding aside the poll in 1970 for the moment, we find that there was a shift towards retentionism in 1971 which is probably indicative of some real realignment of public opinion.[12]

The increase in retentionist sentiment appears to come from those who were previously undecided since the abolitionist sentiment may have changed only slightly[13] between 1966 and 1971. It is important to avoid unwarranted precision when interpreting even the most professionally executed opinion polls. Unfortunately, there have been no other polls of Canada on this question during this period, so corroboration of trends is absent.

The November 1970 Gallup poll asked a slightly more specific question than the general "should we abolish/reinstate the death penalty?" used in other years. It asked, hard on the heels of a widely publicized kidnapping and murder of a politician in Quebec,[14] whether the death penalty should be reinstated for the kidnapping of people in public or political life. This question, at this time, generated the strongest retentionist sentiment in twenty years. Apparently, the hourly reports of the disappearance of the politician, the efforts of the police, including martial law in Canada for a short period, the anguish of his family, and the apparent vulnerability of the nation's leaders to political terrorist groups had a very strong contextual effect on this question. Because one year later, the general question of retention received significantly less support than the specific question had one year earlier.

It is necessary to be cautious in even describing the extent of change in public opinion over time, let alone in analyzing it. The 1970 poll shows the effect of at least three factors on public opinion on capital punishment. A social climate of a heinous crime or one in which there is a sense of powerlessness of the authorities seems to increase retentionist sentiment. This is especially so when the wording of the poll questions captures the essence of that social situation. An apparent increase in general pro capital punishment sentiment had been occurring since some time after the polls of 1965 and 1966.

One interesting feature of the 1970 data is the substantial erosion of abolitionist sentiment (-17 per cent from 1966). This recovers somewhat more (+10 per cent) in the next poll a year later than does retentionist sentiment (-7 per cent). It was previously argued that those who took an abolitionist position on a dichotomous question were more likely to be closer to a pure ideological position of high salience than were their retentionist counterparts who would include more people who had low salience and a complex view of the death penalty. If such an analysis is true, we should expect less change through time among abolitionists than retentionists. However, comparing 1970 to its two temporally contiguous polls shows that there is more change in abolitionists.

One possible explanation is that abolitionist sentiment is not as determined by personality and culture as is retentionist sentiment, although both extreme positions are highly salient to their authors. Rather, the extreme abolitionist is persuaded by a combination of facts and beliefs which may, under extreme circumstances, be open to question. Another explanation is that there is an overlay of abolitionists upon a bedrock abolition position which is much smaller. Although the overlay clings through time, it washes away when an emotional tide on a particular crime occurs.

A plausible guess is that the kinds of people who most support the abolition position in general could identify with the victims of the Quebec tragedy. They are professionals who are urban and highly educated. To the extent that a person can identify with a victim under circumstances where the violence is imagined to be random (as in terrorism), and ordinary authority appears to be powerless to prevent it or protect the victims, his fear may weaken an abolition position.

The pattern of public violence which was widely reported in Canada and the rest of the world in 1973 changed from the 1960's to include airline hijacking, airport and athletic massacres and kidnapping. Middle class professionals could imagine themselves as vulnerable to this violence and powerless to stop it as never before. Although these widely publicized events probably have no effect on the actual chances of an individual in Canada dying, nevertheless, the middle class person may be personally threatened and some may shift away from opposition to the death penalty as a result.[15]

The priority of types of motivation to hold various opinions under various circumstances can be connected to one theme of this book. It may be that in personality matters, as in socio-legal evolution, we find the practical, instrumental approach to deviance replacing an earlier vindictive, expressive response. If a more basic vindictive attitude is progressively suppressed by rational and pragmatic considerations, then the overlay of instrumentality might be strained when a particularly atrocious crime is committed. Unfortunately, there is no empirical evidence for these notions on punishment. So these are only speculations about the personal attitude structure and processes which may underlie a public response on the death penalty.

The best estimate of the trend in public opinion over the past decade is that, in the mid-60's, there was stable approval of the death penalty at between 50 and 58 per cent of Canadians and stable disapproval of it, between 33 and 40 per cent. A period of instability in the late 60's seemed to generate an increase in support of the death penalty to between 60 and 66 per cent of Canadians and a lessening of abolitionist opinion to 27-33 per cent. Those who stated no opinion remained relatively stable, just under 10 per cent.

There are an insufficient number of national polls on the subject to be at all confident about the underlying pattern. It appears that stability followed by rapid fluctuation is indicated. Whether a consistent pattern of long-run decline in support for the death penalty can be discerned or not will depend on the availability of future polls. The trends underlying the recent polls can be a plateau, an increase or a decrease in public support for capital punishment. The best guess is a decline in the 63 per cent in favor in 1971 since, as will be shown shortly, the whole society is becoming more like the people who are, in certain characteristics, more abolitionist.

Education and Opinion on the Death Penalty

One orientation towards understanding different attitudes to legal punishment, in general, and capital punishment, in particular, is to suppose that there are two different, sometimes contradictory, rationales for legal punishment. One is an indignant, moralistic, vindictive, retributive justification which usually leads to harsh punishment. The other is utilitarian, pragmatic, therapeutic in its rationale. These two orientations approximate the expressive versus instrumental orientation to law which is the theme of this book, and the distinction in focusing on the crime, or the criminal, used in legal studies.

The amount of education that a person has received should be related to these distinct orientations. Education in North America typically means that a person is processed through institutions which generally reward rational, calculating, utilitarian, analytic understanding of phenomenon. The culture of science influences most higher education.[16] The prediction is, then, that with more education people will take a more utilitarian view of the death penalty than a retributive view. Since the weight of evidence[17] is that the death penalty probably does not deter murder, we would expect those with more education to be less supportive of the death penalty. In Table 5 we find trends which generally support this hypothesis in all polls of Canadian opinion.[18]

In 1965, there is no difference by educational level in those who would retain the death penalty; however, there is an abolitionist trend among those with higher education. In the other three polls, the differences in the predicted direction are quite consistent and

Table 5:
Public Opinion on the Death Penalty in Canada from 1965 to 1972 by Educational Level
(Percentage)

	1965				1966			
	Retain	Abolish	No Opinion	(N)	Retain	Abolish	No Opinion	(N)
SPS*	57.9	31.6	10.5	(114)	59.1	30.0	10.9	(110)
GPS	56.9	32.3	10.8	(130)	47.6	40.8	11.7	(103)
SHS	56.7	35.4	7.9	(240)	59.0	30.6	10.4	(173)
GHS	54.3	34.9	10.9	(129)	55.4	37.4	7.2	(139)
STS	54.5	36.4	9.1	(11)	33.3	66.7	0.0	(12)
GTS	40.0	50.0	10.0	(10)	50.0	33.3	16.6	(12)
SUN	59.4	40.6	0.0	(32)	34.3	51.4	14.3	(35)
GUN	57.9	36.8	5.3	(38)	40.6	53.1	6.2	(32)
Total	54.8	35.8	9.4	(732)	53.0	37.7	9.3	(658)

	1970				1971			
	Retain	Abolish	No Opinion	(N)	Retain	Abolish	No Opinion	(N)
SPS*	70.1	15.5	14.4	(97)	64.5	19.6	12.0	(92)
GPS	73.8	14.3	11.9	(84)	67.4	25.0	7.6	(92)
SHS	75.8	15.2	9.0	(223)	64.7	24.2	7.1	(238)
GHS	74.3	17.1	8.6	(140)	65.0	31.3	3.7	(163)
STS	47.1	47.1	5.9	(17)	52.6	42.1	5.3	(19)
GTS	66.7	33.3	0.0	(30)	77.8	22.2	0.0	(18)
SUN	56.9	31.4	11.8	(51)	44.9	53.1	2.0	(49)
GUN	51.1	44.4	4.4	(45)	44.2	41.8	14.0	(43)
Total	70.1	20.2	9.7	(692)	63.1	30.1	6.8	(720)

*S= Some; G = Graduate; PS = Public School; HS = High School; TS = Technical School; UN = University

N.B. – Subtotals do not add to grand total for each year as those for whom the information on education is ambiguous or absent have been excluded.

very pronounced. There is about a 20 per cent difference between those with the lowest education (some public school) and those with the highest (graduate of university) on both retention and abolition. Although there is no consistent pattern of those who had no opinion by education, those with the lowest education had a slight tendency to register more "no opinions".

Although the overall change between 1965 and 1966 is so small as to mean that the best guess is that there was no change in public opinion, there was significant changes by educational level. In particular, those at the highest levels became clearly abolitionist. They tend to hold to that tendency through the 70 and 71 polls. However, the tragedy of October 1970 appears to have affected university graduates identically to those with some grade school. Both become more retentionist.[19] Those who were the most affected in 1970 appear to be those in the lower middle educational levels who went to their highest levels of support for hanging.

The lowest education groups appeared to be more permanently affected by the events of 1970. In 1971, they remain high in supporting capital punishment; whereas those with high education recover their abolitionist tendency.

As the proportion of the Canadian population with higher levels of education increase in the future, greater support for abolition of capital punishment should be expected. This depends, of course, on a direct link between education and opinions on legal punishments as theorized earlier. It is difficult to know whether this is truly the case. Various factors can intervene, such as the occupations which educated people have, or their relative position in society which may complicate the effect and, hence, the forecast. Other unknown factors can be the true explanation of the apparent relation between èducation and opinion on legal punishment. The weight of empirical evidence from this and other research supports the importance of education as one ingredient of such opinions.

A similar finding on the relation between education and opinions on criminal law comes from an important study done in 1968 in Quebec.[20] This Prévost Commission report will be taken up in detail when we examine regional differences in Canadian opinion. There appears to be a pronounced difference (12.8 per cent) between those with some higher education (13 or more years) and those with very low education (0-7 years) in their support for the death penalty. A majority of those with high education favour a prison term for convicted murderers. This appears to be consistent with the national findings in 1966.

The overall trend of this poll in Quebec implies that the relatively low retentionist sentiment of 65 and 66 was also identifiable in 68. Thus, the abolitionist direction of the polls may have been stable

Table 6:
Public Opinion on the Appropriate Penalties for Murder by Level of Education in the Province of Quebec*

Type of Penalty	Education			
	0-7 Years	8-12 Years	13 or more Years	Quebec Average
Death Penalty	52.9	40.5	40.1	44.0
Life Imprisonment	35.7	51.2	47.7	45.8
Prison Term	10.3	7.6	10.6	8.9
Other and No Opinion	1.1	.8	1.6	1.3
Sample Size	(382)	(535)	(175)	(1098)

* Prévost Commission, *op. cit.*, p. 142

until October 1970 when the terrorism reversed it. However, the investigation of regional differences in Canada disputes this interpretation.

Regional Differences in Canadian Opinion

"Province" is one of the most widely used categories in common sense, history and journalism in Canada. It is widely believed that there are profound differences in culture and mentality across the various regions of Canada. Canadian humour often depends on the widely understood stereotypic character of these from the Maritimes or Quebec or the West.

The Gallup poll data do not reflect the kind of stability over time in opinion on the death penalty which would support the allegation of important consistencies of opinion within provinces and important differences between them. Either such regional consistency is absent or it does not apply to capital punishment. There are some patterns which will be described cautiously, but the reader is encouraged to bear in mind that differences of less than 6 per cent between comparisons probably reflect no population difference at all.

If, as a summary of Table 7, we rank each province in each poll from high to low on support for retention,[21] the patterns are simplified. Many provinces radically change in their rank from poll to poll. The most retentionist provinces tend to be Quebec and Alberta while those that rank lowest on support for the death penalty are Ontario and Manitoba, followed by Saskatchewan. The Mari-

Figure 3:
Ranking of Provinces on Support for the Death Penalty

	1965	1966	1970	1971
NS.	4	3	9	2
NB.	6	2	1	9
NFLD.	3	9	7	8
QUE.	2	1	4	1
ONT.	7	6	6	6
MAN.	9	7	5	5
SASK.	5	8	8	4
ALTA.	1	5	3	3
BC.	8	4	2	7

From "Retention" Column of Table 7.

time provinces have inconsistent patterns as does British Columbia.

Table 7 shows the specific effect of the Quebec kidnapping on the 1970 polls. On the average, the country increased support for the death penalty by approximately 17 per cent. Surprisingly, Quebec was the least affected. Its support for retention had increased sharply in 1966 and has been increasing steadily since. An irreducible 20 per cent of the Quebeckers polled seemed to be abolitionist.[22]

New Brunswick seemed to be the most affected in the 1970 poll and its neighbour, Nova Scotia, was almost unaffected. However, people in New Brunswick showed the least support for the death penalty only a year later in 1971. In 1970, British Columbia increased its support for hanging remarkably, but this support seemed to disappear one year later.

The inconsistencies and instabilities in these opinions, when compared by province and across time, are very great. The largest populations tend to be more consistent, so some of the variation may be a technical matter accountable to the variable size of the samples drawn in each province. However, one implication is that variations in questions can produce wide differences in results. The specific question on kidnapping used in 1970 produced very different results from adjacent polls in many provinces. One would normally think that the sentiment of populations would not be so variable on a subject. The Prévost Commission question was as general as most capital punishment poll questions (for instance, those of 65, 66, 71), but less extreme in that it asked what is an appropriate punishment rather than, in effect, what is the most extreme punish-

Table 7
Public Opinion on the Death Penalty in Canada, 1965 to 1972, by Province

	1965				1966			
Province	Retain	Abolish	No Opinion	(N)	Retain	Abolish	No Opinion	(N)
NS	55.2	27.6	17.2	(29)	55.9	23.5	20.6	(34)
NB	51.9	37.0	11.1	(27)	56.5	43.5	0.0	(23)
NFLD	60.0	20.0	20.0	(15)	28.6	42.9	28.6	(7)
QUE	63.2	28.4	8.3	(204)	70.1	21.7	8.2	(184)
ONT	51.7	39.4	8.9	(259)	44.9	45.3	9.8	(234)
MAN	44.7	44.7	10.5	(38)	38.9	50.0	11.2	(36)
SASK	53.7	39.0	7.3	(41)	38.2	50.0	11.7	(34)
ALTA	74.0	18.0	8.0	(50)	47.7	34.1	18.1	(44)
BC	44.9	47.8	7.2	(69)	48.2	46.8	4.8	(62)
Total	54.8	35.8	9.4	(732)	53.0	37.7	9.3	(658)

	1970				1971			
	Retain	Abolish	No Opinion	(N)	Retain	Abolish	No Opinion	(N)
NS	61.5	26.9	11.5	(26)	73.3	26.7	0.0	(30)
NB	88.9	3.7	7.4	(27)	44.4	33.3	22.2	(27)
NFLD	62.5	25.0	12.5	(8)	50.0	40.0	10.0	(10)
QUE	71.3	21.3	7.4	(188)	75.0	21.1	3.9	(204)
ONT	66.8	23.2	10.0	(250)	58.4	33.5	8.2	(257)
MAN	70.6	20.6	8.8	(34)	60.0	40.0	0.0	(30)
SASK	62.5	16.7	20.8	(48)	60.7	34.4	4.9	(61)
ALTA	74.4	20.5	5.1	(39)	63.3	23.3	13.3	(30)
BC	77.8	12.5	9.7	(72)	53.5	38.0	8.5	(71)
Total	70.1	20.2	9.7	(692)	63.1	30.1	6.8	(720)

ment you would like to have legally available. It showed 44.0 per cent support for the death penalty in Quebec in 1968, but was surrounded (66 and 70) by support of 70 per cent for the death penalty. Caution in making inferences about the meaning and stability of public sentiment, especially in various regions, is warranted by these data.

Rural and Urban Differences in Capital Punishment Opinion

Along with social class, one of the traditionally potent sociological explanations of a wide range of social phenomena is rural/urban differences. People are sorted and socialized by different occupations and life styles in rural and urban areas. These differences within the same culture and society show up in varying attitudes towards many features of life, including legal sanctions. The differences are not consistent and clear. In 1967, the Harris survey reported that rural people in the United States were more opposed to the death penalty than their urban counterparts.[23] However, in 1968 in Quebec, the Prévost Commission found that people who lived in rural areas were the most positively oriented to the death penalty. Table 8 shows that the respondents from Montreal and from smaller cities were the least supportive of the death penalty, whereas those on farms and in larger cities were more supportive.

Table 8:
Public Opinion on the Appropriateness of the Death Penalty for Murder in Quebec, 1968 by Rural and Urban Areas

Penalty	Montreal	Large Cities	Average Size Cities	Rural Areas	Quebec Total
Death Penalty	38.8	47.7	42.7	50.5	44.0
Life Imprisonment	50.0	44.0	47.9	39.5	45.8
Prison Term	10.1	7.6	8.7	7.7	8.9
Sample Size	(188)	(302)	(309)	(299)	(1098)

There is a slight but fairly consistent trend toward a stronger retentionist sentiment in rural areas than in urban areas as shown in the Gallup polls. While all of these differences are in the predicted direction, they are almost all within the 6 per cent difference which we have set as a rough minimum in estimating a difference in the population. The rural/urban pattern across several opinion polls on the death penalty is uneven and, while the Gallup polls on Canada produce consistent results in the expected direction, the differences are too small to make inferences with confidence.

Table 9:
Public Opinion on the Death Penalty in Canada, 1965-1972, by Rural/Urban Residence

	1965				1966			
Residence Type	Retain	Abolish	No Opinion	(N)	Retain	Abolish	No Opinion	(N)
Rural	66.2	26.0	7.8	(77)	55.7	37.1	7.2	(70)
Rural Non-Farm	63.3	28.9	7.8	(128)	53.5	40.4	6.1	(114)
Urban	52.9	37.4	9.7	(527)	51.9	36.7	11.4	(474)
Total	54.8	35.8	9.4	(732)	53.0	37.7	9.3	(658)
	1970				1971			
	Retain	Abolish	No Opinion	(N)	Retain	Abolish	No Opinion	(N)
Rural	71.2	20.3	8.5	(59)	82.8	12.5	4.7	(64)
Rural Non-Farm	73.0	16.2	10.8	(111)	68.8	25.0	6.2	(112)
Urban	69.3	21.1	9.6	(522)	59.6	33.3	7.2	(544)
Total	70.1	20.2	9.7	(692)	63.1	30.1	6.8	(720)

Capital Punishment and Ethnicity

Whether a person has a French or English origin makes a great deal of difference in attitudes on many topics including capital punishment. Ethnic background in Canada is often and reliably measured by asking prople what language they speak (at home, when they were growing up, etc.), and this is the measure used in the data reported here. It must be remembered that Francophones are concentrated in the province of Quebec and Anglophones elsewhere. Table 10 shows that the French are consistently more retentionist than the English in Canada, with differences in the polls large enough to reflect real differences in the opinion of the population. In addition, French opinion seems to be impressively consistent and stable over time, while English opinion fluctuates.[24]

Table 10
Public Opinion on the Death Penalty in Canada, 1965-1972, by Mother Tongue

	1965				1966			
Mother Tongue	Retain	Abolish	No Opinion	(N)	Retain	Abolish	No Opinion	(N)
English	52.8	37.7	9.5	(464)	44.7	43.9	11.4	(387)
French	64.6	26.5	9.0	(189)	69.0	24.0	7.0	(200)
Other	53.2	39.2	7.6	(79)	50.0	40.0	10.0	(71)
Total	54.8	35.8	9.4	(732)	53.0	37.7	9.4	(658)
	1970				1971			
Mother Tongue	Retain	Abolish	No Opinion	(N)	Retain	Abolish	No Opinion	(N)
English	69.5	20.5	11.0	(400)	58.3	33.1	8.8	(405)
French	75.0	14.6	6.4	(188)	73.9	23.1	3.0	(199)
Other	67.3	22.1	10.6	(104)	61.2	31.9	6.9	(116)
Total	70.1	20.2	9.7	(692)	63.1	30.1	6.8	(720)

French support for the death penalty is not only a regional phenomenon. The English within Quebec are quite different than the French. Table 11 shows the results of the Prevost Commission within Montreal. The English in Montreal were strongly abolitionist in 1968 as opposed to the French who were mildly abolitionist in

Table 11

Public Opinion on the Appropriate Penalty for Murder in Quebec (1968) by Language Spoken (Montreal sub-sample only*)

Penalty		**Language Spoken**	Montreal
	French	English and Other	Average
Death	44.5	29.0	38.8
Life Imprisonment	45.4	58.0	50.0
Prison	9.2	11.6	10.1
Other	.8	1.4	1.1
Sample Size	(119)	(69)	(188)

* Table 96, p. 210, Prévost Commission. The question referred to the language spoken most often in the family. For the sample as a whole, this resulted in almost 90 per cent French which made the analysis of the total sample difficult. Therefore, the analysis was conducted on the Montreal sample where the majority of English-speaking citizens of Quebec live. (Prévost Commission, p. 182.)

that survey. Since the proportion of English outside of Montreal is very small, we can now conclude that the rural/urban difference between Montreal and the rest of the province is largely a consequence of the concentration of English Quebeckers in Montreal. The French in Montreal support hanging at the same proportion as the whole province does.

It is tempting to speculate on punitive elements in French culture, since France is one of the few countries in Western Europe to retain use of the death penalty. This type of explanation is very difficult to sustain in general, but in particular, the histories and legal situation of Quebec and France are so different as to strain the credibility of such speculation. In addition, there is a very limited poll in France reporting less than 40 per cent in favor of the guillotine.[25]

Also, France has moved to a *de facto* abolition status with very few actual executions.

Another plausible explanation emphasizes the Roman Catholic Church, which has never opposed the right of the state to take life.[26] Often the leadership of local priests on public policy questions is important, and they personally have favoured retention. Also, the hierarchical authority orientation of the Church, with an

Table 12:

Public Opinion on Capital Punishment (1966 and 1971*) by Religion

	1966				1971			
Religion	Retain	Abolish	No Opinion	(N)	Retain	Abolish	No Opinion	(N)
Protestant	46.4	42.9	10.7	(308)	63.7	27.1	9.1	(317)
Jewish	20.0	60.0	20.0	(5)	63.6	36.4	0.0	(11)
Roman Catholic	60.2	30.3	9.5	(314)	66.9	28.1	5.0	(302)
Other	41.9	51.6	6.4	(31)	47.8	46.7	5.6	(90)
Total	53.0	37.7	9.3	(658)	63.1	30.1	6.8	(720)

* Questions on religion were not asked in the other (65 and 70) polls under study.

emphasis on obligations and penalties, may encourage a punishment orientation among members. Since the Roman Catholic Church is a major institution in French Canada, it could be argued that what appears to be the effect of French-Canadian culture on attitudes to the death penalty is really the effect of a high concentration of Roman Catholics.[27] Table 12 shows the effect of religious affiliation on death penalty sentiment in Canada. There were large differences between Protestants and Catholics in 1966, but a substantial increase in Protestant sentiment in favour of the death penalty brought the two groups to about the same position in 1971.

Those who are not classified in the major religions remain the most favourable to abolition. These include a large number who report no religion, and their abolitionist tendency is consistent with a secular, instrumental interpretation of their orientation to law. We would expect those who disdain religious affiliation to be less inclined to mobilize a morally expressive stance on law violation. Those with Jewish religious affiliation become unexpectedly supportive of the death penalty in 1971. A substantial change in this conspicuously liberal and humanitarian group would bear close scrutiny if it were not for the very small portion of the sample they constitute. We cannot be at all sure that any change has occurred in Canadian Jewery from these data.

It is impossible to disentangle the separate effects of French ethnicity and Roman Catholic religious affiliation in these data.[28] The best guess is that a cluster of attributes including French ethnicity, Roman Catholic religion, and a regional concentration of these factors at least partly accounts for the relatively strong repressive sentiment in French Canada. It is technically impossible with these data to disentangle the interaction of these factors and specify, with any warranted precision, their independent effects.

Capital Punishment Sentiment and Political Preference

One would expect that any issue of public policy in Canada could be interpreted on some left to right political spectrum and that the national political parties would also be arranged in some fashion across the spectrum.[29] It would not be surprising, then, if the supporters of various parties had quite different views on the death penalty. We would expect a rather common sense hypothesis to hold. Supporters of traditional and conservative parties on the right would be inclined to favour the death penalty more than the progressive or liberal parties on the left. Of course, the 1966-67 debate and vote in Parliament exposed the voting tendencies of MP's and leaders in the various parties to the electorate. The elections of 1968 and 1972 allowed the voters to express any resulting political preference.

In Table 13, we find that the capital punishment issue is less politicized than one might expect. However, the tendency is for the left to right party distinctions to forecast the death penalty opinion. Those who support the Creditiste, Social Credit and Progressive Conservative parties tend to favour hanging more than the Liberal

Table 13:
Public Opinion on Capital Punishment in Canada, 1965 to 1971, by Party Supported in Previous Election

	1965				1966			
Party	Retain	Abolish	No Opinion	(N)	Retain	Abolish	No Opinion	(N)
LIB	53.0	39.0	8.0	(249)	52.8	35.4	11.8	(212)
PC	64.2	27.2	8.7	(173)	55.2	37.6	7.2	(125)
NDP	48.8	44.2	7.0	(43)	48.1	44.3	7.6	(79)
Creditiste	—	—	—		75.0	25.0	0.0	(4)
Soc Cred	51.3	41.0	7.7	(39)	58.3	37.5	4.2	(24)
Total	54.8	35.8	9.4	(732)	53.0	37.7	9.3	(658)

	1970				1971			
Party	Retain	Abolish	No Opinion	(N)	Retain	Abolish	No Opinion	(N)
LIB	73.5	19.5	6.7	(268)	65.6	28.0	6.4	(218)
PC	82.7	11.8	5.5	(110)	67.8	18.3	13.9	(115)
NDP	47.4	35.4	16.7	(48)	55.8	44.2	0.0	(43)
Creditiste	90.9	9.1	0.0	(11)	77.8	27.2	0.0	(9)
Soc Cred	88.9	11.1	0.0	(9)	100.0	0.0	0.0	(16)
Total	70.1	20.2	9.7	(692)	63.1	30.1	6.8	(720)

N.B. Columns do not add to total N because some miscellaneous categories such as 'refused to answer', "don't know", "don't remember", and "too young to vote" are excluded.

and New Democratic Party supporters. There is a clear tendency for New Democrat supporters to be less favourable under all conditions to the death penalty than the country as a whole. But these supporters are by no means clearly abolitionist. Their large proportion of abolitionists seems to be firm, however, withstanding the swing to favouring hanging evident in the 1970 poll. The Conservative supporters of abolition appeared to shrink in 1970 and 1971 being reduced to less than 20 per cent from their high of 37 per cent in 1966. Although there is relatively small overall differences in the supporters of the Liberals and Conservatives on the death penalty, the Liberals seem to have a stronger core of abolitionists.

The supporters of the Creditiste Party have extremely strong retentionist views, as do the remaining supporters of the dwindling Social Credit Party.

Overall, the two center parties' supporters tend to differ slightly in the predicted direction; the New Democrats' large majority of abolitionists are anchored, probably by liberal political ideology, to an irreducible 40 per cent, and the Quebec Creditistes are strong retentionists.

Summary

The national polls in Canada on the death penalty question must be interpreted cautiously. It is particularly important for legislative representatives to attend to the variability over time of these indicators of the public mood. The interpretation of polls for impact on the legislative process must take into account many considerations including the enlightenedness of the opinion and its stability over time. If people change their opinions rapidly (there is some evidence in the 1970 polls that they do), legislative responsiveness to the public will should be cautious.

Canadian opinion on the legal availability of capital punishment as a maximum penalty is favourable. It appears that most people do not want it used very much, if at all, and that people tend to allow that experts should decide on its use. The saliency of opinion on the death penalty is relatively low for the majority of Canadians. It seems to be a legislative issue which taps conflicting and incoherent feelings rather than coherent and consistent opinions in the public. It changes over time and seems to be responsive to widely publicized crimes. There is some regional difference in Canada which may be attributed to other factors. People who live in Quebec and Alberta seem to be consistently more inclined to favour the death penalty than people elsewhere who are less consistent. This discernable pattern in an otherwise confusing array of regional inconsistency is probably best explained by religion. The concentration of a relatively authoritarian Roman Catholic Church in Quebec and a relatively high proportion of authoritarian Fundamentalist religious sects in Alberta may be the partial cause of death penalty support in these areas.

Those voting for the socialist NDP tended to be the least in favour of the death penalty and to be impressively consistent over several opinion polls. Supporters of the Ralliement des Creditistes were also consistent, but for retention. Because of their concentration in rural Quebec, it is difficult to interpret their support of the death penalty as an ideology separate from the influences of rural, French Catholic life. In the case of NDP support, an ideological basis for their position is more plausible. However, the support for abolition is unexpectedly weak (between 35.4 per cent and 44.3 per cent) in this consciously humanitarian political party. The major parties seem to encompass approximately the same range of opinion on the death penalty. The issue is unusually apolitical.

Protestants and Catholics, English and French Canadians have differences on the question of the death penalty. The French and Catholic populations support it more. However, these differences are sometimes not large and seem to be unstable. Those who profess no religion are consistently the least in favour of the death penalty.

Finally, unlike the United States, there is a tendency for people who live in rural areas of Canada to support the death penalty more than their urban counterparts.

The tendency for the irreligious, socialist voter, highly educated, urban dweller to be least inclined to support the death penalty is consistent with the interpretation made in this book that such support requires more of a non-rational, expressive, moralistic orientation to law.

Some Sources of Public Opinion

The preceding discussion has attempted to acquaint the reader with a description and analysis of what is reliably known about Canadian public opinion on the death penalty. The discussion has, unfortunately, been full of disclaimers, qualifiers and cautions. It is a matter ultimately of judgement and guess work when the murky "facts" of public opinion are subjected to quantitative analysis intended to point to associated social patterns and, ultimately, to some prediction and explanation. There is grave danger in going too far on too little when public policy and legislative decisions may be involved.

There has been some empirical research which is oriented to the psychological study of attitudes towards the death penalty. We can feel much more confident about the "facts" of these studies since the sampling and measurement techniques are typically explicit and detailed. Of necessarily limited generality, these studies can shed light on some of the personality factors which may lie behind the tendency for a person to take a more or less severe stand towards law violators. There are very few of these studies in Canada. The concept of the authoritarian personality serves to unify several studies on this topic in the United States. To quote Vidmar:[30]

> . . . there is a substantial body of psychological literature showing that samples of U.S. adults who favour the death penalty are more likely to be authoritarian, dogmatic and conservative in their political views than persons who are against the death penalty.[31]

Other studies have shown authoritarian persons to be more punitive toward others[32] and to express greater degrees of retributive motives in attitudes toward criminal punishment[33] than non-authoritarian persons. Vidmar goes on to argue the relation of capital punishment endorsement to a relatively low regard for values such as equality, forgiving and loving.[34] In addition, he links pro-capital punishment sentiment to prejudice, ethnocentrism and a low evaluation of the value of equality through the research on the authoritarian personality.

It is important to note that these attributes which tend to cluster in particular personalities are conceived, by experts in this research, to be dimensions. They are thought of in terms of more or less, rather than present or absent. Thus, these characteristics are tendencies which can be more or less pronounced in various people.

Vidmar classifies respondents who support the death penalty on the basis of their reasons for supporting it. Some support it for utilitarian reasons; that is, they believe it reduces crime. Others supported it for retributive reasons.[35] After careful analysis of a variety of measures of this motivation to support the death penalty, Vidmar concludes that over half of those supporting it had a largely retributive motive as their basis of support. This retribution tendency extended to other areas such as school discipline. In addition, those who supported the death penalty were inclined toward being dogmatic, punitive and prejudiced against French Canadians, Indians and hippies. Vidmar found a surprisingly small and inconsistent relation between the fear of crime and death penalty opinion. This widely assumed explanation may be more complicated than previously supposed.

The thrust of Vidmar's important research is that opinions on capital punishment are located in broader orientations toward deviance. This orientation could be seen as being punitive, repressive and retributive. It is an orientation which emphasizes the evaluative and symbolic rather than the practical or utilitarian reasons for legal punishment. This orientation seems to have a consistent pattern with other attitudes such as ethnocentrism and dogmatism.

It is here that two themes are imposed on Vidmar's research. One is the problem raised early in this chapter which is the neglected area of attitudinal saliency in capital punishment research. Vidmar's research points the way to a theory of the intensity of capital punishment opinion. We would expect that attitudes toward the death penalty would be strongly held to the extent that they were a facet of a broader personality organization having as its theme higher than normal levels of authoritarianism.

The second and more important theme relaxes a radical psychological assumption that attitudes are features of personality which, in adults, are largely unresponsive to the socio-cultural milieu. When we find wide differences in support for the death penalty over time and in different regions, religions, ethnic and education groups, we must conclude that these attitudes are open to at least partial modification or even, determination by the social environment. One theme of this research, explored in detail in Chapter 4, is that social homogeneity creates the social response of repression of deviance. The situation of ethnocentrism, dogmatism, prejudice, punitiveness and a concern for the evaluative and symbolic seem to be precisely what Durkheim had in mind in the simple society with mechanical solidarity. Similarly, in the theory of moral indignation, as a consequence of lower middle class life, Ranulf intepretes these punitive motives as emanating from a social situation. Sutherland argues that punitiveness is more characteristic of relations between adjacent social classes than those that are removed from each other. Ross argues the opposite of Durkheim, in that he thinks that societies that are more complex and conflictive will generate more repression than homogeneous ones.[36]

The important point is that a wide variety of theorizing at both the psychological and social levels of analysis can be joined. A fusion of evidence gathered with psychological assumptions and with sociological assumptions is possible.[37] In spite of the different traditions, the evidence forms a pattern of variation in both personality and social correlates to death penalty support.

The element of indignation, envy, authoritarianism and punitiveness which emerges from both traditions illuminates our search for a theory of saliency or intensity of attitudes to the death penalty. A cursory glance at letters to newspapers and reports from Canadian Members of Parliament indicate that there is often substantial intensity in the views of those who wish to retain the death penalty. The theme of moral indignation and law as primarily an expression of evaluation predicts not only to those who will hold particular versions of the range of opinion on the question but also to the intensity with which it will be held.

Thus, theories of both the distribution and the salience of death penalty public opinion can be adduced. Some classic formulations not only appear to satisfy the basic sociological propensity to locate cause in social structure, but also to forecast to both distribution and intensity of repressive sentiment. The Durkheimian formulation of Chapter 4 on repressive sentiment also appears to bear up under empirical examination.

Footnotes

[1] A detailed discussion of the variety of orientations to the elected representative's role occurs in Chapter 3.

[2] The conditions under which legislation is more or less reflective of a "majority" sentiment are discussed in Chapter 3.

[3] Hugo Adam Bedau, *The Death Penalty in America*, (New York: Doubleday & Company, Inc.), 1967.

[4] Edmund Burke (1774) is the most widely cited advocate of the independence of the elected office holder.

[5] The Gallup poll selects areas at random within pre-selected regions of Canada. Thus, all provinces and rural and urban areas are included. Then, interviewers are required to fill quotas of age and sex groups in these areas. Error estimates become larger as analysis reduces the size of the group being analyzed.

[6] Sometimes the psychological and cultural correlates of a death penalty opinion are used to discredit it. For example, some abolitionists are successfully accused of being socialist ideologues. Often retentionist opinion is associated with authoritarianism. The demonstration that retentionism is "unenlightened" public opinion is one research strategy of abolitionists in the United States. This strategy focusses on attempting to show that those who favour retention also tend to favour an unacceptable position on more basic values, like the restriction of democratic rights.

[7] A major theory of repression connects the rise of the lower middle class to punitiveness. See Svend Ranulf, *op. cit.*

[8] All sources and research procedures are described in Appendix I. Important data sources and analytic procedures will be indicated when they are raised.

[9] Joseph K. Balogh and Mary Anne Mueller, "A Scaling Technique for Measuring Social Attitudes Toward Capital Punishment", *Sociology and Social Research* (Oct. 1960), p. 24.

[10] For an example of this type of research done outside of North America, see: Podgorecki, "Prestige of Law", *Acta Sociologica*, no. 10 (1966).

[11] Craig L. Boydell and Carl F. Grindstaff "Public Opinion and the Criminal Law: An Empirical Test of Public Attitudes Towards Legal Sanctions". in *Deviant Behaviour and Societal Reaction* (edited by C. L. Boydell, C. F. Grindstaff and P. C. Whitehead) (Toronto: Holt, Rinehart and Winston of Canada Limited, 1972).

[12] When comparing the percentages in various years, it is important to remember that each percentage reflects an estimate of the population percentage if everyone were asked the question. Thus, in 1966, between 56.0 and 50 per cent of the population favored the death penalty, between 34.7 and 40.7 per cent opposed it. In 1971, between 66.1 and 60.1 per cent of the population favored it and between 27.1 and 33.1 per cent opposed it. A difference of more than 6 per cent can be considered as reflecting a real population difference. Less than a 6 per cent difference cannot be so considered.

[13] Of course, this yields the most conservative estimate of real population differences. The real differences might be at the other extreme of the range of sampling variation. There might have been a 16.1 per cent increase in retentionist sentiment or a 4.1 per cent increase.

[14] James Cross, the British Ambassador, was kidnapped and later released.

Pierre Laporte, a Minister of the Quebec Government, was kidnapped and later killed. Both crimes were committed by a radical separatist organization in Quebec.

[15] Vidmar's research reports a complex relation between fear or perceived threat and death penalty attitudes. (See the section later on in this chapter under the heading "Some Sources of Public Opinion".)

[16] Although education is alleged to have an independent effect on opinion, there is some possibility that, as the educational level of the total population increases over time, comparing people on years of education also sorts them into age groups. The ideal way to check this is to control on education and test the effect of age. We have an indication that age has no continuous effect on opinion on the death penalty. The Prevost Commission finds that 26 per cent of those between 18 and 24 years support the death penalty but above that age, each age group approximates the provincial average of 44 per cent support.

[17] An important problem is implied here which is also discussed in the introduction. There are roughly three sources of evidence on the question under deterrent effect. One is the quantitative reporting of murder rates under varying conditions of penalties which almost universally show no effect of punishment on murder rate. Another is the authoritative opinion of someone who has contact with crime and murders. Such people as policemen and prison superintendents fall into this category. In the past in North America, these authorities have supported capital punishment more than they have opposed it. And finally, there is personal experience and the judgement based on projecting oneself into an experience or situation. Most personal judgement on this takes the view that "I would think twice about murdering someone if I knew I might be hanged". When both authority and personal judgement tend to produce conclusions on the death penalty which are contrary to scientific, empirical evidence, those who have not been taught to value the superiority of objective information in arriving at conclusions will tend to be swayed by authority and personal experience. The "scientific" critical training of higher education should foster reliance on objective information as well as increase the utilitarian orientation to legal punishment.

[18] Vidmar (*op. cit.* p. 44) reports a statistically significant relation between having more education (some university) and being against the death penalty.

[19] It is difficult to marshall these data to clearly bear on the forecast made earlier. As abolitionists, those with high education should not be moved by the October kidnapping; as professionals identifying with the victims, they should be. These may countervail each other and produce the average effect noted in Table 5.

[20] La société face au Crime, Annexe 4, La justice criminelle. Sondage d'opinion publique sur la justice criminelle au Québec (Montreal, 1969), p. 142.

[21] These ranks are derived from the retention column of Table 7. One is the highest percentage for retention and 9 is the lowest.

[22] It should be pointed out here that, although these findings for Quebec are

impressively consistent, the Prévost Commission, with scientifically selected samples and a more detailed question, find that only 44 per cent of Quebeckers think the death penalty is an appropriate penalty for murder in 1968.

[23] Hugo Bedau, *The Death Penalty in America* (Anchor Paperback, 1967), p. 241.

Opinion on Death Penalty by Size of Place, USA. Language Spoken (Percentage)

Size of Place	Favor	Oppose	Not Sure
City	37	46	17
Suburb	48	37	15
Town	30	56	14
Rural	33	52	15
Total	38%	47%	15%

[24] This may reflect the fact that French opinion tends to be geographically concentrated, while English opinion will contain regional variation.

[25] Goyer, *op. cit.*, p. 22.

[26] This has been a traditional argument which is often repeated in debates in the House of Commons. However, the Canadian Catholic Conference, which is the association of Roman Catholic Cardinals, Archbishops and Bishops, took a position favouring the suspension of the death penalty in January, 1973.

[27] The factor of the *concentration of* religion of ethnicity, apart from the content of the beliefs and values, is part of an important theory of repression. It is examined in detail in Chapter 4.

[28] The ideal way to examine these explanations is to examine the effect of both religion and ethnicity together on death penalty opinion. However, there are several problems with this under these conditions. First, there is the implication of more precision in these population estimates than is warranted by these polls. Secondly, the size of some cells in the analysis would be too small for reliable comparisons to be drawn. When Tables 10 and 12 are compared, the French support of the death penalty is always higher than the total Roman Catholic support (69.0 and 60.2 in 1966 and 73.9 and 66.9 in 1971), and the English support is always lower (44.7 and 46.4 in 1966 and 58.3 and 63.7 in 1971) than the total Protestant support. This indicates that, if all French are Roman Catholic, non-French Catholics are less retentionist. Although Catholics may be more retentionist than Protestants (there is no significant difference in 1971) these differences probably do not explain the French/English differences.

[29] Most Canadian political commentators generally agree that the small So-

cial Credit and Creditiste parties are right wing politically, and that the New Democratic Party is on the left. The other two parties are wide ranging, accommodative parties in which each occupies a substantial and overlapping portion of the centre. The Progressive Conservatives, however, lean to the right and the Liberals to the left.

30 N. Vidmar, *op. cit.*

31 V. R. Boehm, "Mr. Prejudice, Miss Sympathy, and the Authoritarian Personality: An Application of Psychological Measuring Techniques to the Problem of Jury Bias." *Wisconsin Law Review*, 1968, pp. 734-750; R. F. Crosson, *An Investigation into Certain Personality Variables among Capital Trial Jurors*. Unpublished Ph.D. Dissertation, Western Reserve University, 1966; F. Goldberg, "toward Expansion of Witherspoon: Capital Punishment, Jury Bias and Use of Psychological Data to Raise Presumptions in Law," *Harvard Civil Rights Law Review*, 1970, 5, p. 53; G. Y. Jurow, "New Data on the Effect of a Death Qualified Jury on the Guilt Determination Process," *Harvard Law Review*, 1971, 84, pp. 567-611; M. Rokeach and D. D. McLellan, "Comment: Dogmatism and the Death Penalty: A Reinterpretation of the Duquesne Poll Data," *Dequesne Law Review*, 1970, 125; A. H. Roberts and R. Jessor, "Authoritarianism, Punitiveness, and Perceived Social Status," *Journal of Abnormal and Social Psychology*, 1958, 55, pp. 311-314; as cited in N. Vidmar, *op. cit.*

32 R. Epstein, "Authoritarianism, Displaced Aggression, and Social Status of the Target," *Journal of Personality and Social Psychology*, 1965, 2, pp. 585-589; R. Epstein, "Aggression Toward Outgroups as a Function of Authoritarianism and Imitation of Aggressive Models," *Journal of Personality and Social Psychology*, 1966, 3, pp. 574-579; H. E. Mitchell and D. Byrne, "Minimizing the Influence of Irrelevant Factors in the Courtroom: The Defendant's Character, Judge's Instructions and Authoritarianism," Paper presented at the Midwestern Psychological Association Convention, Cleveland, Ohio, May, 1972; H. E. Mitchell and D. Byrne, "The Defendant's Dilemma: Effects of Juror's Attitudes and Authoritarianism on Judicial Decision," *Journal of Personality and Social Psychology*, 1973, 25, pp. 123-129; A. H. Roberts and R. Jessor, "Authoritarianism, Punitiveness, and Perceived Social Status," *Journal of Abnormal and Social Psychology*, 1958, 55, pp. 311-314; as cited in N. Vidmar, *op. cit.*

33 N. Vidmar and L. Crinklaw, "Retribution and Utility as Motives in Sanctioning Behavior," Paper presented at the Midwestern Psychological Association convention, Chicago, Illinois, May, 1973.

34 M. Rokeach and N. Vidmar, "Testimony Concerning Possible Jury Bias in a Black Panther Murder Trial," *Journal of Applied Social Psychology*, 1973, 3, pp. 19-29.

35 The 1971 Gallup poll finds (The Gallup Report, Feb. 2, 1972) that, of those who reject capital punishment, most do so for "moral" reasons, in the sense that two wrongs dont make a right. Only 13 per cent believe that it has no deterrent effect. However, 64 per cent of those favouring it specify its deterrent effect as their reason for supporting it. Vidmar pro-

perly points out both the superficiality of these responses as well as their "acceptability" in discussing his own data which depart from this tendency.

[36] These are taken up in more detail in Chapter 4.

[37] For a fine example of this type of integrative research on a related topic, see S. M. Lipset, *Political Man* (Anchor Books, 1963), especially Chapter 4, "Working Class Authoritarianism," pp. 87-116.

Chapter 3: The Representative and the Constituency

The Assumption that the Representative Represents

Chapter four of this research project is the examination of the Durkheimian based notion that sentiment in areas in which the population is homogeneous would be more repressive. This classic notion is examined with the assumption that the elected Member of Parliament would reflect this sentiment in his vote on the death penalty. And this is the most reasonable of all assumptions about the relations of the representative to his constituents. It does not mean that in every case, and for all issues, the MP will reflect popular sentiment. Much of the time he won't know what that sentiment is. Even on issues which he has some feeling about the mood of his constituents, he will have little precise information on the distribution of the opinion or how strongly it is held.

It should matter a great deal, in practical politics, if the public policy is strongly dividing a constituency or whether those who feel strongly about an issue always vote against you anyway.[1]

There are endless combinations of the distribution and saliency of public opinion (see Chapter 2 on public opinion polls) and strategies, trade-offs and obfuscations that the representative can employ to survive. But for most issues and over the aggregate of Members of Parliament, it is reasonable to assume a tendency to congruence in the vote of the MP and the policy preference of the constituency. He will have been elected and his party will have been supported at least in part because of policy similarities to a plurality of the constituency. In this section, we marshal evidence to decompose and examine this assumption, on the capital punishment votes of 1966 and 1973 in Canada.

Western democracies have assumed the normative propriety and factual truth of substantial constituency influence over the legislative representative.

Two of the major controversies in both normative political theory and in empirical political science polarize on this problem. To what extent should, and is, the legislative representative an instructed delegate of his electors? Is he elected, or should he be elected, to represent the constituents' interests but not their will, as Edmund Burke proposed. Another controversy opposes the instructed delegate to the representative of a national party with a national policy and constituency of which the local riding is but a numeric component. We leave the normative controversy to others and turn to the scientific.

As one would expect, the empirical legislative world contains elements of all three orientations. A major study[2] of this problem in the United States uncovers some association between an emphasis on each of the three facets of the representative's role and the public policy issue. Miller and Stokes found that the instructed-delegate was most pronounced for civil rights' matters, the responsible national party orientation for welfare policy, and the Burkean independence characterized foreign policy legislation. To the extent that a capital punishment debate is like a civil rights debate in its moral concerns, there is indirect support for the assumption in this research that the Canadian MP will see himself as responsible to his constituents on this issue.

A cautionary note is in order here lest the false impression of certainty on these facets of the legislator's orientation be conveyed. The work of Miller and Stokes is only part of an era of decomposition and testing of these relationships. For example, the dynamic by which a legislator comes to represent his constituency on civil rights matters is found to be more a matter of his altering his attitudes (and voting behavior) in response to his accurate perception of his constituency opinion, than his being elected in the first place because of similar attitudes.[3] For our purposes, it is sufficient to see the major outlines of theory on the legislator's behavior.[4]

The Canadian Representative

The Canadian situation differs in some important ways from the problem of representativeness in the legislatures of the United States. In Canada there appears to be stronger party discipline, especially in a minority government situation, than in the United States Congress, where there is considerable individual voting. However, there are more parties in Canada, so regional and other differences in political ideology can find more avenues of expression. Because there are more parties, a Member can be elected with a plurality which may be as low as 30 per cent of the total vote in a general election. The specification of the effective constituency in Canada must consider the possibility that the MP may need to represent only a minority of his constituents.

A major study of representation in Canada was published in 1967 on the 25th Parliament (Sept. 1962 – Feb. 1963).[6] In this study, Kornberg organizes his research under the assumption that legislative behavior is a product of the interaction between the individual legislator, the influence of his society (constituency), and the legislative institutions *per se*. After extensive interviews with Canadian Members of Parliament, Kornberg's analysis reveals that about one half of these legislators described their own role as that of delegate or servant to their constituency at least some of the time.[7] He reports that this contrasts quite sharply with the very low proportion of Congressmen who evidence this view of themselves.

A later study of the 26th Parliament (1963-65) corroborates and extends these notions about the representativeness of Canadian legislators.[8] It distinguishes several role orientations[9] of the MP through the analysis of self-reports gathered in interviews:

a) The "constituency delegate" expresses as faithfully as he can the wishes of his constituents. Neither personal nor party considerations interfere with a commitment to express the constituency view on public policy.
b) The "party delegate" expresses the position of the political party and takes only personal or constituency views into the collective formation of the party policy. After the policy is formed, he follows it.
c) The "trustee" is either unaware or indifferent to constituency and party and will vote independently. If necessary, he will vote against either's wishes.
d) The "mixed type" varies in behavior depending on the issue. This Member is inclined to his own views but allows constituency or party to affect his attitudes.

Table 14:
How Back Bench MP's See Their Representative Role by Region*
(Percentages)

Region	Constituency Delegate	Party Delegate	Trustee	Mixed	Total
BC & Yukon	0	27	64	9	100
Prairies & NWT	12	23	34	41	100
Ontario	16	24	30	30	100
Quebec	12	14	37	37	100
Atlantic	13	0	25	62	100
N	(14)	(21)	(38)	(42)	(115)

* Hoffman and Ward, *op. cit.*, p. 72.

The patterns of the relation between endorsing these orientations and other characteristics, reported, in Table 14, have relevance for our interest in representativeness. Those MP's from BC and the Yukon see themselves as most clearly independent of their constituency and, to some extent, most freed from party constraints. Although they affirm the largest party obedience (27 per cent), they have the smallest (9 per cent) mixed orientation which can, under varying circumstances, be properly considered as part of either the constituent or party delegate orientation.

MP's from Quebec emphasize the trustee role (33 per cent) and de-emphasize the party (14 per cent). Those from the Atlantic area de-emphasize party and trusteeship. Ontario MP's have the strongest affirmation of constituency delegate orientation. It is possible in all cases except BC and the Yukon to consider the MP's constituency or party delegate role to increase to about 50 per cent of all back benchers by adding the mixed role to each. Where there is a "free vote", for example, we would expect the mixed orientation to shift to constituency delegate.

Table 15
How Back Bench MP's See Their Representative Role by Political Party*
(Percentages)

Party	Constituency Delegate	Party Delegate	Trustee	Mixed	Total
LIB	10	24	25	41	100
PC	13	12	34	41	100
NDP	0	11	78	11	100
SC	20	20	40	20	100
RC	50	0	33	17	100
N	(14)	(21)	(38)	(42)	(115)

* Hoffman and Ward, *op. cit.*, p. 71.

The New Democrats consider themselves to be predominantly trustees (78 per cent) in representational role, and the Ralliement des Creditistes consider themselves to be predominantly constituency delegates (50 per cent). There is more emphasis on the constituency and on trusteeship amongst PC Members and more emphasis on the party among Liberals. All but the NDP could approximate 50 per cent of their members attending to either party or constituency opinion under various circumstances.

An important finding is that no more than 24 per cent of any party's MP's say they will follow party policy exclusively. It is widely alleged in parliamentary systems that party discipline is a crucial component to the working of the system. Although in their voting on most issues most MP's vote along with the party, they report substantial subjective independence from it. When they were asked what position they would take if their own views appeared to conflict with the views of their party, the break-down by party shows that the NDP MP's would remain consistent with their own (78 per cent).

Table 16:
Disposition of Respondents to Stick to their Own Views in Conflict with Those of their Party*
(Percentages)

Party	Own View	Go with Party	No Answer	Total
LIB	26	71	3	100
PC	49	39	12	100
NDP	78	22	0	100
SC	80	20	0	100
RC	50	50	0	100
N	(49)	(66)	(7)	(112)

* Hoffman and Ward, *op. cit.*, p. 74.

Additional data in this report shows that urban MP's would take an independent role in conflict with the party, and that MP's from the Atlantic Provinces would be most inclined to move towards constituents in any conflict situation. Hoffman and Ward find no important differences between French and English MP's on representational orientation. Nor do they find any differences between urban and rural areas.

For our purposes in the analysis of capital punishment votes in 1966 and 1973, we should remember that there is some regional and party variation in self-reported representational roles. Of the major parties, the Liberals tend to emphasize party and the Conservatives, trusteeship. However, no party has more than one quarter of its members who say they will follow policy. Of course, the votes to be analyzed here were declared to be "free" votes, in which party discipline was removed.

The conclusion to these separate reports on two Parliaments is that up to one half of the Members report that, under various circumstances, they follow constituency or party opinion. So the self-characterization of Canadian MP's must be as predominantly issue-oriented mixtures of the various orientations.[10]

It is important to distinguish between studies which examine the self-reports of representatives on their perception of the degree of control their constituency exercises over them, and those studies which do not depend on self-reports. Although self-reports are the easiest and most plausible way of examining the degree to which a constituency exercises control over a representative, they are subject to the bias that few representatives would say they totally disregard their constituency even if they do. This unknown bias must be taken into account in conducting and evaluating studies using self-report data.

A more indirect and difficult to interpret approach to the same problem is to use more objective measures of the representative's behavior, and compare that with indicators of the sentiment of his constituency. This allows judgements on the relative representativeness of legislators to be made through inference.

Both approaches have advantages and difficulties but the second approach avoids any self-interested, self-report bias. This approach will be used to assess the representativeness of MP's on the capital punishment votes of 1966, 1967 and 1973.

The Representativeness of the Canadian MP on Death Penalty Legislation

This section is oriented to the political sociology question of when, to what extent, and under what conditions, political representatives reflect their constituents' views and when they do not on the question of the abolition of the death penalty.

The legislative issue of capital punishment commends itself as a research case for the general question of representativeness for several reasons. Unlike many legislative issues, some estimates of public sentiment can be made from the public opinion polls which are typically taken as the issue becomes a legislative topic. The clarity of the choices over the issue reduce the possibility of obfuscation and equivocation by public figures. The history of capital punishment debates in Britain, the United States and Canada has been that there is relatively high rates of legislative and public participation. Editorials, petitions, bipartisan testimony from churches, public organizations and other evidence of arousal are common. While it is true that legislators are supposed to represent their constituents to a greater or lesser degree, the moderate level of public interest in most political decisions usually allows legislators a substantial amount of independence. In contrast to this, the death penalty debates seem to attract relatively close public scrutiny of legislators.

While the death penalty itself is seen as an important moral and practical issue in a society, the issue also appears to have a lightning rod quality of attracting related issues of the coddling of criminals, crime prevention, the alleged moral breakdown of the family and other controls as well. Kornberg remarks that legislative activity sometimes performs the function of facilitating a catharsis of societal grievances by providing a forum for their expression. Any capital punishment debate seems to qualify as an example of this catharsis.

And finally, as an issue which represents the combination of emotion and practical concern which occurs on most legislative issues, the death penalty is an excellent example. Questions of the value of life and the level of civilization are mixed with scientific analysis of deterrence and practical problems of judicial application.

For these reasons, legislative activity on the question of the death penalty is an important case for the student of law makers. While few other issues are similar to it in all respects, it does highlight and maybe, even caricature, important elements in all legislative topics.

The Canadian Death Penalty Debates

The Canadian Parliament has been considering the death penalty periodically for many years. Not until 1966 was there sufficient support for abolition or modification of the death penalty to warrant extensive parliamentary debate. As in most countries, this was preceded by several decades of a sharp reduction in the number of executions and, indeed, in Canada there have been none since 1962.

In this setting of *de-facto* abolition, the Parliament debated and narrowly defeated a Private Members abolition bill in 1966. A government bill which abolished the death penalty for a five year trial period, except for the murder of prison guards and policemen, was passed in a free vote in 1967 and a similar bill was renewed in a free vote by only 13 votes in 1973. At both debates, an unusually large number of Members spoke on both sides of the issue. There was heavy mail from the public. The mass media provided extensive coverage. Editorial opinion was widely offered on the question of the purpose and value of the death penalty.

The Department of Justice provided the Members of Parliament with extensive and objective scientific evidence and expert opinion on the death penalty in Canada, and other countries, in two papers, prepared before each debate. In response to the 1966/67 debate over the deterrent effect of the death penalty, the government commissioned an independent study of the deterrent effect in Canada which was available before the most recent parliamentary consideration of capital punishment in late 1973.

The Canadian Gallup Poll included questions on the death penalty at periods around these two debates and many less reliable polls were taken by newspapers, interested organizations and some Members of the House. So, in both the 1966/67 period and in 1973, Canadian public opinion could be estimated on the death penalty. It was a relatively clear issue, publicly discussed, and it enjoyed high levels of public and legislative participation.

In this research we analyze the 1966 and the 1973 debates and votes. The earlier date is preferable in that a larger number (80) of MP's were present and voting in 1966, allowing a more comprehensive comparison with 1973.[11]

The best estimate of public sentiment on the death penalty in Canada is that in 1966 at least 50 per cent of the people approved of it in some form. Later, although the period of the poll (1971) and the vote (1973) do not closely correspond, the best estimate is that at least 60 per cent of Canadians approved of it.

We will make several simplifying assumptions about the distribution of this opinion in this section. Here, we are attempting to marshal evidence to the question of how much elected representatives represent constituency opinion on the death penalty question. This is a complicated question to answer with empirical evidence, and a series of assumptions which simplify this complexity are required.

The first assumption is that each constituency mirrors the opinion of the country as a whole. Thus, in 1966, 50 per cent or more of each constituency approved the death penalty. Similarly, in 1973, we assume that 60 per cent or more of each constituency approved it. If, in addition, we assume that there are no other influences on the MP but his constituency, we would expect that all MP's in both time periods would vote for retention. However, 112 in 1966 and 119 in 1973 voted against retention. We would expect that these MP's would then be less likely to assume a delegate role and would have the characteristics that scholars in this area have found to be associated with relative independence from constituency influences. Several of these factors are examined in the first section.

In the second section, rather than assuming opinion to be evenly distributed in each constituency, we assume that constituencies will vary in support for retention or abolition. For evidence of this variation, we use information in the Gallup Poll to estimate the type and magnitude of these variations. We still assume that representatives are responsive exclusively to their constituents, but now we do not necessarily expect that all who vote against retention will be voting against the majority of their electorate. Finally, in this section we release the representative from our analytic assumption of representing the total electorate of the constituency. By checking the party preferences of those with various sentiment on the death penalty, we can see whether MP's tend to represent their own electors more than their constituents.

In the third section, we discard the first two assumptions and treat the MP as an individual. We assume, here, that the MP is not playing a representative or party role. The MP's are now just like any other group of 264 individuals discussing the death penalty, but are encouraged to come to a decision. Here, we examine individual characteristics of MP's and their vote. However, political affiliation is taken into account as if it were an individual characteristic which draws individuals into influence groups.

In the final section, we replace the preceding assumption with the view of the legislature as a small society. MP's in this view are responsive to their party's influence and ideology as well as other features of the legislative system. Under this assumption, they bring no personal view nor any obligation to represent a constituency to this debate.

This series of assumptions is intended to highlight each of the variety of constituency, party, and individual factors involved in this complex legislative process. These procedural assumptions allow an orderly empirical examination of the question. They are not intended to produce fundamentally different perspectives on the same problem, as would occur if a variety of theoretical assumptions were used. Rather they facilitate the presentation of a series of simplified empirical analyses of an otherwise prohibitively complex process.

The MP as Representing Evenly Distributed Opinion

Over 50 per cent of Canadians supported the death penalty in 1966, while only 35 per cent opposed it. In 1973, approximately 60 per cent supported it and 30 per cent opposed it. In 1966, 56 per cent of MP's rejected a pure abolition bill; in 1967, 60 per cent of MP's supported a partial and temporary abolition bill and in 1973, 53 per cent of the MP's renewed this bill. In 1967 and 1973, the MP's appeared to be more abolitionist than the people.[12]

The several votes in Parliament which indicate at least majority support in modified and temporary abolition must mean that some, if not all, of the abolitionist Members are defying the will of the people. Their speeches also reflect this. Retentionist speakers frequently refer to constituency opinion, whereas abolitionist speakers rarely, if ever, do. We shall now examine some of the factors which may account for this disparity between public sentiment and parliamentary voting.

If we assume that public opinion was uniformly retentionist across all constituencies, it would mean, in 1966-67 that 50 to 55 per cent of the population of each constituency favoured the death penalty. Thus, those who voted in favour of full abolition, 44 per cent of the MP's would be in disagreement with the majority of their constituents. In 1973, between 60 and 65 per cent of the public opposed abolition but only 47 per cent of their MP's did.

We should expect that these 112 MP's in 1966 and 119 in 1973 will differ from those that followed the will of their constituents. We expect, for example, that those MP's who are more closely bound to their electorate should support hanging to a greater extent than their less involved counterparts.[13]

Local Birth and Representativeness

We expect that MP's who were born in their riding, for example, would be more likely to vote to retain capital punishment. Table 17 shows that there was a strong tendency for Members who were born in their constituencies to favour retention in 1966. Over 65 per cent of them favoured hanging in 1966, whereas less than half of their counterparts born outside of their constituency favoured it.

Table 17

Vote on Capital Punishment (1966) and Birthplace of M.P. (Percentages)

	Birthplace									
Vote on Capital Punishment	No Information	(N)	In Constituency	(N)	In Canada	(N)	Foreign Born	(N)	Total	(N)
No Vote	.0	(0)	5.1	(5)	3.8	(5)	.0	(0)	3.8	(10)
Abolition	36.4	(4)	29.6	(29)	49.6	(66)	56.5	(13)	42.3	(112)
Retention	63.6	(7)	65.3	(64)	46.6	(62)	43.5	(10)	54.0	(143)
Total	4.2	(11)	37.0	(98)	50.2	(133)	8.7	(23)	100.0	(265)

In 1973, the same pattern holds to a much reduced extent, as seen in Table 18. The additional categories used in coding 1973 birthplace of MP's allows us to see that movement within the same province does not liberate the MP from his constituents, whereas movement across provincial lines does. 56 per cent of those born in a different province than the one they represent favour abolition; whereas only 41 per cent of their colleagues born in or near their own constituency favoured it. It seems plausible that "local" representatives would have a more accurate perception of the constituency viewpoint and would have more local bonds with political support groups and community associations. Under these circumstances, he would tend to follow his constituency more closely in his voting in Parliament.

Table 18:
Vote on Capital Punishment (1973) and Birthplace of M.P.
(Percentages)

	Birthplace									
Vote on Capital Punishment	No Infor-mation	(N)	In Consti-tuency	(N)	In Same Province	(N)	Out Of Province	(N)	Total	(N)
No Vote	15.8	(3)	15.0	(15)	18.5	(17)	9.6	(5)	15.2	(39)
Abolition	42.1	(9)	42.0	(42)	41.3	(38)	55.8	(29)	44.7	(119)
Retention	42.1	(8)	43.0	(43)	40.2	(37)	34.6	(18)	40.2	(106)
Total	7.2	(19)	37.9	(100)	34.8	(92)	19.7	(52)	100.0	(264)

Political Security and Representativeness

Democratic legislatures depend on electoral competition at some minimal level to afford choice to the electorate. In an excellent review of the impact of constituency competitiveness in Canada, Lovink asserts that the basic proposition which informs this research is that competitiveness increases politicians' responsiveness to the electorate's needs and wishes.[14] It seems sensible that, as the candidates and parties are more evenly balanced in popularity, then the successful candidate would protect his position by attending more faithfully to the people's wishes.

We measured popularity by dividing the winning candidate's vote by the total vote cast in the last election in his constituency. This could be considered as an index of the degree of inter-party competition in each constituency. With a low proportion of the

Table 19:
Vote on Capital Punishment (1966) by Political Popularity of M.P. (Percentages)

Vote on Capital Punishment	POPULARITY Low	(∠50%)	High	(⦣50%)	Total	
No Vote	4.0	(6)	3.6	(4)	3.8	(10)
Abolition	44.0	(66)	40.0	(46)	42.3	(112)
Retention	52.0	(78)	56.5	(65)	54.0	(143)
Total	56.6	(150)	43.4	(115)	100.0	(265)

* Popularity is measured by dividing the winning Member's vote by the total vote in the last election. See following table for popularity distribution.

Percent of Vote

	26-35%		36-45%		46-55%		56-65%		66+%		Total	
1965 Election	3.0	(8)	29.8	(79)	47.5	(126)	17.4	(46)	2.3	(6)	100.0	(265)
1972 Election	3.0	(8)	35.6	(94)	40.5	(107)	25.4	(67)	3.0	(8)	100.0	(264)

total vote, a successful MP could see his constituency as sharply contested, and, therefore, tend to vote to retain the death penalty.

The evidence in Tables 19 and 20 does not support this hypothesis. In both the 1966, and to a greater extent, in the 1973 votes, those MP's who had relatively low proportions of the total vote

Table 20:
Vote on Capital Punishment (1973) by Political Popularity of M.P. (Percentages)

Vote on Capital Punishment	POPULARITY Low	(∠50%)	High	(⦣50%)	Total	
No Vote	15.7	(24)	14.1	(16)	15.2	(39)
Abolition	49.0	(75)	38.7	(43)	44.7	(119)
Retention	35.2	(54)	46.8	(52)	40.2	(106)
Total	57.9	(153)	42.0	(111)	100.0	(264)

tended to support abolition, but their more popular colleagues were more likely to reflect their constituents' wishes and vote to retain it. Popularity with voters does not seem to provide the "elbow room" that would be expected on the capital punishment issue. Rather, it reflects a closer correspondence of the MP's behavior with the sentiment of the people. This may be part of the cause of his popularity rather than a consequence of it. The more closely contested constituencies tend to be three-way contests with the allegiances of most voters solidified. In these areas where a few swing voters make the difference in success or failure, the MP may not attend to the whole constituency but only his supporters. He may have very little to lose by taking an unpopular stand. We discuss this in more detail later in this section when we release ourselves from the assumption of an even distribution of public opinion on the death penalty question.

General considerations worth noting are that the rational course for an MP in a highly competitive constituency is not followed. And that what appears, at first, to be a simple and common sense view of how a more secure Member would differ from an insecure Member on the capital punishment vote is very complex and counter-intuitive.

Following the intuitive notion that political security generates

Table 21:
Vote on Capital Punishment (1966) by Number of Times Elected (Percentages)

Vote on Capital Punishment	Times Elected: One		Two		Three		Four	
No Vote	.0	(0)	6.1	(2)	6.8	(5)	.0	(0)
Abolition	50.9	(28)	57.6	(19)	49.3	(36)	21.2	(7)
Retention	49.1	(27)	36.4	(12)	43.8	(32)	78.8	(26)
Total	20.8	(55)	12.5	(33)	27.5	(73)	12.5	(33)

	More Than Four		Other Combination		Total	
No Vote	5.8	(3)	0.0	(0)	3.8	(10)
Abolition	25.0	(13)	47.4	(9)	42.3	(112)
Retention	69.2	(36)	52.6	(10)	54.0	(143)
Total	19.6	(52)	7.2	(19)	100.0	(265)

freedom for the Member to stray on some issues from the public sentiment, we checked the electoral history of Members against their vote. We would expect that those who had been re-elected several times to be more abolitionist than those who did not have a confidence inspiring record of re-elections. Table 21 shows a tendency which is contrary to this prediction. Those who are recently elected are more inclined to depart from the mood of the country than their colleagues who have been elected more than three times. These, who were first elected in 1958 and before, are more retentionist than the country is.

Table 22, showing the same relations for 1973, presents a different picture. The most recently elected MP's (1972) and those first elected more than a decade earlier (1962 or earlier) were the most retentionist. The rest were quite strongly abolitionist. There is no clear conclusion that can be drawn from this evidence. It seems that highly competitive constituencies do not generate a delegate orientation as Kornberg found. In the same vein, the security of being re-elected also does not generate clear-cut abolitionist patterns as might be expected.

Table 22:

Vote on Capital Punishment (1973) by Number of Times Elected (Percentages)

Vote on Capital Punishment	Times Elected: No Information		One		Two		Three		Four	
No Vote	.0	(0)	7.7	(8)	17.9	(10)	16.7	(5)	55.6	(5)
Abolition	.0	(0)	45.2	(47)	50.0	(28)	50.0	(15)	33.3	(3)
Retention	100.0	(1)	47.1	(49)	32.1	(18)	33.3	(10)	11.1	(1)
Total	.4	(1)	39.4	(104)	21.2	(56)	11.4	(30)	3.4	(9)

	Five		More Than Five		Other Combination		Total	
No Vote	25.0	(7)	5.0	(1)	25.0	(4)	15.2	(39)
Abolition	53.6	(15)	25.0	(5)	31.3	(5)	44.7	(119)
Retention	21.4	(6)	70.0	(14)	43.8	(7)	40.2	(106)
Total	10.6	(28)	7.6	(20)	6.1	(16)	100.0	(264)

MP's Background and Representativeness

Kornberg finds that, of his "prior experience" variables, only education and occupation affected the degree to which Members assumed delegate or trustee orientations. He finds that the more education an MP has, the less he focusses on his constituents. In addition, he found that businessmen and professionals were less likely to take a delegate orientation than were farmers, white collar and blue collar workers.

Education

Those MP's with a high level of education depart more from the prevailing pro capital punishment sentiment of the public. A majority of the highly educated MP's favoured abolition of the death penalty, whereas only one-third of those with relatively low education favoured its abolition in 1966 (see Table 23). Abolitionist sentiment increases in both groups in 1973 but more so in the group with lower education (see Table 24). It appears that the effect of education on representativeness is complex. Those with high education depart from the public mood the most. However, those with lower education seem to resist the public opinion swing of the 1970's. If we note the large number (92) of MP's for whom we do not have precise educational information, there is a plausible technical explanation. The coding of education in 1966 included the use of inferences about education from job and last school attended. In 1973, a more strict coding produced a classification only where there was direct evidence of years of schooling. If the large number of MP's in this "no information" category are fairly assumed to be more likely to have low, rather than high, education, then the 1973 table (Table 24) shows relatively little change from 1966. Those with lower education reflect constituency sentiment more accurately.

Table 23:
Vote on Capital Punishment (1966) by Education of M.P.
(Percentages)

Vote on Capital Punishment	Education: No Information		Two or More University Degrees		One University Degree		No Degree		Total	
No Vote	.0	(0)	2.0	(2)	.0	(0)	7.3	(8)	3.8	(10)
Abolition	55.6	(5)	58.8	(60)	36.4	(16)	28.2	(31)	42.3	(112)
Retention	44.4	(4)	39.2	(40)	63.6	(28)	64.5	(71)	54.0	(143)
Total	3.4	(9)	38.5	(102)	16.6	(44)	41.5	(110)	100.0	(265)

Table 24:
Vote on Capital Punishment (1973) by Education of M.P.
(Percentages)

Vote on Capital Punishment	Education: No Information	Two or More University Degrees	One Degree Or Evidence Of Attendence	No Degree	Total
No Vote	18.6 (21)	20.0 (17)	3.4 (2)	.0 (0)	15.2 (39)
Abolition	33.6 (38)	52.9 (45)	57.6 (34)	14.3 (1)	44.7 (119)
Retention	47.8 (54)	27.1 (23)	39.0 (23)	85.7 (6)	40.2 (106)
Total	42.8 (113)	32.2 (85)	22.3 (59)	2.7 (7)	100.0 (264)

Occupation

As Kornberg finds, professional occupations seem to allow a wider departure from public sentiment. In 1966, a strong majority of professionals were for outright abolition, whereas their non-professional colleagues were clearly retentionists (see Table 25). Table 26 shows that the professionals increased their abolitionist strength in 1973, with farmers, blue collar workers and, departing from Kornberg's findings, businessmen, being more sympathetic to

Table 25
Vote on Capital Punishment (1966) by Occupation of M.P.
(Percentages)

Vote on Capital Punishment	Occupation: No Information	Lawyer	Professional	Clergy	Business	White Collar
No Vote	.0 (0)	2.9 (2)	3.7 (2)	.0 (0)	5.9 (4)	.0 (0)
Abolition	38.5 (5)	53.6 (37)	57.4 (31)	66.7 (2)	20.6 (14)	63.2 (12)
Retention	61.5 (8)	43.5 (30)	38.9 (21)	33.3 (1)	73.5 (50)	36.8 (7)
Total	4.9 (13)	26.0 (69)	20.4 (54)	1.1 (3)	25.7 (68)	7.2 (19)

Vote on Capital Punishment	Skilled Blue Collar	Farmer	Unskilled Blue Collar	Retired	Total
No Vote	.0 (0)	3.8 (1)	14.3 (1)	.0 (0)	3.8 (10)
Abolition	75.0 (3)	15.4 (4)	57.1 (4)	.0 (0)	42.3 (112)
Retention	25.0 (1)	80.8 (21)	28.6 (2)	100.0 (2)	54.0 (143)
Total	1.5 (4)	9.8 (26)	2.6 (7)	.8 (2)	100.0 (265)

the constituents' views. In addition, those with high education and professional occupations resisted the trend in the country between 1966 and 1973 to become more retentionist, by increasing their abolitionist tendency.

Table 26
Vote on Capital Punishment (1973) by Occupation of M.P. (Percentages)

Vote on Capital Punishment	Occupation: No Information		Lawyer		Professional		Clergy		Business	
No Vote	7.7	(2)	17.9	(12)	8.5	(5)	.0	(0)	19.2	(15)
Abolition	57.7	(15)	50.7	(34)	59.3	(35)	75.0	(3)	28.2	(22)
Retention	34.6	(9)	31.3	(21)	32.2	(19)	25.0	(1)	52.6	(41)
Total	9.8	(26)	25.4	(67)	22.3	(59)	1.5	(4)	29.5	(78)

Vote on Capital Punishment	White Collar		Skilled Blue Collar		Farmer		Unskilled Blue Collar		Total	
No Vote	25.0	(2)	.0	(0)	20.0	(3)	50.0	(1)	15.2	(39)
Abolition	50.0	(4)	20.0	(1)	20.0	(3)	50.0	(1)	44.7	(119)
Retention	25.0	(2)	80.0	(4)	60.0	(9)	.0	(0)	40.2	(106)
Total	3.0	(8)	1.9	(5)	5.7	(15)	.8	(2)	100.0	(264)

Summary

In the 1966-67 period, and later in 1973, the majority of the Canadian public supported the death penalty. Yet many Members of Parliament voted for abolition. If we assume that there was an even distribution of this sentiment in Canada, then many Members voted against the majority of their constituents and, thus, did not represent them. Members who were born in their constituencies conformed to the pattern of representing the wishes of the people. Likewise, Members who were not subjected to the cosmopolitan influences of extensive education and professionalized occupations were more likely to reflect the public mood. However, the apparently rational behavior of reflecting constituency sentiment more when there is more political insecurity is not borne out in our data. Insecure MP's tend to oppose public sentiment. If we combine some of these findings, we get a preliminary picture of the relatively independent "Burkean" trustee. He is more of a stranger to his constituency, not having been born or raised in or near it. He is highly educated and holds a professional occupation which may reduce his ties to his constituency, and provide him with an alternative reference group. In addition, his constituency will tend to be sharply contested which may not be of great concern to him since, with his high status occupation, he may be less enthralled being an MP.

Our preliminary picture is based on the obviously wrong, but necessary, simplifying assumption of an even distribution of public opinion in Canada.

The MP as Representative of Unevenly Distributed Opinion

An addition of complexity and reality occurs when we release ourselves from the assumption that the public opinion on the death penalty is evenly distributed across political constituencies.

In this section, we still assume that the MP's vote is solely influenced by a desire to reflect constituency opinion. Neither personal belief nor political group influences are assumed to affect his vote. However, the 264 political constituencies are now allowed to vary in the distribution and intensity of opinion on the death penalty. The MP's, therefore, should reflect these differentials in constituency influence.

An analysis of Gallup poll data in 1966 and 1971 allows us to make some inferences about the kind of constituency which might be more in favour of retention of the death penalty than others at each time period.

Regional Variation in Public Opinion and Legislative Vote on the Death Penalty

We must remember that in this section we are comparing sample survey data, with its sampling variation, to the behavior of the population of Members of Parliament. The Gallup poll suggests plus or minus 3 per cent when making population estimates from their polls. There was considerable variation in the degree of support for the death penalty in different regions of Canada.

Table 27 shows that support for hanging ranges from a high of 70 per cent in favour in Quebec to a low of 50 per cent against in Manitoba and Saskatchewan in 1966. In 1971, Quebec (see Table 29) is again the most supportive of the death penalty, but New Brunswick becomes the least retentionist with only 44 per cent in favour of retaining it. It should be pointed out that detailed analysis of public opinion *per se* occurs in Chapter 2. Here, we concern ourselves only with the relation between regional variations in public opinion and regional variations in MP's' vote (see Tables 28 and 30).

Ranking provinces on the extent of support for the death penalty, as indicated in public opinion, and also on the proportion of their MP's who voted for retention in 1966 and 1973, simplifies interpretation of any correspondence between the two. In 1966, there is no relation between the public opinion rank and the Members' voting rank (see Figure 1). This pattern is preserved in 1973.[16]

Figure 1:
Ranking of Support for Retention of the Death Penalty, for Provinces by Public Opinion and MP Vote

Province	1966 Public Opinion Rank	1966 MP Vote Rank	1971 Public Opinion Rank	1973 MP Vote Rank
NS	3	4	2	2
NB	2	5	9	4.5
NFLD	9	8	8	9
QUE	1	3	1	6
ONT	6	7	6	7
MAN	7	6	5	3
SASK	8	2	4	8
ALTA	5	1	3	1
BC	4	9	7	4.5

1 = most support for death penalty; 9 = least support

		1966 MP's Vote Above 5	1966 MP's Vote 5 and Below
Public Opinion 1966	Above 5	3	2
	5 and Below	2	2

		1973 MP's Vote Above 5	1973 MP's Vote 5 and Below
Public Opinion 1971	Above 5	2	3
	5 and Below	2	2

(Data from Figure 1.)

Table 27:
Public Sentiment on Capital Punishment by Province (1966)
(Percentages)

Opinion on Capital Punishment	Province									
	NFLD		NS		NB		QUE		ONT	
Abolish	42.9		23.5		43.5		21.7		45.3	
Retain	28.6		55.9		56.5		70.1		44.9	
No Opinion	28.6		20.6		0.0		8.2		9.8	
Total	1.1	(7)	5.2	(34)	3.5	(23)	28.0	(184)	35.6	(234)
	MAN		SASK		ALTA		BC		TOTAL	
Abolish	50.0		50.0		34.1		46.8		37.7	(246)
Retain	38.9		38.2		47.7		48.2		53.0	(346)
No Opinion	11.2		11.7		18.1		4.8		9.3	(66)
Total	5.5	(36)	5.2	(34)	6.7	(44)	9.4	(62)	100.0	(658)

Table 28:
Vote on Capital Punishment by Province (1966)
(Percentages)

Vote on Capital Punishment	Province: NFLD & PEI		NS		NB		QUE		ONT	
No Vote	9.1	(1)	8.3	(1)	10.0	(1)	0.0	(0)	7.1	(6)
Abolish	54.5	(6)	25.0	(3)	30.0	(3)	32.0	(24)	51.8	(44)
Retain	36.4	(4)	66.7	(8)	60.0	(6)	68.0	(51)	41.2	(35)
TOTAL	4.2	(11)	4.5	(12)	3.8	(10)	28.3	(75)	32.1	(85)

	MAN		SASK		ALTA		BC, YUK NWT		TOTAL	
No Vote	7.1	(1)	0.0	(0)	0.0	(0)	0.0	(0)	3.8	(10)
Abolish	50.0	(7)	29.4	(5)	23.5	(4)	66.7	(16)	42.3	(112)
Retain	42.9	(6)	70.6	(12)	76.5	(13)	33.3	(8)	54.0	(143)
Total	5.3	(14)	6.4	(17)	6.4	(17)	9.1	(24)	100.0	(265)

Table 29:
Public Sentiment on Capital Punishment by Province (1971)
(Percentages)

Opinion on Capital Punishment	Province									
	NFLD		NS		NB		QUE		ONT	
Abolish	40.0		26.7		33.3		21.1		33.5	
Retain	50.0		73.7		44.4		75.0		58.4	
No Opinion	10.0		0.0		22.2		3.9		8.2	
TOTAL	1.4	(10)	4.2	(30)	3.8	(27)	28.3	(204)	35.7	(257)
	MAN		SASK		ALTA		BC		TOTAL	
Abolish	40.0		34.4		23.3		38.0		30.1	(217)
Retain	60.0		60.7		63.3		53.5		63.1	(454)
No Opinion	0.0		4.9		13.3		8.5		6.8	(49)
TOTAL	4.2	(30)	8.5	(61)	4.2	(30)	9.9	(71)	100.0	(720)

*Source: C.I.P.O. Poll #350, Conducted in December, 1971

Table 30:
Vote on Capital Punishment by Province (1973)
(Percentages)

Vote on Capital Punishment	Province									
	NFLD & PEI		NS		NB		QUE		ONT	
No Vote	0.0	(0)	18.2	(2)	10.0	(1)	23.0	(17)	10.2	(9)
Abolish	81.8	(9)	18.2	(2)	50.0	(5)	39.2	(29)	54.5	(48)
Retain	18.2	(2)	63.6	(7)	40.0	(4)	37.8	(28)	35.2	(31)
TOTAL	4.2	(11)	4.2	(11)	3.8	(10)	28.0	(74)	33.3	(88)
	MAN		SASK		ALTA		BC, YUK NWT		TOTAL	
No Vote	15.4	(2)	30.8	(4)	15.8	(3)	8.0	(2)	15.2	(39)
Abolish	30.8	(4)	38.5	(5)	15.8	(3)	52.0	(13)	44.7	(119)
Retain	53.8	(7)	30.8	(4)	68.4	(13)	40.0	(10)	40.2	(106)
TOTAL	4.9	(13)	4.9	(13)	7.2	(19)	9.5	(25)	100.0	(264)

It is interesting to note some patterns over the two periods. MP's from Quebec tend to be less retentionist, relatively, than their constituents, whereas MP's from Alberta have the opposite pattern. They are more retentionist than Albertans generally. Although there is variation in regional sentiment and regional voting on the death penalty, the two do not seem to be strongly related. In addition, there is inconsistency between 1966 and 1973 in both regional variation in public opinion and MP's' votes.

Rural and Urban Variations in Public Opinion and Legislative Vote on the Death Penalty

Rural-urban differences in public opinion are generally alleged and usually found on issues like capital punishment. There appear to be surprisingly small differences in rural and urban sentiment in the 1966 Gallup poll data on the death penalty in Canada (see Table 31). However, in 1971 (Table 33), a more expected pattern of rural areas favouring retention appears. The greatest increase in public sentiment to approve of retaining the death penalty occurs in rural areas. However, the MP's from non-metropolitan areas appear to reduce their support for retention between 1966 and 1973. While public support for the death penalty increased somewhat in urban areas, the urban MP's remained as abolitionist as they had been in 1966.

In 1966, the MP's' vote exaggerated slight urban-rural differences in public sentiment. In 1973, the urban MP's exaggerated the urban dwellers' relatively mild retentionist opinion into a strong

Table 31
Public Sentiment on Capital Punishment by Rural and Urban Residence (1966)
(Percentages)

Opinion on Capital Punishment	Residence: Farm		Rural Non-Farm		Urban		Total	
Abolish	37.1		40.4		36.7		37.7	(246)
Retain	55.7		53.5		51.9		53.0	(346)
No Opinion	7.2		6.1		11.4		9.3	(66)
Total	10.6	(70)	17.3	(114)	72.0	(474)	100.0	(658)

Table 32
Vote on Capital Punishment by Rural-Urban Area (1966)
(Percentages)

Vote on Capital Punishment	Non-metropolitan Area		Metropolitan Area		Total	
No Vote	4.7	(9)	1.4	(1)	3.8	(10)
Abolish	34.2	(66)	63.9	(46)	42.3	(112)
Retain	61.1	(118)	34.7	(25)	54.0	(143)
Total	72.8	(193)	27.2	(72)	100.0	(265)

Table 33:
Public Sentiment on Capital Punishment by Rural and Urban Residence (1971)
(Percentages)

Opinion on Capital Punishment	Residence Farm		Rural Non-Farm		Urban		Total	
Abolish	12.5		25.0		33.3		30.1	(217)
Retain	82.8		68.8		59.6		63.1	(454)
No Opinion	4.7		6.2		7.2		6.8	(49)
Total	9.5	(65)	16.7	(112)	81.1	(544)	100.0	(720)

Table 34:
Vote on Capital Punishment by Rural-Urban Area (1973)
(Percentages)

Vote on Capital Punishment	No Information		Area Non-metropolitan Area		Metropolitan Area		Total	
No Vote	0.0	(0)	18.1	(33)	8.7	(7)	15.2	(39)
Abolish	0.0	(0)	36.8	(67)	63.8	(51)	44.7	(119)
Retain	100.0	(2)	45.1	(82)	27.5	(22)	40.2	(106)
Total	.8	(2)	68.9	(182)	30.3	(80)	100.0	(264)

abolitionist vote and the MP's with more rural constituencies muted the strong retentionist, rural public opinion. Rural-urban differences in public sentiment reached a parliamentary vote in a very distorted rendition. But the basic trend is that public opinion differences are reflected in the vote in Parliament.

Religious Variations in Public Opinion and Legislative Vote on the Death Penalty

There was for some time the view that, since the Roman Catholic Church did not discourage the use of the death penalty in contrast to Protestant churches, Catholics and Protestants would differ as individuals in the same way their churches differed. In 1966 (Table 35), this pattern holds. In 1971 (Table 38), however, both groups have become more retentionist. The Protestants have changed substantially in outlook. There is, by 1971, no significant difference between Catholic and Protestant death penalty opinion. The United Church and other major Protestant churches still maintain an abolitionist position. They have been joined by prestigious Roman Catholic organizations in 1973. But both population groups do not grow together in a swing to abolition with their organizations. Rather, they both become more retentionist. The other categories in this table are quite small, but the Jews have apparently moved from a traditional abolitionist position and the remainder, typically those who report no religion, retain their abolitionist pattern.

Table 35: Public Sentiment on Capital Punishment by Religion (1966) (Percentages)

	Religion									
Opinion on Capital Punishment	Protestant		Roman Catholic		Jewish		Other		Total	
Abolish	42.9		30.3		60.0		51.6		37.7	(246)
Retain	46.4		60.2		20.0		41.9		53.0	(346)
No Opinion	10.7		9.5		20.0		6.4		9.4	(66)
Total	46.8	(308)	47.7	(314)	.8	(5)	4.7	(31)	100.0	(658)

Table 36:
Vote on Capital Punishment by Proportion of Protestants*
in Constituency (1966)
(Percentages)

Vote on Capital Punishment	Percent Protestants 0-9		10-19		20-29		30-39		40-49	
No Vote	.0	(0)	.0	(0)	9.1	(1)	13.6	(3)	3.7	(1)
Abolish	27.3	(15)	35.7	(5)	36.4	(4)	59.1	(13)	70.4	(19)
Retain	72.7	(40)	64.3	(9)	54.5	(6)	27.3	(6)	25.9	(7)
Total	20.8	(55)	5.3	(14)	4.2	(11)	8.3	(22)	10.2	(27)

	50-59		60-69		70-79		80-89		90-100		Total	
No Vote	3.6	(1)	2.1	(1)	4.0	(2)	14.3	(1)	.0	(0)	3.8	(10)
Abolish	46.4	(13)	47.9	(23)	36.0	(18)	14.3	(1)	33.3	(1)	42.3	(112)
Retain	50.0	(14)	50.0	(24)	60.0	(30)	71.4	(5)	66.7	(2)	54.0	(143)
Total	10.6	(28)	18.1	(48)	18.9	(50)	2.6	(7)	1.1	(3)	100.0	(265)

* Those who report affiliation with Major Protestant Churches (Anglican United, Baptist, Lutheran and Presbyterian) to the 1961 Census.

Table 37:
Vote on Capital Punishment by Proportion of Roman Catholics in Constituency (1966)
(Percentages)

Vote on Capital Punishment	0-9		10-19		20-29		30-39		40-49	
No Vote	33.3	(1)	3.3	(2)	3.3	(2)	.0	(0)	7.1	(1)
Abolish	.0	(0)	41.7	(25)	45.9	(28)	56.5	(13)	57.1	(8)
Retain	66.7	(2)	55.0	(33)	50.8	(31)	43.5	(10)	35.7	(5)
Total	1.1	(3)	22.6	(60)	23.0	(61)	8.7	(23)	5.3	(14)

	50-59		60-69		70-79		80-89		90-100		Total	
No Vote	10.0	(2)	22.2	(2)	.0	(0)	.0	(0)	.0	(0)	3.8	(10)
Abolish	55.0	(11)	66.7	(6)	42.9	(3)	31.3	(5)	25.0	(13)	42.3	(112)
Retain	35.0	(7)	11.1	(1)	57.1	(4)	68.8	(11)	75.0	(39)	54.0	(143)
Total	7.5	(20)	3.4	(9)	2.6	(7)	6.0	(16)	19.6	(52)	100.0	(265)

Table 38:
Public Sentiment on Capital Punishment by Religion (1971)
(Percentages)

Opinion on Capital Punishment	Religion					
	Protestant		Roman Catholic		Jewish	
Abolish	27.1		28.1		36.4	
Retain	63.7		66.9		63.6	
No Opinion	9.1		5.0		0.0	
Total	44.0	(317)	41.9	(302)	1.5	(11)

	Other		Total	
Abolish	46.7		30.1	(217)
Retain	47.8		63.1	(454)
No Opinion	5.6		6.8	(49)
Total	12.5	(90)	100.0	(720)

Members of Parliament from constituencies where there is a concentration of each major religious group generally exaggerate the constituency sentiment. Those from predominantly Protestant constituencies reacted to the swing in sentiment in these areas quite severely. Tables 36 and 39 show that MP's from predominantly Protestant constituencies strongly endorsed the death penalty and increased this support in 1973. Their colleagues in ridings where there was a concentration of Roman Catholics (Tables 37 and 40) became less retentionist than their electorate in 1973. There is a tendency for MP's from homogeneous constituencies, whatever the religion, to be more retentionist than all other Members. This important fact is taken up in Chapter 4. The religion of a constituency does not have a clear and powerful influence on the MP. Possibly, the dramatic change in Protestant opinion is seen in the very strong retentionism in constituencies where over 60 per cent of the popula-

Table 39:
Vote on Capital Punishment by Proportion of Protestants*
in Constituency (1973)
(Percentages)

Vote on Capital Punishment	Percent Protestants 0-9		10-19		20-29		30-39		40-49	
No Vote	26.2	(16)	6.7	(1)	18.2	(2)	11.5	(3)	5.7	(2)
Abolish	37.7	(23)	60.0	(9)	72.7	(8)	65.4	(17)	57.1	(20)
Retain	36.1	(22)	33.3	(5)	9.1	(1)	23.1	(6)	37.1	(13)
Total	23.1	(61)	5.7	(15)	4.2	(11)	9.8	(26)	13.3	(35)

	50-59		60-69		70-79		80-89		90-100		Total	
No Vote	8.5	(5)	19.0	(8)	25.0	(3)	.0	(0)	.0	(0)	15.2	(39)
Abolish	49.2	(29)	26.2	(11)	8.3	(1)	.0	(0)	.0	(0)	44.7	(119)
Retain	42.4	(25)	54.8	(23)	66.7	(8)	100.0	(2)	100.0	(1)	40.2	(106)
Total	22.3	(59)	15.9	(42)	4.5	(12)	.8	(2)	.4	(1)	100.0	(264)

* Those who report affiliation with Major Protestant Churches (Anglican, United, Baptist, Lutheran and Presbyterian) to the 1971 Census.

Table 40:
Vote on Capital Punishment by Proportion of Roman Catholics in Constituency (1973)
(Percentages)

Vote on Capital Punishment	Percent Roman Catholics 0-9		10-19		20-29		30-39		40-49			
No Vote	.0	(0)	9.5	(4)	16.2	(11)	10.7	(3)	.0	(0)		
Abolish	20.0	(1)	28.6	(12)	39.7	(27)	50.0	(14)	72.7	(16)		
Retain	80.0	(4)	61.9	(26)	44.1	(30)	39.3	(11)	27.3	(6)		
Total	1.9	(5)	15.9	(42)	25.8	(68)	10.6	(28)	8.3	(22)		
	50-59		60-69		70-79		80-89		90-100		Total	
No Vote	12.5	(2)	22.2	(2)	22.2	(2)	12.5	(2)	28.6	(14)	15.2	(39)
Abolish	81.3	(13)	66.7	(6)	66.7	(6)	56.3	(9)	28.6	(14)	44.7	(119)
Retain	6.2	(1)	11.1	(1)	11.1	(1)	31.3	(5)	42.9	(21)	40.2	(106)
Total	6.1	(16)	3.4	(9)	3.4	(9)	6.1	(16)	18.6	(49)	100.0	(264)

tion is Protestant, but we must look to other factors to explain the reduction in support for the death penalty in predominantly Roman Catholic constituencies.

Ethnic Variation in Public Opinion and Legislative Vote on Capital Punishment

In 1966, English Canadians were more abolitionist than French Canadians (Table 41). By 1971, both groups had become more inclined to retention but the English had changed more (Table 44). There has been dramatic reduction in support for the death penalty among MP's from predominantly French constituencies (Tables 42 and 45), and small increase in the comparable MP from a predominantly English origin constituency (Tables 43 and 46). All other MP's from areas where there is neither a French nor an English concentration tend to support abolition more.[17]

The concentration of single ethnic groups in a constituency seems to affect the MP's vote on the death penalty. Whether it is English or French ethnicity which is concentrated has differing effects in each study period. Chapter 4 examines this phenomenon in theoretical and empirical detail.

Table 41
Public Sentiment on Capital Punishment by Ethnicity (Mother Tongue) 1966
(Percentages)

Opinion on Capital Punishment	Mother Tongue							
	English		French		Other		Total	
Abolish	43.9		24.0		40.0		37.7	(246)
Retain	44.7		69.0		50.0		53.0	(346)
No Opinion	11.4		7.0		10.0		9.4	(66)
Total	58.8	(387)	30.4	(200)	10.8	(71)	100.0	(658)

Table 42:
Vote on Capital Punishment by Proportion of French in Constituency (1966)
(Percentages)

Vote on Capital Punishment	Percent French 0-9		10-19		20-29		30-39		40-49	
No Vote	4.5	(6)	6.7	(2)	11.1	(1)	.0	(0)	11.1	(1)
Abolish	45.9	(61)	43.3	(13)	66.7	(6)	60.0	(6)	66.7	(6)
Retain	49.6	(66)	50.0	(15)	22.2	(2)	40.0	(4)	22.2	(2)
Total	50.2	(133)	11.3	(30)	3.4	(9)	3.8	(10)	3.4	(9)

	50-59		60-69		70-79		80-89		90-100		Total	
No Vote	.0	(0)	.0	(0)	.0	(0)	.0	(0)	.0	(0)	3.8	(10)
Abolish	33.3	(1)	66.7	(2)	35.7	(5)	22.2	(4)	22.2	(8)	42.3	(112)
Retain	66.7	(2)	33.3	(1)	64.3	(9)	77.8	(14)	77.8	(28)	54.0	(143)
Total	1.1	(3)	1.1	(3)	5.3	(14)	6.8	(18)	13.6	(36)	100.0	(265)

Table 43:
Vote on Capital Punishment by Proportion of English in Constituency (1966)
(Percentages)

Vote on Capital Punishment	Percent English 0-9		10-19		20-29		30-39		40-49			
No Vote	2.1	(1)	.0	(0)	.0	(0)	8.3	(2)	2.9	(1)		
Abolish	27.1	(13)	36.8	(7)	40.0	(8)	41.7	(10)	55.9	(19)		
Retain	70.8	(34)	63.2	(12)	60.0	(12)	50.0	(12)	41.2	(14)		
Total	18.1	(48)	7.2	(19)	7.5	(20)	9.1	(24)	12.8	(34)		
	50-59		60-69		70-79		80-89		90-100		Total	
No Vote	.0	(0)	.0	(0)	8.1	(3)	11.8	(2)	16.7	(1)	3.8	(10)
Abolish	51.5	(17)	66.7	(18)	32.4	(12)	23.5	(4)	66.7	(4)	42.3	(112)
Retain	48.5	(16)	33.3	(9)	59.5	(22)	64.7	(11)	16.7	(1)	54.0	(143)
Total	12.5	(33)	10.2	(27)	14.0	(37)	6.4	(17)	2.3	(6)	100.0	(265)

Table 44:
Public Sentiment on Capital Punishment by Ethnicity (Mother Tongue) 1973 (Percentages)

Opinion on Capital Punishment	Mother Tongue English		French		Other		Total	
Abolish	33.1		23.1		31.9		30.1	(217)
Retain	58.3		73.9		61.2		63.1	(454)
No Opinion	8.8		3.0		6.9		6.8	(49)
Total	56.3	(405)	27.6	(199)	16.1	(116)	100.0	(720)

Education Level Variation in Public Opinion and Legislative Vote on the Death Penalty

Tables 47 and 49 show that, over both periods, people with higher education tend to have less support for the death penalty. When constituencies are compared on the proportion of people in them with relatively high education (Tables 48 and 50), we see that MP's do reflect this feature in the correct direction in their vote although the effect is more pronounced in 1966.

In 1973, MP's from highly educated areas (those with over 55 per cent of the population with high school or university training) were clearly abolitionist. In constituencies where a low proportion (less than 34 per cent) had this level of education, the MP was more abolitionist than those with middle levels of education in their constituency. In 1966, the effect of educational level on the MP's vote was more uniform.

Political Party Variation in Public Opinion and Legislative Vote on the Death Penalty

To end this section, we turn to a special problem. In the foregoing, we assume that the MP will be affected by his whole constituency. Any characteristic of this collectivity, such as rurality or ethnicity which is related to public opinion, should, therefore, affect his vote. This is what is supposed to happen in western democracies. Even if elected by some specialized minority in the constituency, the MP should reflect the interests and wishes of all the people.

It is possible, however, to imagine that a representative might

Table 45:
Vote on Capital Punishment by Proportion of French in Constituency (1973)
(Percentages)

Vote on Capital Punishment	Percent French 0-9		10-19		20-29		30-39		40-49	
No Vote	13.7	(20)	.0	(0)	.0	(0)	28.6	(2)	.0	(0)
Abolish	40.4	(59)	68.4	(13)	72.7	(8)	57.1	(4)	85.7	(6)
Retain	45.9	(67)	31.6	(6)	27.3	(3)	14.3	(1)	14.3	(1)
Total	55.3	(146)	7.2	(19)	4.2	(11)	2.7	(7)	2.7	(7)

Vote on Capital Punishment	50-59		60-69		70-79		80-89		90-100		Total	
No Vote	16.7	(1)	16.7	(1)	10.0	(1)	28.6	(6)	29.0	(9)	15.2	(39)
Abolish	50.0	(3)	50.0	(3)	80.0	(8)	28.6	(6)	25.8	(8)	44.7	(119)
Retain	33.3	(2)	33.3	(2)	10.0	(1)	42.9	(9)	45.2	(14)	40.2	(106)
Total	2.3	(6)	2.3	(6)	3.8	(10)	8.0	(21)	11.7	(31)	100.0	(264)

Table 46:
Vote on Capital Punishment by Proportion of English in Constituency (1973)
(Percentages)

Vote on Capital Punishment	Percent English 0-9		10-19		20-29		30-39		40-49	
No Vote	21.2	(11)	35.7	(5)	10.0	(2)	13.6	(3)	13.9	(5)
Abolish	32.7	(17)	42.9	(6)	70.0	(14)	50.0	(11)	63.9	(23)
Retain	46.2	(24)	21.4	(3)	20.0	(4)	36.4	(8)	22.2	(8)
Total	19.7	(52)	5.3	(14)	7.6	(20)	8.3	(22)	13.6	(36)

	50-59		60-69		70-79		80-89		90-100		Total	
No Vote	10.8	(4)	10.3	(3)	14.8	(4)	10.5	(2)	12.5	(1)	15.2	(39)
Abolish	43.2	(16)	48.3	(14)	25.9	(7)	31.6	(6)	50.0	(4)	44.7	(119)
Retain	45.9	(17)	41.4	(12)	59.3	(16)	57.9	(11)	37.5	(3)	40.2	(106)
Total	14.0	(37)	11.0	(29)	10.2	(27)	7.2	(19)	3.0	(8)	100.0	(264)

Table 47:
Public Sentiment on Capital Punishment by Education (1966)
(Percentages)

Opinion on Capital Punishment	Education: Up to Public School Graduation		Up to High School Graduation		Up to University Graduation		Total	
Abolish	35.2		33.7		51.7		37.7	(228)
Retain	53.5		57.3		38.5		53.0	(330)
No Opinion	15.2		8.9		9.9		9.3	(71)
Total	33.9	(223)	47.4	(312)	13.8	(91)	100.0	(658)

Table 48:
Vote on Capital Punishment by Educational* Level of Constituency (1966)
(Percentages)

Vote on Capital Punishment	Percent of Population with High School or University Education 0-24		25		30-34		35-39		40-44			
45-49												
No Vote	.0	(0)	.0	(0)	4.5	(1)	.0	(0)	7.1	(3)		
Abolish	28.6	(4)	15.4	(2)	36.4	(8)	33.3	(10)	38.1	(16)		
Retain	71.4	(10)	84.6	(11)	59.1	(13)	66.7	(20)	54.8	(23)		
Total	5.3	(14)	4.9	(13)	8.3	(23)	11.3	(30)	15.8	(42)		
	45-49		50-54		55-59		60-64		65 & Over		Total	
No Vote	3.4	(1)	12.5	(4)	.0	(0)	5.3	(1)	.0	(0)	3.8	(10)
Abolish	41.4	(12)	43.8	(14)	48.6	(18)	42.1	(8)	74.1	(20)	42.3	(112)
Retain	55.2	(16)	43.8	(14)	51.4	(19)	52.6	(10)	25.9	(7)	54.0	(143)
Total	10.9	(29)	12.1	(32)	14.0	(37)	7.2	(19)	10.2	(27)	100.0	(265)

*Proportion of population of constituency 15 years and older, not attending school, who had completed some or all of high school and some or all of university, as reported to the 1961 Census.

Table 49:
Vote on Capital Punishment by Educational* Level of Constituency (1973)
(Percentages)

Vote on Capital Punishment	Percent of Population with High School or University Education											
	0-24		25-29		30-34		35-39		40-44			
No Vote	26.3	(5)	15.4	(4)	13.2	(5)	19.2	(10)	17.5	(11)		
Abolish	31.6	(6)	38.5	(10)	55.3	(21)	44.2	(23)	33.3	(21)		
Retain	42.1	(8)	46.2	(12)	31.6	(12)	36.5	(19)	49.2	(31)		
Total	7.2	(19)	9.8	(26)	14.4	(38)	19.7	(52)	23.9	(63)		
	45-49		50-54		55-59		60-64		65 & Over		Total	
No Vote	7.7	(2)	10.0	(2)	.0	(0)	10.0	(1)	.0	(0)	15.2	(39)
Abolish	57.7	(15)	50.0	(10)	80.0	(4)	30.0	(3)	100.0	(5)	44.7	(119)
Retain	34.6	(9)	40.0	(8)	20.0	(1)	60.0	(6)	.0	(0)	40.2	(106)
Total	9.8	(26)	7.6	(20)	1.9	(5)	3.8	(10)	1.9	(5)	100.0	(264)

*Proportion of population of constituency who had completed some or all of high school and some or all of university as reported to 1971 Census. Note difference from 1961 data in Table 48. Levels of education in all constituencies are depressed by the inclusion of school children in 1973.

Table 50:
Public Sentiment on Capital Punishment by Education (1971)
(Percentages)

Opinion on Capital Punishment	Education: Up to Public School Graduation	Up to High School Graduation	Up to University Graduation	Total
Abolish	24.7	29.4	43.4	30.1 (216)
Retain	75.3	64.8	50.4	63.1 (454)
No Opinion	10.0	5.0	6.0	6.8 (48)
Total	22.7 (184)	54.9 (401)	17.7 (129)	100.0 (720)

attend to the wishes of political supporters more assiduously than others. By examining the capital punishment opinions of those who support various parties, we can make an estimate of direction of influence of particular supporters on the MP. Tables 51 and 53 show that there is almost no difference between Liberal and Conservative voters in their views on the death penalty. Both tend to support it. Quebec Social Credit voters are substantially more retentionist than the supporters of the two major parties and the New Democratic Party supporters tend to be somewhat less retentionist. These patterns are quite stable over the two time periods. The Progressive Conservative MP's closely reflect the distribution of opinion in their supporters in their rates over two periods (see Tables 52 and 54). The Ralliement des Creditistes MP's over-represent in the correct direction the retentionist sentiment of their supporters. The Liberals in 1966 voted counter to their supporters in the House and almost reversed them in 1973. The New Democratic Party is consistently abolitionist when their supporters are only slightly less retentionist than other Canadians.

In general, there is not a great difference in the supporters of various parties' views on the death penalty. People's opinion does not seem to be associated with political ideology as strongly as it is for MP's. MP's tend to exaggerate the tendencies of their supporters when they vote in the Commons.

Summary

In this section, we are still holding to the temporarily useful assumption that individual and party characteristics do not determine an MP's vote on the death penalty question. Rather he reflects constituency sentiment. We expect, then, that variations in the patterns of public opinion should be reflected in the votes of MP's from constituencies subject to these patterned variations. This is a complex and tentative task of inference. These patterns of variation

Table 51:
Public Sentiment on Capital Punishment (1966) by Party Supported in 1965 Election (Percentages)

Opinion on Capital Punishment	Political Party* LIB		PC		SC	
Abolish	35.4		37.6		37.5	
Retain	52.8		55.2		58.3	
No Opinion	11.8		7.2		4.2	
Total**	32.2	(212)	18.9	(125)	3.6	(24)

	NDP		RC		TOTAL	
Abolish	44.3		25.0		37.7	(246)
Retain	48.1		75.0		53.0	(346)
No Opinion	7.6		.0		9.4	(66)
Total	12.6	(79)	.6	(4)	100.0	(658)

*LIB = Liberal; PC = Progressive Conservative; SC = Social Credit; NDP = New Democratic Party; RC = Ralliement des Creditistes.
**Refusal to answer, too young to vote, don't remember, etc. are excluded from Table.

in opinion are conceived of as indicators of the climate of opinion an MP might find himself in. Only the weakest inference is intended here since the methodological problems in this inference are important.[18]

There appears to be some correspondence between public opinion and MP's vote for these selected characteristics. Regional variation in opinion is inconsistent over time as is regional variation in MP's voting. Only the small number of Members from Newfoundland and P.E.I. seem to consistently reflect the abolitionist sentiment of these areas. Similarly, the moderate views of Ontarians and their MP's are stable. MP's from Alberta are consistently more retentionist than Albertans and MP's from Quebec are consistently more abolitionist than Quebeckers.

Rural repressive opinion is muted and the urbanites' abolitionism is extended by their respective MP's.

On the cultural attributes of religion and ethnicity, a complicated

Table 52: Vote on Capital Punishment by Political Party (1966) (Percentages)

Vote on Capital Punishment	Political Party: No Information		LIB		PC		SC	
No Vote	.0	(0)	5.4	(7)	3.1	(3)	.0	(0)
Abolish	100.0	(1)	54.6	(71)	17.3	(17)	20.0	(1)
Retain	.0	(0)	40.0	(52)	79.6	(78)	80.0	(4)
Total	.4	(1)	49.1	(130)	37.0	(98)	1.9	(5)

	NDP		RC		Liberal Labor		Total	
Abolish	.0	(0)	.0	(0)	.0	(0)	3.8	(10)
Retain	100.0	(21)	.0	(0)	100.0	(1)	42.3	(112)
No Opinion	.0	(0)	100.0	(9)	.0	(0)	54.0	(143)
Total	7.9	(21)	3.4	(9)	.4	(1)	100.0	(265)

Table 53 Public Sentiment on Capital Punishment (1971) by Party Supported in 1968 Election (Percentages)

Opinion on Capital Punishment	Political Party: LIB		PC		NDP	
Abolish	28.0		18.3		44.2	
Retain	65.6		67.8		55.8	
No Opinion	6.4		13.9		.0	
Total	31.1	(218)	16.4	(115)	6.1	(43)

	RC		OTHER		TOTAL	
Abolish	22.2		36.1		30.1	(217)
Retain	77.8		63.9		63.1	(454)
No Opinion	.0		.0		6.8	(49)
Total	1.3	(9)	45.1	(316)	100.0	(720)

picture of representation which changes over time emerges. Roman Catholic and French people tend to favour the death penalty. MP's from predominantly French and Catholic constituencies are moving away from retention over time. On the other hand, Protestant and English People are becoming relatively more repressive over time and MP's representing their constituencies are voting in correspondence with this shift. Homogeneity of these cultural characteristics in a constituency is associated with a retentionist vote.

The expected relation of education to opinion and its impact through the constituency on the MP's vote occurs. Highly educated people and MP's representing their constituencies tend to vote for abolition. And finally, the left right political spectrum, which has a minor effect on public opinion has an exaggerated effect in the voting of MPs.

None of these factors appears to be, in itself, very powerful. While MP's seem to respond to these differences in the climate of opinion, they do so inconsistently.

Constituencies which are rural in Quebec or Alberta, with a concentration of one religious and ethnic group, and in which the population has relatively low levels of education and has voted Social

Table 54
Vote on Capital Punishment by Political Party (1973)
(Percentages)

Vote on Capital Punishment	Political Party LIB		PC		SC	
No Vote	17.6	(19)	13.9	(15)	13.3	(2)
Abolish	63.9	(69)	20.4	(22)	.0	(0)
Retain	18.5	(20)	65.7	(71)	86.7	(13)
Total	40.9	(108)	40.9	(108)	5.7	(15)

	NDP		INDEP		TOTAL	
No Vote	9.7	(3)	50.0	(1)	15.2	(39)
Abolish	87.1	(27)	.0	(0)	44.7	(119)
Retain	3.2	(1)	50.0	(1)	40.2	(106)
Total	11.7	(31)	.8	(2)	100.0	(264)

Credit, produce a retentionist climate of opinion which the MP responds to. The opposite characteristics in combination produce the opposite effect.

Cross pressure effects of mixed ethnicity or relatively high education in rural areas confuse the climate and probably the MP.

A final word on the status of political party as a variable in this section is in order. A vote for a particular party is not like ethnicity or rurality. It can be changed easily. Ethnic and rural-urban characteristics of constituencies can also be changed through redistricting, of course. But political preference may *summarize* these other attributes rather than being an independent addition to them. Rural Alberta and Quebec constituencies have supported the Social Credit party more than any other area of Canada. We have no way of knowing whether the Social Credit MP was elected because of his retentionist position, or whether he takes a retentionist position because of the constituency he was elected in. This problem is particularly knotty for the major parties where the differences in public opinion of their supporters is for practical purposes non-existent.

The Personal Characteristics of MP's and their Vote on Capital Punishment

In this section, we treat the Members of Parliament as if they might be any other collection of people who were asked for their view on capital punishment. That is, we assume that the constituencies' opinion and party organization have no influence on their vote. This is a useful, oversimple assumption to check some ideas about individual attitudes and the death penalty. We, of course, have no data on the psychologies of the individual MP's. But we have indicators of a few characteristics which have been found to be associated with punitiveness.[19]

In both the 1966 and the 1973 debates, the party affiliation of MP's made a substantial difference in their vote on the death penalty. Although the formal discipline of the party whip was removed in these "free" votes, the members of each party tended to vote alike.

In the following discussion of some individual characteristics of MP's and their effect on death penalty vote, the political affiliation of the Member is taken into account.

Age, Political Party and Death Penalty Vote

Those MP's who have joined political parties which stand for more conservative policies should be more inclined to support the retention of capital punishment. Although the Social Credit and Progressive Conservative parties cannot be designated as to the right of the Liberals and the NDP on every issue, they have, and encourage, the reputation of being more conservative than the other two. The New Democratic Party is recognized as being on the left of the Canadian political spectrum. We would assume a tendency for individual Members to be reflective of the general political view of their party. Thus, even in a free vote, we can predict that individual MP's will tend to be conservative and support the death penalty in

Table 55:
Vote to Retain Capital Punishment by Age of MP and Political Party (1966) (Percentages)

	Political Party							
	LIB		PC		SC		NDP	
Age								
18-27	.0	(0)	.0	(0)	.0	(0)	.0	(0)
8-37	33.3	(21)	62.5	(8)	.0	(1)	.0	(1)
38-47	40.8	(49)	71.0	(31)	100.0	(1)	.0	(7)
48-57	43.2	(37)	84.8	(33)	100.0	(3)	.0	(7)
58-67	45.5	(11)	90.0	(20)	.0	(0)	.0	(4)
68-77	20.0	(5)	80.0		.0	(0)	.0	(2)
No Information	42.9	(7)	100.0	(1)	.0	(0)	.0	(0)
Total	40.0	(130)	79.6	(98)	80.0	(5)	.0	(21)

	RC		INDEP		TOTAL	
Age						
18-27	.0	(0)	.0	(0)	.0	(0)
28-37	100.0	(1)	.0	(1)	39.4	(33)
38-47	100.0	(3)	.0	(0)	50.5	(91)
48-57	100.0	(4)	.0	(0)	60.7	(84)
58-67	100.0	(1)	.0	(0)	66.7	(36)
68-77	.0	(0)	.0	(0)	41.7	(12)
No Information	.0	(0)	.0	(1)	44.4	(9)
Total	100.0	(9)	.0	(2)	54.0	(265)

increasing proportions as one moves from NDP through Liberal and Conservative to the Social Credit Party.

Tables 55 and 56 show this trend quite clearly in the two separate Parliaments. Only one NDP Member voted in favour of the death penalty and over 80 per cent of the Social Credit and Ralliement des Creditistes MP's did. 40 per cent of the Liberal MP's were retentionists in 1966 but only 18 per cent were retentionists in 1973. The PC's also lost retentionists from 79.6 per cent in 1966 to 66.0 per cent in 1973. The conservative to liberal political spectrum is

**Table 56:
Vote to Retain Capital Punishment by Age of MP and Political Party (1973)
(Percentages)**

Age	LIB		PC		SC	
18-27	.0	(0)	67.0	(3)	.0	(0)
28-37	.0	(15)	67.0	(15)	100.0	(2)
38-47	10.0	(40)	76.0	(24)	100.0	(2)
48-57	24.0	(34)	63.0	(38)	100.0	(3)
58-67	42.0	(12)	60.0	(15)	66.0	(6)
68-77	100.0	(1)	100.0	(2)	.0	(0)
No Information	29.0	(7)	33.0	(6)	100.0	(2)
Total	18.0	(109)	66.0	(107)	87.0	(15)

Age	NDP		INDEP		TOTAL	
18-27	.0	(1)	.0	(0)	50.0	(4)
28-37	.0	(6)	.0	(0)	32.0	(38)
38-47	.0	(5)	.0	(0)	37.0	(76)
48-57	.0	(10)	.0	(1)	41.0	(85)
58-67	14.0	(7)	.0	(0)	48.0	(40)
68-77	.0	(1)	.0	(0)	75.0	(4)
No Information	.0	(1)	100.0	(1)	41.0	(17)
Total	3.0	(31)	50.0	(2)	40.0	(264)

then one of the factors which is associated with variations in support for the death penalty.

It also appears in these tables that the older MP's in all parties tend to be more favourable to hanging. This trend is noted with a few anomalies, over two Parliaments. Within the largest age groups in Parliament, those from 28-67 years of age, the overall trend is a uniform increase in support for the death penalty with age. This trend is preserved within the Liberal MP's where the younger ones are fully abolitionist and the older ones tend to vote for retention in greater numbers, although the majority always favour abolition. Of the two minority parties, there is a tendency for the Scoial Credit Members to be older and the NDP younger, but their left-right differences seem to account for their almost unanimous positions on the death penalty.

The effect of age within the Progressive Conservative party varies over the years and tends in the opposite direction to the overall pattern in 1973. Those Progressive Conservative MP's under 47 years of age were more retentionist than their older colleagues in 1973. Increases in age and political conservativism both tend to have an independent, consistent and favourable effect on support for the death penalty.

Education, Political Party and Death Penalty Vote

Because the party affiliation of MP's is closely related to their vote, we shall continue to examine it as we look at other plausible personal influences. Education is thought to encourage a more rational and pragmatic world view as well as to reduce emotionalism and the reliance on unexamined belief. Those who vote for the death penalty are thought to be more punitive, authoritarian and emotional in decision making. It should follow that the greater the amount of education and an MP has received, the less he is likely to vote for retention of the death penalty.

Tables 57 and 58 show the overall effect of education on death penalty vote as well as its effect within each party. The overall trend in both years is consistent, with those MP's having the highest education, 2 or more university degrees, supporting abolition more than their less educated colleagues. This effect is also consistent in the predicted direction within the major parties, over the two Parliaments. So education itself affects the support of individual MP's on the death penalty. There is some tendency for the Liberals and NDP to have more highly educated Members than the other parties.

Table 57:
Vote to Retain Capital Punishment by Education of MP and Political Party (1966)
(Percentages)

	Political Party													
Education	LIB		PC		SC		NDP		RC		INDEP		TOTAL	
2 Degrees	28.8	(59)	65.6	(32)	.0	(1)	.0	(8)	100.0	(2)	.0	(0)	39.2	(102)
1 Degree	55.0	(20)	78.9	(19)	100.0	(1)	.0	(2)	100.0	(1)	.0	(1)	63.6	(44)
0 Degree	47.7	(44)	89.1	(46)	100.0	(3)	.0	(11)	100.0	(6)	.0	(0)	64.5	(110)
No Information	42.9	(7)	100.0	(1)	.0	(0)	.0	(0)	.0	(0)	.0	(1)	44.4	(9)
Total	40.0	(130)	79.6	(98)	80.0	(5)	.0	(21)	100.0	(9)	.0	(2)	54.0	(265)

Table 58:
Vote to Retain Capital Punishment by Education of MP and Political Party (1973)
(Percentages)

Education	LIB		PC		SC	
			Political Party			
2 Degrees	7.0	(41)	59.0	(32)	100.0	(1)
1 Degree	9.0	(23)	70.0	(30)	.0	(0)
0 Degrees	100.0	(1)	80.0	(5)	100.0	(1)
No Information*	32.0	(44)	68.0	(40)	85.0	(13)
Total	18.0	(109)	66.0	(107)	87.0	(15)

Education	NDP		INDEP		TOTAL	
2 Degrees	.0	(11)	.0	(11)	27.0	(85)
1 Degree	.0	(6)	.0	(0)	39.0	(59)
0 Degrees	.0	(0)	100.0	(1)	75.0	(8)
No Information*	7.0	(14)	.0	(0)	49.0	(111)
Total	3.0	(31)	.0	(0)	40.0	(264)

* A more stringent criteron on educational attainment was employed in analyzing the biographical data in 1973 (The Canadian Parliamentary Guide) as compared to 1966. All categories of education are reduced in 1973 but those with "no degree" are deflated the most.

Religion, Political Party and Death Penalty Vote

The public positions of the major religious organizations on the death penalty are quite well known. The large Protestant denominations such as the United Church of Canada, has been publicly opposed to hanging for many years. Until the 1973 debate, the Roman Catholic Church did not oppose it. But recently, one prom-

Table 59
Vote to Retain Capital Punishment by Religion of MP and Political Party (1966)
(Percentages)

Religion	LIB		PC		SC		NDP		RC		INDEP		TOTAL	
Roman Catholic	52.8	(72)	85.7	(14)	.0	(0)	.0	(1)	100.0	(9)	.0	(1)	60.8	(97)
Protestant	21.7	(46)	80.5	(77)	75.0	(4)	.0	(10)	.0	(0)	.0	(0)	54.7	(137)
Jewish	.0	(2)	.0	(0)	.0	(0)	.0	(3)	.0	(0)	.0	(0)	.0	(5)
Protestant Sect	.0	(0)	60.0	(5)	100.0	(1)	.0	(0)	.0	(0)	.0	(0)	66.7	(6)
No Information	40.0	(10)	50.0	(2)	.0	(0)	.0	(7)	.0	(0)	.0	(1)	25.0	(20)
Total	40.0	(130)	79.6	(98)	80.0	(5)	.0	(21)	100.0	(9)	.0	(2)	54.0	(265)

Table 60
Vote to Retain Capital Punishment by Religion of MP and Political Party (1973)
(Percentages)

Religion	Political Party LIB		PC		SC	
Roman Catholic	18.0	(62)	56.0	(16)	85.0	(13)
Protestant	17.0	(24)	70.0	(74)	.0	(0)
Jewish	.0	(2)	.0	(1)	.0	(0)
Protestant Sect	.0	(1)	67.0	(6)	.0	(0)
No Information	.0	(19)	55.0	(11)	100.0	(2)
Total	18.0	(109)	66.0	(107)	87.0	(15)

Religion	NDP		INDEP		TOTAL	
Roman Catholic	.0	(1)	50.2	(2)	34.0	(94)
Protestant	.0	(12)	.0	(0)	51.0	(110)
Jewish	.0	(3)	.0	(0)	.0	(6)
Protestant Sect	.0	(1)	.0	(0)	50.0	(8)
No Information	7.0	(14)	.0	(0)	30.0	(46)
Total	3.0	(31)	.0	(0)	40.0	(264)

inent Roman Catholic organization endorsed the renewal of the 5 year trial period.[20]

We would expect, then, that religious affiliation should make a difference in the MP's vote on a moral issue like the death penalty. In Tables 59 and 60, the relationship of religion to the capital punishment vote and to political party is shown. Overall, it appears that Jews and those that do not report religious involvement are the least retentionist over the two Parliaments. MP's who belong to small Protestant sects and churches tend to be consistently more retentionist. The most striking feature of these data is the reversal of Roman Catholic and Protestant MP's between 1966 and 1973. Roman Catholic MP's become much less retentionist than their Protestant colleagues. This reduction in Roman Catholic punitive sentiment occurs almost equally in both major parties (about 30 per cent reduction). The public position of religious organizations does not have a clear effect on the votes of MP's who affiliate with various religious organizations.

MP's who are atheists, agnostics or who for various reasons do not report a religious affiliation, tend not to support the death penalty as do Jewish MP's The positive effect of Roman Catholic religion on a retention vote in 1966 erodes substantially by 1973.

Considering the theme of this book, it is tempting to consider the possibility of a secularizing of Catholic opinion in this period from a previous emphasis on the sacred. It can be argued that public policy debate in a religiously plural society on such matters as criminal sanctions, reproductive technology & church state relations, forces a more rational, instrumental and secular orientation to public policy discussion on organizations which normally give priority to the moral and expressive orientation.

Occupation, Political Party and Death Penalty Vote

In addition to summarizing some background characteristics, such as education, the occupation of an MP indicates differences in life-style between MP's which may have an effect on punitiveness. One might forecast that professions, with their affiliations which cut across the immediate setting of an MP, would tend to produce a more contextual orientation to punishment for deviance. Practicality, rationality and expedience should also characterize the orientation of businessmen and farmers to such problems as law violation. These should be consistent with norms of decision making operative in these occupations.

Tables 61 and 62 present variations in MP's vote on the death penalty by the occupations they hold. Of the large occupational groups, farmers and businessmen support the death penalty more than professionals including lawyers. This pattern holds over time and weakly within political parties. It is difficult with these data to disentangle the effect of education and occupation. All the professions have 2 or more degrees and, therefore, any independent effect of occupation is obscure. It does appear that businessmen and farmers in any party are relatively repressive. The guess that rationality norms should transfer from business to politics, and that they predict to a less repressive orientation, appears faulty.

Table 61:
Vote to Retain Capital Punishment by Occupation of MP and Political Party (1966)
(Percentages)

Occupation	Political Party LIB		PC		SC	
Lawyer	30.0	(40)	72.0	(25)	.0	(0)
Other Professionals	26.7	(30)	62.5	(16)	50.0	(2)
Clergy	.0	(0)	.0	(0)	100.0	(1)
Businessman	60.6	(33)	85.7	(28)	.0	(0)
White Collar	46.7	(15)	.0	(1)	.0	(0)
Skilled Blue Collar	.0	(0)	.0	(0)	.0	(0)
Farmer	.0	(3)	95.2	(21)	100.0	(1)
Unskilled Blue Collar	.0	(1)	50.0	(2)	100.0	(1)
Retired	.0	(0)	100.0	(2)	.0	(0)
No Information	62.5	(8)	100.0	(3)	.0	(0)
Total	40.0	(130)	79.6	(98)	80.0	(5)

Occupation	NDP		RC		INDEP		TOTAL	
Lawyer	.0	(4)	.0	(0)	.0	(0)	43.5	(69)
Other Professionals	.0	(3)	100.0	(2)	.0	(1)	38.9	(54)
Clergy	.0	(2)	.0	(0)	.0	(0)	33.3	(3)
Businessman	.0	(1)	100.0	(6)	.0	(0)	73.5	(68)
White Collar	.0	(0)	.0	(0)	.0	(0)	36.8	(7)
Skilled Blue Collar	.0	(3)	.0	(1)	.0	(0)	25.0	(4)
Farmer	.0	(1)	.0	(0)	.0	(0)	80.8	(26)
Unskilled Blue Collar	.0	(3)	.0	(0)	.0	(0)	28.6	(7)
Retired	.0	(0)	.0	(0)	.0	(0)	100.0	(2)
No Information	.0	(1)	.0	(0)	.0	(1)	61.5	(13)
Total	.0	(21)	100.0	(9)	54.0	(265)	.0	(2)

Birthplace, Political Party and Vote on the Death Penalty

The distinction between people for whom moral indignation is a dominating response to deviance and those who tend to emphasize relativity, contextuality, and expediency in such matters is important in this book. One predictor of this difference is the extent to which people change cultural and social settings. Those who have stayed in one social milieu will be more likely to exhibit moral indignation and punitiveness than those who have had a more varied set of experiences. To examine this notion, Tables 63 and 64

Table 62:
Vote to Retain Capital Punishment by Occupation of MP and Political Party (1973)
(Percentages)

	Political Party					
Occupation	LIB		PC		SC	
Lawyer	.0	(31)	66.7	(30)	100.0	(1)
Other Professional	16.0	(25)	65.0	(20)	100.0	(2)
Clergy	.0	(0)	50.0	(2)	.0	(0)
Businessman	31.3	(32)	66.7	(33)	87.5	(8)
White Collar	.0	(2)	66.7	(3)	.0	(0)
Skilled Blue Collar	75.0	(4)	100.0	(1)	.0	(0)
Farmer	.0	(3)	90.0	(10)	.0	(1)
Unskilled Blue Collar	.0	(0)	.0	(1)	.0	(0)
No Information	27.3	(11)	37.5	(8)	100.0	(3)
Total	18.0	(109)	66.0	(107)	87.0	(15)

Occupation	NDP		INDEP		TOTAL	
Lawyer	.0	(4)	.0	(1)	31.3	(67)
Other Professionals	.0	(12)	.0	(0)	32.2	(59)
Clergy	.0	(2)	.0	(0)	25.0	(4)
Businessman	25.0	(4)	100.0	(1)	52.6	(78)
White Collar	.0	(3)	.0	(0)	25.0	(8)
Skilled Blue Collar	.0	(0)	.0	(0)	80.0	(5)
Farmer	.0	(1)	.0	(0)	60.0	(15)
Unskilled Blue Collar	.0	(1)	.0	(0)	.0	(2)
No Information	.0	(4)	.0	(0)	34.6	(26)
Total	3.0	(31)	50.0	(2)	40.0	(264)

Table 63
Vote to Retain Capital Punishment by Birthplace of MP and Political Party (1966)
(Percentages)

	Political Party					
Birthplace	LIB		PC		SC	
In Constituency	47.9	(48)	92.3	(39)	.0	(1)
In Canada	30.9	(68)	71.4	(49)	100.0	(3)
Foreign	50.0	(6)	66.7	(9)	100.0	(1)
No Information	62.5	(8)	100.0	(1)	.0	(0)
Total	40.0	(130)	79.6	(98)	80.0	(5)

	NDP		RC		INDEP		TOTAL	
In Constituency	.0	(4)	100.0	(5)	.0	(1)	65.3	(98)
In Canada	.0	(10)	100.0	(3)	.0	(0)	46.6	(133)
Foreign	.0	(7)	.0	(0)	.0	(0)	43.0	(23)
No Information	.0	(0)	100.0	(1)	.0	(1)	63.6	(11)
Total	.0	(21)	100.0	(9)	.0	(2)	54.0	(265)

Table 64
Vote to Retain Capital Punishment by Birthplace of MP and Political Party (1973
(Percentages)

	Political Party					
Birthplace	LIB		PC		SC	
In Constituency	20.0	(55)	81.0	(32)	100.0	(5)
In Province	17.0	(29)	59.0	(46)	83.0	(6)
Out of Province	13.0	(16)	68.0	(22)	0.0	(1)
No Information	25.0	(8)	38.0	(8)	100.0	(3)
Total	18.0	(109)	66.0	(107)	87.0	(15)

	NDP		INDEP		TOTAL	
In Constituency	.0	(7)	100.0	(1)	43.0	(100)
In Province	.0	(10)	.0	(1)	40.0	(92)
Out of Province	8.0	(13)	.0	(0)	35.0	(52)
No Information	.0	(1)	.0	(0)	29.0	(28)
Total	3.0	(31)	50.0	(2)	40.0	(264)

were constructed, comparing those MP's who were born in ridings they represent to those who were not. Data from both the 1966 and 1973 Parliamentary debates show that those who were born in their own constituency are slightly more retentionist than those born in the same province or in Canada. Those born outside the province of their constituency and outside Canada are the least retentionist. This overall effect is not faithfully preserved within each party. However, the MP's who were born in their own riding always tend to be among the most repressive in both the major parties. This difference is more pronounced in 1966 than in 1973.

Some General Comments on Individual Factors in MP's Votes on the Death Penalty

In spite of the declaration of a free vote in both 1966, 1967 and 1973 debates of the death penalty, Members of each political party tended to vote alike. This effect was more pronounced in the major parties in 1973. Even in a free vote on an issue of individual conscience such as this one, we would expect some similarity in voting within parties. These Members are, after all, drawn into party organizations in part because of shared beliefs, values and ideology about public policy. They also spend time together, and depend on each other and the organization for support in their political roles. These influences will be examined in more detail in the next section.

It does appear that independent of these group influences, some individual factors of background and life experience do influence the vote.

Localism versus cosmopolitanism may summarize one cluster of these attributes. Those born outside their constituency, with high levels of education, and who have professional occupations, tend to vote against the death penalty more than their more "local" colleagues who do not have these attributes. They would tend to have experienced a wider range of social contexts and have a more pragmatic, instrumental approach to deviance. Similarly, those who are younger and less religious would tend to be less ethnocentric and moralistic. While all these attributes can be conceived as indicators of psychological dispositions in the individual MP to vote for or against the death penalty, and are so conceived in this section, they can be interpreted otherwise.

The cosmopolitan cluster can be interpreted as an insulator of the MP from the sentiment of his constituency. Of this were true, we should expect more difference between locals and cosmopolitans in 1973 when the sentiment for retention in the country was stronger than in 1966. We do not find any strong or consistent difference in the effect of these local-cosmopolitan attributes which changes between 1966 and 1973.

The Legislature and Party Influence

In this section, we assume that the individual MP enters the social world of the legislature and its party organizations with neither a personal view on the death penalty nor any understanding that he is to express the views of others such as his constituency's. Here, we will speculate and marshall whatever evidence seems appropriate to describe the group and institutional influences which may affect the MP's vote on the death penalty. This evidence will be of a variety of sources. First, let us examine the quantitative materials on the 1966 and 1973 votes to see whether they illuminate this problem.

We know that party affiliation is closely associated with voting behavior in 1966 and more so in 1973. The minority parties are almost unanimous in their positions in both years. The MP's from the larger parties tend strongly in opposite directions on the issue. Since there is no public party policy on this issue, and the leadership of both major parties tends to be abolitionist, then a tendency for MP's to influence each other through their party affiliations, must exist. In this case, we might expect there to be a relationship between length of time in the House and vote on the death penalty. The longer period would permit more complete socialization and influence into the group's beliefs on the death penalty question. For the Liberals, it would be in the abolitionist direction and for Progressive Conservatives, in the retentionist direction. As aggregates, both parties have become more divided over time on this question.[21] The question is, does time have the same impact on individuals? The Social Credit and NDP clearly socialize new Members to their positions. Most of the NDP (20), were elected since the 1966-67 debate, and almost half (8) of the Social Credit, so the group influence within the minority parties seems to be strong.

Tables 65 and 66 are necessarily complex. The length of tenure in the House is, of course, associated with age. We know that age has some effect on capital punishment vote. In 1966, there was an even increase in support for the death penalty with increases in age of the Member. However, only 42 per cent of the oldest Members (over 68 years) supported it. In 1973, the same pattern emerges; however, the small group of young Members (18-27) are anomalous. They show unexpected support for the death penalty. The effects of age, alone, and for each party, on the vote are shown in the total col-

Table 65:
Vote to Retain Capital Punishment by Political Party, Electoral History and Age of MP (1966) (Percentages)

Age	Liberal Electoral History (Year First Elected)						
	1965	1963	1962	1958	Before (58)	Combination	Total
18-27	—	—	—	—	—		
28-37	28.6 (7)	33.3 (6)	28.6 (7)	—	—	100.0 (1)	33.3 (21)
38-47	38.5 (13)	40.0 (10)	40.9 (22)	—	66.7 (3)	.0 (1)	40.8 (49)
48-57	75.0 (8)	14.3 (7)	35.7 (14)	100.0 (2)	33.3 (3)	33.3 (3)	43.2 (37)
58-67	—	—	50.0 (6)		40.0 (5)		45.5 (11)
68-77	—	—	.0 (1)	.0 (1)	50.0 (2)	.0 (1)	20.0 (5)
No Information	50.0 (2)	.0 (1)	.0 (2)		100.0 (2)		42.9 (7)
Total	46.7 (30)	29.2 (24)	36.5 (52)	66.7 (3)	53.3 (15)	66.7 (6)	40.0 (130)

Age	Progressive Conservative Electoral History (Year First Elected)						
	1965	1963	1962	1958	Before (58)	Combination	Total
18-27							
28-37	33.3 (3)	100.0 (1)		66.7 (3)	100.0 (1)		62.5 (8)
38-47	57.1 (7)	100.0 (1)	.0 (2)	71.4 (7)	83.3 (12)	100.0 (2)	71.0 (31)
48-57	100.0 (4)	75.0 (4)	80.0 (5)	87.5 (8)	88.9 (9)	66.7 (3)	84.8 (33)
58-67	100.0 (2)	.0 (1)	100.0 (1)	87.5 (8)	100.0 (7)	100.0 (1)	90.0 (20)
68-77				100.0 (2)	66.7 (3)		80.0 (5)
No Information			100.0 (1)				100.0 (1)
Total	68.8 (16)	71.4 (7)	66.7 (9)	82.1 (28)	87.5 (32)	83.3 (6)	79.6 (98)

Vote to Retain Capital Punishment by Political Party, Electoral History and Age of MP (1966) [Continued] (Percentages)

Age	1965		1963		1962		1958		Before 1958		Combination		Total	
	Social Credit and Ralliement des Creditistes|Electoral History (Year First Elected)													
18-27					—		—					(58)	—	
28-37	.0	(1)			—		100.0	(1)	—		—		50.0	(2)
38-47	100.0	(1)	—		100.0	(2)	—		—		100.0	(1)	100.0	(4)
48-57					100.0	(5)	—		—		100.0	(2)	100.0	(7)
58-67	100.0	(1)	—				—		—				100.0	(1)
68-77			—		—		—		—				—	
No Information	—		—		—		—		—				—	
Total	66.7	(3)		(0)	100.0	(7)	100.0	(1)		(0)	100.0	(3)	92.9	(14)

Age	1965		1963		1962		1958		Before (58)		Combination		Total		GRAND TOTAL	
	New Democratic Party,Electoral History (Year First Elected)															
18-27	—		—		—		—		—		—		—			
28-37	.0	(1)	—		—		—		—		—		.0	(1)	40.6	(32)
38-47	.0	(2)			.0	(3)	—		.0	(2)	—		.0	(7)	50.5	(91)
48-57	.0	(1)	.0	(1)	.0	(1)	—		.0	(1)	.0	(3)	.0	(7)	60.7	(84)
58-67	.0	(1)	.0	(1)	.0	(1)	—		.0	(1)	—		.0	(4)	66.7	(36)
68-77	—		—		—		—		.0	(1)	.0	(1)	.0	(2)	41.7	(12)
No Information	—		—		—		—		—		—		—		50.0	(8)
Total	.0	(5)	.0	(2)	.0	(5)		(0)	.0	(5)	.0	(4)	.0	(21)	54.4	(263)

N.B. Independents are excluded.

Retention votes by electoral history are: 1965 = 50:0 (54); 1963 = 36.6 (33); 1962 = 43.8 (73); 1958 = 81.3 (32); 4+ = 69.2 (52); C = 52.6 (19)

Table 66:
Vote to Retain Capital Punishment by Political Party, Electoral History and Age of MP (1973)
(Percentages)

	Liberal Electoral History (Year First Elected)															
Age	1972		1968		1965		1963		1962		Before (62)		Combination		Total	
18-27	—		—		—		—		—		—		—		—	
28-37	.0	(8)	.0	(5)	.0	(2)	—		—		—		—		.0	(15)
38-47	.0	(9)	10.0	(10)	20.0	(10)	.0	(4)	.0	(6)	—		100.0	(1)	10.0	(40)
48-57	40.0	(5)	27.3	(11)	33.3	(6)	.0	(1)	.0	(6)	100.0	(1)	.0	(3)	24.2	(33)
58-67	.0	(1)	100.0	(3)	33.3	(3)	50.0	(2)	.0	(3)	—		—		41.7	(12)
68-77	100.0	(1)	—		—		—		—		—		—		100.0	(1)
No Information	40.0	(5)	.0	(1)			.0	(1)	—		—		—		28.6	(7)
Total	17.2	(29)	23.3	(30)	23.8	(21)	12.5	(8)	.0	(15)	100.0	(1)	25.0	(4)	18.3	(109)

	Progressive Conservative Electoral History (Year First Elected)															
Age	1972		1968		1965		1963		1962		Before (62)		Combination		Total	
18-27	66.7	(3)	—		—		—		—		—				66.7	(3)
28-37	66.7	(12)	100.0	(2)	.0	(1)	—		—		—		—		66.7	(15)
38-47	82.3	(17)	50.0	(4)	75.0	(4)	—		—		100.0	(3)	.0	(1)	75.9	(29)
48-57	67.0	(21)	.0	(2)	100.0	(1)	.0	(1)	.0	(1)	75.0	(8)	75.0	(4)	63.1	(38)
58-67	100.0	(1)	66.7	(3)	—		—		33.3	(3)	60.0	(5)	66.7	(3)	60.0	(15)
68-77			100.0	(1)	—		—		—		100.0	(1)	—		100.0	(2)
No Information	33.3	(6)	—		—		—		—		—		—		66.7	(6)
Total	68.3	(60)	58.3	(12)	66.7	(6)	.0	(1)	25.0	(4)	76.5	(17)	62.5	(8)	66.3	(107)

Table 66: (continued)

Vote to Retain Capital Punishment by Political Party, Electoral History and Age of MP (1973)

(Percentages)

Social Credit — Electoral History (Year First Elected)

Age	1972		1968		1965		1962		Before (62)		Total	
	—		—		—		—		—		—	
18-27	100.0	(1)	100.0		—		—		—		100.0	(2)
28-37	—		—		100.0	(1)			.0	(1)	100.0	(2)
38-47	—		100.0	(2)	—		100.0	(1)	—		100.0	(3)
48-57	—		.0	(2)	—		100.0	(3)	100.0	(1)	66.7	(6)
58-67	—		—		—		—		—		—	
68-77											100.0	(2)
No Information	100.0	(2)	—		—		—	—	—			
Total	100.0	(3)	.0	(5)	100.0	(1)	100.0	(4)	50.0	(2)	86.7	(15)

New Democratic Party — Electoral History (Year First Elected)

Age	1972		1968		1965		1962		Before (62)		Combination		Total		GRAND TOTAL	
			.0	(1)									.0	(1)	50.0	(4)
18-27	.0	(5)	.0	(1)									.0	(6)	31.6	(38)
28-37	.0	(4)	.0	(1)									.0	(5)	36.8	(76)
38-47	.0	(2)	.0	(3)	.0	(2)	.0	(1)	.0	(2)			.0	(10)	41.7	(84)
48-57			.0	(2)			50.0	(2)			.0	(3)	14.2	(7)	47.5	(40)
58-67							.0	(1)					.0	(1)	75.0	(4)
68-77																
No Information	.0	(1)											.0	(1)	37.5	(16)
Total	.0	(12)	.0	(8)	.0	(2)	25.0	(4)	.0	(2)	.0	(3)	3.2	(31)	40.5	(262)

1963 is deleted for Social Credit and NDP as none began their careers in 1963.
N. B. — 2 Independents are excluded, which reduces the total to 262.

Retention votes by electoral history are: 1972 = 47%; 1968 = 31%; 1965 = 33%; 1963 = 11%; 1962 = 22%; 5+ = 70%; C = 41%.

umns. The effects of electoral history alone and for each party is shown in the total rows. The support within each party, age group and electoral history type is shown in each cell.

Overall, we find that support for the death penalty is higher for new Members and long-term Members, those enjoying several terms seem to be more abolitionist. Interestingly, those who came into Parliament in 1962 and 1963, of both Liberals and Conservatives, are the most abolitionist.

For the major parties, there is no clear pattern of increasing longevity leading to increasing endorsement of the group tendency on capital punishment. New Members of the major parties, those elected for the first time in 1972 and in 1965, have about the same proportion of support for retention as everyone else in the party. Age seems to have different effects on the death penalty vote of MP's at different times and in each of the major parties. Only 4 (7.3 per cent) of the 55 Liberal MP's under 47 years voted for the death penalty in 1973. There was a slight tendency for PC members over 47 years to support it less than their younger colleagues. However, in 1966 the younger PC Members were less retentionist and there was very little relation of age to vote for Liberals in the same year.

There is some evidence of the "law and order" mandate which some PC's claim was the basis of their 1972 electoral gains. At all age levels, the PC's elected in 1972 support the death penalty slightly more than their PC colleagues who were first elected earlier. However, this difference is very small. The opposite pattern holds for PC's in 1966.

Although the predicted pattern of socialization into a party cannot be sustained on these data, another pattern worthy of speculation emerges. Those MP's elected in 1962 and 1963 for both Liberals and PC were less retentionist than their party. Those who still sit in the House in 1973 are less retentionist. It may be that candidates are sorted and socialized in the eras in which they are first elected on major issues and values. They may then carry these attributes in a relatively unchanging pattern as long as they serve in the Commons.

Some Impressions of the Legislative and Party Influence on the Death Penalty Vote

Informal interviews with some Members of the House on how they voted as well as their perception of the events of the 1973 debate were conducted. Another source of data on this legislative phenomenon is the *verbatim* reports of the debates in Parliament for 1966 and 1973. A less rigorous, but probably more "lifelike" view of the legislative and party setting of these debates comes from this.

The first impression one gets when exposed to MP's in their place of business is the sense of special people going about special and important business. MP's of all parties tend to be drawn together into a comradeship, which while more intense within parties, cuts across party lines. This is reinforced by lore, humour and heroics about MP's and their adventures. It is clear they depend on respected and honest experts among them for opinion on public policy both in session and privately. There seems to be substantial sharing of political advice and inside information about the plans and secret intentions of others.

In the 1973 debate, there was an informal group of abolitonists from all parties, except the Social Credit, which advised and was consulted by the Solicitor General and his staff throughout the debate. This group used the caucus of each party to get information about the position of each MP on the bill to extend the five year ban on the death penalty. Those who were identified as in a quandry on it would be contacted by an abolitionist MP who knew them personally and would reassure them on the merits of the abolition position.

The usual ambivalence was claimed to be the tendency for MP's to be mildly abolitionist in sentiment but having a constituency which appeared to be strongly retentionist. Several abolitionist MP's sent out questionnaires which they regretted doing. They usually got a small return (5 to 10 per cent of those sent out) which ran heavily 80 to 90 per cent in favour of retention (see Chapter 1). In addition, all MP's spoken to reported relatively heavy mail, both from constituents and others running between 60 to 90 per cent in favour of retention. Most MP's were getting mail from party workers and long-time political supporters favouring retention. The strength and emotion of retentionist letters was much greater than the more measured and qualified abolition letters. Hence most abolitionists were in a position to at least guess that they might be voting against strong retentionist sentiment in the constituency. Although MP's are aware that those who write to them are not in any sense reflective of the distribution of opinion in the constituency, they do have a theory that the number and intensity of letters do reflect something to be reckoned with. None of the MP's interviewed took an arrogant version of the Burkean position. Most felt that they got close to their constituency opinion on most issues, and hoped to persuade them on issues where they disagreed.

Those MP's who were leaning to abolition but were concerned about constituency sentiment were counselled with several neutralizing beliefs which MP's seem to share. One is that elections generally turn, not on such idealistic issues as the death penalty, but on more "bread and butter" issues like taxes. Running counter to a constituency was, therefore, not as politically dangerous as it seemed. Also, all the party leaders, except the Social Credit leader, were open abolitionists and, therefore, the electorate had no symbolic leader for a retentionist vote.

Many MP's were concerned about the apparent laxity in the prison and parole systems in Canada at the time of this debate. There had been several flagrant and widely publicized escapes while prisoners were on temporary passes, one at a hockey game, for example, which were ammunition for a more general attack on penal policy under the Liberal government. These MP's were reassured that the Solicitor General had plans to tighten up on some of the excesses and abuses.

Although the sentiment of Parliament appeared to be swinging to a more retentionist position in 1973 in the first portion of the debate, the Solicitor General decided to try to amend the bill in committee. This backfired. After several days of debate, the bill to extend the five year moratorium on the death penalty, except for the killing of policemen and prison guards, was sent to committee by a vote of 138 to 114. At this second reading stage, the tradition is that the bill is approved or disapproved in principle, and, if approved, is sent to Committee for minor changes preparatory to the third round of debate in the House and the final vote.

The Solicitor General, his staff and other abolitonists in the House interpreted much of the debate as being in favour of full abolition of the death penalty if accompanied by tougher sentencing provisions and better public security from convicted capital offenders. They offered such a two-part amendment to the Committee of the House which was deliberating on the bill. This was widely reported in the press as only an attempt to fully abolish the death penalty. It was apparently surprising to the Committee and other Members of the House, as no advance consultations with prominent Members had occurred. In consequence of this, some Members bridled at the discourtesy of the surprising move. The Committee failed to modify the bill, deciding that it changed its intent.

This plan and the Solicitor General's motives generated some largely partisan debate on third reading of the original bill. It was regarded by some as a kind of trick. While the nature of the bill was to be changed with the amendments, it was by no means substantially out of the ordinary for the Committee, after the second reading, to accommodate the criticism of proposed legislation and alter proposals to meet these criticisms.

However, once viewed as a breach of custom and procedure,

compounded by the uncertain etiquette of surprising the Committee, and subjecting it to a windstorm of publicity and advice, the debate turned more partisan and critical of the original bill.

The setting of the House debate was conducive to a more partisan debate than in 1966-67. The Liberals had only two more seats than the opposition Conservatives and were in a minority government situation, being supported by the NDP. They were being criticized for not bringing forward legislation to deal with rising inflation and were accused of using the death penalty debate to occupy Parliament's time when more important economic matters waited. Also, some MP's in the Progressive Conservative party saw the opinion in the country as strongly retentionist and the Liberals as so out of phase with it that they wanted to force an election on the matter. Others counselled against that, however, within the PC group.

The generally partisan atmosphere of a minority government situation tended to polarize the Liberals and Conservatives. The party whips were not used and the deviance of a large minority of party members attests to that. There would be a tendency for Liberal Members to follow their leadership; the Cabinet voted abolition because of their moral leadership and strategic influence. However, the relatively large number of Liberal MP's who spoke against the bill was interpreted by one MP as providing the back bencher with an opportunity to show his constituents that he is not only a party delegate as he is obligated to be, most of the time, and particularly in a minority government situation.[22]

Retentionist MP's did not seem to be as organized as the abolitionists. Even those mentioned by others as prominent retentionists claimed not to have any substantial influence or contact with other MP's. One did finally allow that several had sought out his advice and that, while not encouraging them to vote retentionist, they were "comforted" by the knowledge that others shared their view. Usually, the retentionists took pride in their non-organization and mildly complained about the "unethical" organization on the other side. A free vote is relatively unusual in the Canadian Parliament and the distinction between party discipline and levels of organized influence seems unclear.

The "manoeuvres" of the government were also criticized. In addition to the abortive attempt to modify the bill in Committee, it was believed that the government had sent more retentionists out of the country on legislative committee business than abolitionists.

Overall, both retentionist and abolitionist MP's seemed to think that the death penalty was personal and moral. Both took pains to express understanding of their adversaries.

Some retentionist MP's (usually from rural areas) felt that those "sophisticated" abolition MP's (usually from big cities) had become confused about basic values and needed to be persuaded of the more grassroots and fundamental moral position on the vote. But others claimed to be open to changing their view. Members on both sides expressed concern for images. Abolitionists disclaimed the "bleeding heart" image and one retentionist said that he wasn't a "hardnosed, red necked, hanging Tory".

Many retentionists allowed as how the aboliton MP was taking a courageous moral leader position and was to be ruefully admired. The abolitionists also seemed to feel that the other side was morally committed. Only a few MP's were viewed by the abolitionists as cowering fearfully before ill-informed public opinion and voting contrary to their personal beliefs.

The rare personal antipathy and bitterness seemed to be reserved for MP's who had changed their mind at the last minute. Several MP's were counted as supporters by both sided before the vote. It is surprising that, on an issue of such moral intensity (Members sometimes wept during the Canadian death penalty votes), personal and collective bitterness could be avoided. Since the major parties are cross cut by death penalty opinion, the divisiveness of the issue may be muted. The minority NDP and Quebec Social Credit groups are so different in political philosophy, language and regional concentration that their death penalty differences are not unexpected.

The influence structure of the parties on this issue is unclear. Because many individuals in a party vote the same way on a free vote, we cannot assume either socialization into a party philosophy on the death penalty or some form of covert party discipline. There is no evidence for the pressure of either factor although both are quite plausible.

Conclusion

Party similarity in voting can be a result of the mutual selection of political affiliations by political aspirants and their supporters. Constituency opinion can foster the general success of a party and indirectly influence an MP's vote from the party.[23] The multitude of factors which may be operating together or in countervailing directions, alone or in interaction, to produce the capital punishment vote are depicted in footnote 23.

It is difficult to specify the independent and interactive influences adequately. Localism seems to foster not only individually based tendencies to retain the death penalty, but also connects the MP more firmly to his constituency making him more susceptible to their influences and opinion. If the constituency has the characteristics which encourage the MP to see it as retentionist, then the more local and less insulated the Member is, that is, the more he is a constituency delegate, the more he will express this sentiment. This will be especially true if the issue presents an opportunity, as in the case of some Liberal MP's, to show independence from the party elite, and accommodation to constituency opinion. If such an MP finds himself in a network of party and legislative colleagues who support retention, then the integration and weight of influences is very conducive to retentionist vote.

Most MP's are not in such an integrated situation. They affiliate with a party which is at least divided on the death penalty question, with respected Members including the three national leaders publicly in favour of abolition. They are generally better educated than their constituents, travel in their jobs, and deal with a wide variety of legislative topics. Although "cosmopolitan" is a relative term, the MP will tend to be more cosmopolitan than most constituents.

Abolition support depends on the proportion of MP's who are younger, less religious, highly educated, high status professionals, and who are socially and geographically mobile. These factors both insulate the MP from retentionist opinion in the constituency and move him as an individual towards a more rational, instrumental view of deviance.

As constituencies become culturally heterogeneous, urban, highly educated and supportive of liberal political philosophy, their opinion will become abolitionist. Under these conditions, the Burkean trustee abolitionist can live in closer harmony with his constituency.

Footnotes

[1] See footnote, Table 19 for distribution of popularity of Canadian MP's. Most MP's receive less than 50 per cent of the popular vote.

[2] Warren Miller and Donald Stokes, "Constituency Influence in Congress," *American Political Science Review*, 57 (1963), pp. 45-56.

[3] Charles Cnudde and Donald McCrone, "The Linkage between Constituency Attitudes and Congressional Voting Behavior: A Causal Model," *American Political Science Review* (December 1966), p. 66.

[4] For an outstanding review of theories of this area as well as a summary of empirical findings, see Malcolm Jewell, "Attitudinal Determinants of Legislative Behavior: The Utility of Role Analysis", in Alan Kornberg (ed.) *Legislatures in Developmental Perspective* (Duke University Press, 1970).

[5] The manifold and important differences between a parliamentary system and the United States' system will not be discussed here.

[6] Alan Kornberg, *Canadian Legislative Behavior* (New York, 1967).

[7] Kornberg, *op. cit.*, p. 108.

[8] David Hoffman and Norman Ward, "Documents of the Royal Commission on Bilingualism and Biculturalism".

[9] Hoffman and Ward, *op. cit.*, p. 67.

[10] For a recent critical review of this area of research on representational roles in Canada, see Robert Jackson and Michael Atkinson, *The Canadian Legislative System*, (Canada: MacMillan of Canada, in press).

[11] This analysis relies on data from The Canadian Parliamentary Guide, Statistics Canada, The Canadian Institute of Public Opinion and interviews with Canadian Members of Parliament. In 1966, 255 MPs voted on the death penalty bill, in 1967, 175 MPs voted and in 1973, 225 MPs voted.

[12] This is more difficult to conclude than it would appear at first glance. Public opinion, while favouring the death penalty, seems to favour a sharply restricted usage of it (see Chapter on Public Opinion). The modified death penalty bill of 1967 and 1973 may accord with public sentiment quite closely.

[13] The comparison between 1966, 1967 and 1973 involves very few Members who actually changed their vote. Of the MP's present and voting in 1973, 1 changed from retentionist to abolitionist, and 5 changed in the opposite direction. 9 abolitionists did not vote in 1973 as did 4 retentionists. The comparison between 1966 and 1967 of these Members (in the House in 1973) yields a similar finding, with 7 shifting to abolition from 1966 to 1967 and 1 the opposite way. So, the comparison between the periods does not describe individual changes.

[14] J. A. A. Lovink, "Is Canadian Politics to Competitive?" *Canadian Journal of Political Science*, 7, No. 3, September, 1973, p. 341. See also Malcolm Jewell, *op. cit.*, and Kornberg, *op. cit.*

[15] In this chapter, some evidence is reported more than once, under a variety of theoretical assumptions. For example, MP's education can be viewed as an insulating condition which releases him from a "delegate" role, as above. Later, education is used as an independent variable with a direct effect on death penalty opinion.

[16] Rank of Public Opinion by Rank of M.P. vote for Provinces

[17] It must be remembered that constituencies which have a low percentage of one religion will tend to have a high percentage of the other.

[18] Since the problem of how much correspondence there is between MP's, votes and public opinion is important and interesting and these data provide some clues to this correspondence, it is worthwhile to proceed in spite of some important but insoluble problems.

Characteristics of individuals and their attitudes from a sample of all Canada are used to make an inference about the climate of opinion in all or part of a political constituency which is characterized, as a collectivity. This form of evidenciary chain is unorthodox and determined by the limited availability of empirical data on the topic, rather than by design. Rather more detail is presented in these data than is usual because of this. This allows the reader a chance to examine more of this phenomenon.

[19] Vidmar, *op. cit.*, reports from studies of authoritarianism that those who are older or are less educated or who are politically conservative tend to be more authoritarian.

[20] Canadian Catholic Conference, January 26, 1973.

[21] Tables 52 and 54 show a 21.5 per cent reduction in retentionist votes for Liberals and a 13.9 per cent reduction in retentionist votes for PC's from 1966 to 1973. But in 1966, there was a 39.6 per cent difference between Liberal and PC retention; in 1973 this had increased to 47.2 per cent difference.

[22] Hoffman and Ward report that many MP's disassociate themselves with their party role. One MP informant said that a government back bencher is vulnerable to criticism, that he is only a rubber stamp for the government leadership and relishes opportunities to get his independence into the record.

[23] The classes of variables explored in this chapter and their relationships are sketched below

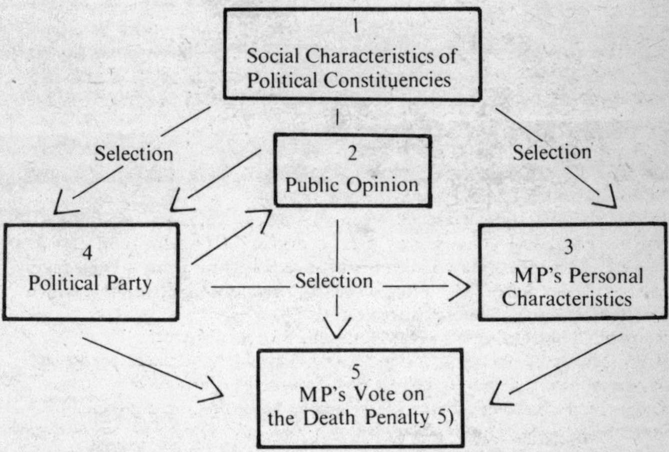

1) These characteristics of the political constituency such as rurality or ethnicity are seen as determinants of the public opinion and also selective of political parties and types of individual MP's. Homogeneity is a characteristic which is examined theoretically and empircally in Chapter 4.

2) Public opinion is largely determined by 1) but can be influenced by the party and the individual MP. The opinion on various matters (possibly the death penalty but not importantly) influences the selection of

certain MP's with various backgrounds and their party affiliations and processes. It should directly effect MP's behavior such as a vote on the death penalty.

3) These characteristics are largely selected by the party and the characteristics of the constituency. There may be some selection through public opinion. The characteristics directly influence the MP's vote and the party influence structure. The MP may lead public opinion in his constituency.

4) Parties are selected by constituency characteristics which may be mediated by public opinion. Individual MP's can influence the party to varying degrees. The MP's vote can be influenced by the party, as can a selection of his characteristics. Parties may influence constituency opinion.

5) The MP's vote is directly affected by public opinion, personal characteristics and political influence.

Chapter 4: Durkheim and Repressive Law

This chapter introduces the work of a major sociologist to the question of law and its relation to society. Because Durkheim's thought is central to modern sociology, and his work on law is central to his thought in general, this chapter deals with substantial theoretical and empirical detail. In addition, no comprehensive empirical examination of his ideas on repressive law has been undertaken, although these ideas are widely cited as if they have been empirically verified. This chapter undertakes an empirical examination of an hypothesis, based on Durkheim's thought on the relationship between social homogeneity and repressive law. Marshalling evidence to test this notion is also a convenient way of describing and analysing the wide variety of data we have collected on the social characteristics which are associated with support for repressive law.

Although non-intuitive, Durkheim's ideas add a dimension to our potential understanding of the legislative process in society. It is not that other ideas about the underlying dynamic of this process are clearer, more elegant and proveable, and that Durkheim's are more mysterious and metaphoric. Indeed, part of the purpose of this study is to debunk some simplistic "common knowledge" about the very complex legislative process. Because of this complexity, all our "explanations" about where law comes from are partial, conditonal and often metaphoric. Even in the apparent simplicity of an absolute monarchy, the analyst speculates about the King's breakfast and its relation to law.

Considerable attention has been paid in this section to a description of Durkheim's sociological style, assumptions and vocabulary since he departs substantially from common sense understandings of society in his work. Still it is to Durkheim that most sociologists trace the roots of their discipline. In 1893, his analysis of suicide began an era of scientific method sociology,[1] but his seminal ideas on law and punishment and their correlated social conditions concern us here.

Theories of Punishment

There are many difficulties which have been recognized by scholars in their efforts to understand the phenomenon of punishment. One of the difficulties is that punishment can be conceptualized at least at two levels. At the psychological or interpersonal level, an event may be defined as punishment if a person defines the event as unpleasant and, most importantly, intended to be so by someone else. This leads to great difficulty in obtaining conceptual closure on the empirical events which can be included under an interpersonal definition of punishment. It is clear that a very wide variety and a great many events in any society can fall under this purview.

At the sociological level, conceptual closure is enhanced because individual definitions of punishment are precluded. What is of concern at this level is official definitions of deviation and official definitions of punishment. Thus, the variety of events which can be punitive to the individual is reduced to only those events which are institutionalized as punitive. There are still problems at this level of analysis, for as Malinowski[2] points out, it is often difficult in the study of a society to identify anything like a court or to distinguish law from custom, so the type and form of institutionalization is also problematic. However, as Lindesmith indicates in discussing punishment "confusion is likely to follow from the failure to distinguish between the sociological and the psychological frames of reference".[3]

There are several hypotheses on the conditions in a society which lead to a greater or milder official punishment. Lindesmith outlines several of these. He reports that Ranulf argues that the lower middle class is particularly punitive towards crime and sin because of the frustrations generated by belonging to this class.[4] This social psychological argument is supported by historical examples and is similar to the contemporary arguments used to explain the particular support for "law and order" policies among the white lower middle classes in America.

What appears to be a contradictory hypothesis to this is reported from Sutherland and Cressey by Lindesmith. They argue that the brutality of punishment is directly related to social distance between the punisher and the punished.[5] Since it is typically the lower classes who are being officially punished, then it would seem that these two hypotheses are contradictory. The first argues for the punitiveness of a category of people close to the lower class and the second would predict that the upper classes would be the most punitive. Lindesmith concludes that there is inadequate empirical evidence at this time to support general theories of punishment.[6]

Some have argued that the sanctioning of deviance is best described as a curve in its relation to social class.[7] This formulation describes the upper and lower strata of any group or society as sanctioning and being sanctioned less than their middle level counterparts. It is those in the middle who have the most to gain through conformity. Those at the top have no incentive to increase conformity and sanctions, and those at the bottom cannot lose any more.

E. A. Ross, who introduced the term "social control" to American sociology, was interested in the regulative institutions of society. In particular, he was interested in public opinion, the informal force of sustaining social order, and law, the formal force. He saw these two sources of control as varying in society as other conditions of the society varied. In particular, he says that political instruments, such as law, will be preferred "in proportion as the population elements held together are antipathetic and jarring"; in short, heterogeneous. He says that ethical instruments of control, such as public opinion, will be preferred in proportion as its (society's) culture is uniform and diffused;[8] in short, homogeneous. Since he saw the ethical instruments of control as more mild and suasive, and law as repressive, it could be argued that he saw repression to be more likely where the population is more heterogeneous. Ross' theory is of particular interest here since it appears to be precisely the converse to Durkheim's theory of punishment, which is the subject of this chapter.

The best rendition of this problem in legal studies occurs in the fine work of Herbert Packer.[9] His study of the moral and social purposes of criminal justice includes a discussion of the difference between the moralistic, judgemental, retributive (repressive) rationale and the pragmatic, utilitarian justification of criminal punishment. However, most scholars who address themselves to the understanding of punishment do so with the very apparent bias of seeing punishment as an ignoble part of the primitive legacy of modern societies. This fits with the more general perspective that deviance is not "normal" in society but a result of either psychic or social pathologies. Other scholars have not assumed this bias, but rather have treated this assumption as a question to be answered through research.

The Functional View of Punishment

One of the most important developments in social science was the recognition that facts can have a variety of interpretations and explanations. This variety can be classified into levels of explanation, for instance, psychological, sociological, biological, and so on, each of which are distinct and legitimate. Facts can also be interpreted in an evaluative mode, such as, moral, aesthetic, etc., or in a scientific mode which is more or less free of evaluation.[10]

The functional view of punishment attempts to distinguish these modes, and for some functionalists, to maintain a single level of explanation. It is possible then to consider crime and punishment as normal in a society and still abhor it. Just as we can point out how pain is necessary for the survival of an organism without "approving" of it, we can understand punishment while disapproving of it aesthetically or humanistically.

G. H. Mead is one scholar who has interpreted the social and psychological causes and consequences of punishment in this way. He points out that punishment of criminals which is, an "attack upon the enemy of ourselves and of society", "also awakens in law-abiding members of society the inhibitions which make rebellion impossible to them".[11] He seems to indicate in this article that criminality is necessary for the cohesion of society and that criminal activity in itself does not seriously endanger the structure of society. He points out that courts of criminal jutice "may be essential to the preservation of society even when we take into account the impotence of the criminal against society and the clumsy failure of criminal law in the repression and suppression of crime".

In short, crime and punishment are normal properties of social systems.

Durkheim's View of Punishment

The scholar who emphasized, perhaps more than any other, the functional analysis of punishment was Emile Durkheim. He saw punishment, its frequency, the form it took, and the behavior to which it was applied, as a crucial indicator of the nature of a society. In the section of his famous, *The Rules of Sociological Method*, where he examines the normal and the pathological in society, he concludes on criminality that "there is then no phenomenon that presents more indisputably all the symptoms of normality, since it appears closely connected with the conditions of collective life."[12]

In an untranslated article, Durkheim illustrates his generalizations about punishment.[13] In this article, he puts forward two laws which describe the change in punishment from, in the language of the day, less elevated to more elevated societies. These two laws, which appear to be more correctly empirical generalizations on the legal systems he was comparing, described two aspects of the evolution of punishment. The law of quantitative variation states that the intensity of punishment for any crime is reduced as a society becomes more complex.[14] The law of qualitative variation states that punishment shifts from corporal and capital to the loss of liberty or imprisonment, as society becomes more complex.[15] Durkheim recognized the empirical unity of these two aspects but found it useful to separate them conceptually. He describes how these generalizations apply to the history of several societies such as Athens and the ancient Hebrews, and adds important discussion of government, religion, and the family to his arguments about penal evolution. But for Durkheim, the significance of punishment lay in its indicative power. Because the forms and intensity of punishment were intimately connected to the structure of society, and because punishment was observable, he found great analytic utility in it.

Durkheim said "what we avenge, what the criminal expiates is the outrage to morality".[16] Moral phenomena, or what he sometimes called the collective states of mental life, were one of his most important concepts in analyzing society. In contemporary language, these collective states of mental life are equivalent to values, morals, ideology; in short, culture.

Durkheim's View of Punishment and Social Structure

Since his major interest in *The Division of Labour* was social solidarity, Durkheim was interested in the states of collective mental life which contributed to the social solidarity of various types of social structure. This contribution varied with the type of social structure. In societies which were simple, that is, in which the division of labour was low, social solidarity depended upon the strength and similarity of values that people in that society shared with each other. Because of the importance of this state of collective morality for social cohesion, these societies could not afford violations of this basis of solidarity. In these societies, which Durkheim characterized as having mechanical solidarity, deviance was punished severely. The empirical indicator of this type of society was repressive law. These societies appeared to need (in a functional sense) to prevent the demoralization of upright consciences through a strong collective reaction to violations of the collective sentiment. Crime was an event which shocked sentiments, and this outrage to morality determined the reaction. He points out that punishment in these societies bore no relation to the objective danger to the society of the particular offense. Rather, punishment appeared to be a reaction of collective revulsion to the act.

The comparative lack of these reactions in more complex societies led Durkheim to the conclusion that there was, in more complex societies, a different basis of social cohesion. It appeared to him that the basis of social cohesion was inherent in the structure of a more complex society itself. In complex societies, solidarity or cohesion depends on the interdependence of the units of the structure. Durkheim called this type of solidarity "organic". These societies were characterized by restitutive laws, which tended to redress grievances by stipulating that the offender make restitution to the aggrieved. These societies were not as dependent on collective sentiment for cohesion. Therefore, there would be less need (in the functional sense) for repressive sanctions.[17]

To summarize Durkheim's investigations: Systems which are more simple in their structure will depend on the similarity of strongly held sentiments for social solidarity. This will be evident in a strong and repressive reaction to deviant behavior. The more complex the social structure, the less it will depend for solidarity on strongly held and similar sentiments. This will be evident in a more lenient and restitutive reaction to deviant behavior.

Durkheim's Sociology

It is necessary to understand Durkheim's approach to sociology in order to understand his interests and how he formulated his thought. Durkheim's approach has been described as "sociologistic". This describes a category of social theory which explains social or psychic phenomena by referring to their correlated social conditions. These social conditions are seen as more than the sum of individuals actions or beliefs; in fact, individual psychological phenomena are seen as deriving from these social conditions. Durkheim's famous methodological dictum that social facts must be explained with reference to other social facts[18] is primarily aimed at those who accept the use of psychological variables to explain social phenomena. In short, Durkheim is a sociological realist. He sees society as real, external to, and constraining on individuals, and an appropriate object in itself of scientific study.

There are, of course, those who disagree with all, or part of, the sociologism perspective. The debate about the logic of the approach or the utility and sensibility of its assumptions should not foreclose the examination of its empiric or theoretic contribution to the fundamental curiosity about social life. It seems reasonable to consider the contribution of a theoretical perspective at least partly in terms of the information it produces. It has been argued that Durkheim's contribution lies in his empirical studies, which he used to support his perspective, rather than in the general utility or validity of the perspective.

Sorokin suggests that the criteria that Durkheim used of externality and constraint for distinguishing phenomena as social, is particularly useful for the study of moral and juridical phenomena.[19]

Durkheim's Variables

In the first part of *The Division of Labour in Society*, Durkheim uses social differentiation, or the division of labour, as an independent variable and specifies its consequences for other social phenomena. He focuses particularly on its consequences for the dependent variable of solidarity. In the second part of this work, Durkheim treats social differentiation as a dependent variable and locates its causes in the degree of dynamic density of a population. Only the first part of his formulation is of concern here.

Differentiation: Differentiation for Durkheim was the extent to which a social structure was comprised of interdependent parts. His meaning of this concept does not seem to differ from contemporary usage. A society can have subgroups within it, but the extent of their dependence on each other for survival, determines the degree of differentiation. A society composed of many, autonomous, self-sufficient clans is not differentiated. A society in which there is interdependence for survival is more differentiated. Differentiation, then, is the number and interdependence of units in a social system.

Durkheim saw societies in evolution. He conceived of them as systems that moved from being less differentiated to more differentiated or more "elevated". The empirical indicator he focussed on to compare societies on this variable was the degree of division of labour or specialization in occupation.

Solidarity: Solidarity, which he variously referred to as cohesion or integration is somewhat more elusive in his writings. Although he refers to cooperation and men being drawn together which seems straightforward, he also insists that solidarity "is a completely moral phenomenon which taken by itself does not lend itself to exact observation".[20]

What is observable and, as he calls it, an "external index" of solidarity, is law. He argues that the sanctions attached to legal rules are indicators of their precepts (appropriate moral conduct). He sees these sanctions as indicative of "the gravity attributed to the precepts, the place they hold in the public conscience, the role they play in society".[21] He then goes on to classify sanctions into two broad types. First, *Repressive Sanctions*: When loss of life, liberty, property, honour, in short, suffering, is inflicted on the deviant, he calls the sanction repressive. *Restitutive Sanctions*, on the other hand, are intended to return relations in society to their original state, without necessarily inflicting suffering, he calls the sanctions restitutive.

Collective Sentiment: Durkheim was particularly interested in the concept of collective sentiment. The terms he used have been variously translated from his writing as "collective conscience", a term which connotes the idea of morality and control, "collective consciousness", a term which connotes the idea of being aware of belonging to a group and "collective representation", which connotes the idea of shared definition of reality, which is also the most literal translation from the French. Although this concept is vague and apparently, highly connotative in his writing, a reasonable contemporary equivalent is the moral and sacred aspects of culture.

These are the variables with which Durkheim was particularly concerned in his study of societal evolution from primitive to modern. He was interested in how solidarity was maintained as the division of labour increased.

Interpretation of Durkheim

His hypothesis was that, as societies became more complex, the basis of solidarity changed from mechanical to organic. In societies with a low level of differentiation, solidarity was based on the collective allegiance to a strong and homogeneous culture which penetrated everyday activities. This culture must be homogeneous, that is, there must be widespread agreement on certain values and their importance, because as he conceives mechanical solidarity, it is based on "likeness". The use of "agreement" in the foregoing must be qualified. Durkheim emphasized sentiment, so the agreement we speak of is both overt and unrecognized. One of the functions of crime is to make the unrecognized, unconscious morality overt through the drama of punishing its violator.

Durkheim's model is at this point interpreted as follows: A social system which has a low level of interdependence of its units will have a homogeneous culture which permeates everyday life with morality and this results in social solidarity. This system will be characterized by repressive as opposed to restitutive sanctions on deviant behavior. A social system in which there is a high level of interdependency amongst units will have a more heterogeneous (pluralistic) culture in which everyday activities are less sacred. Deviant behavior will occasion less repressive and more restitutive sanctions.

We need not look very far for contemporary examples of this situation. Home or family relations, in which the division of labour is low, are characterized by repressive sanctions. These are relations in which the social bond is shared sentiment and the existence of the group depends exclusively on this. Deviance in these groups is monitored closely and punished severely. This implies the symbolic rather than the practical significance of the offense. The orientation to punishment is thus expressive rather than instrumental.

Empirical Evidence to the Contrary

Malinowski takes issue with Durkheim and others who take the "exaggerated view" that order and solidarity in a primitive society are based on "unselfish, impersonal, unlimited group loyalty". His investigations lead him to conclude that "the savage is neither an extreme 'collectivist' nor an extreme 'individualist'—he is like man in general, a mixture of both".[22]

More recently, a more rigorous empirical work on this topic has appeared. It may be that either or both Malinowski and Durkheim had correctly interpreted an unrepresentative sample of ethnographies.

A cross cultural test by Schwartz and Miller disconfirmed Durkheim's hypothesis that division of labour is related to the type of sanction.[23] This study focussed on restitutive sanctions and found in an examination of 51 societies that restitutive sanctions were sometimes more frequent in simple societies than in more complex ones. This appears to be the only rigorous test of the restitutive law hypothesis.

Durkheim appears to conceive of the evolution of mechanical to organic solidarity as being shown in a changing ratio of restitutive to repressive sanctions. If it is assumed that the amount of sanctions in a society is constant between simple and complex, then there is a zero-sum system in which the decrease or increase in one type of sanction is automatically accompanied by a compensatory variation in the other type. The model changes if the assumption of constancy is not made. Then it would be possible to have one type of sanction change and the other remain constant and still preserve the changing ratio that Durkheim hypothesized. It would be, for example, that repressive sanctions diminish with increasing complexity and no difference occurs in the amount of restitutive sanction. This would be possible if the total amount of sanctions in a society decreased as it became more complex. If this assumption is held, then findings of no difference between simple and complex societies on restitutive sanctions but simple societies having more repression would not be inconsistent with his hypothesis.

Durkheimian Method

Durkheim used the comparative method to examine social solidarity. His explanation was functionalist. He examined the structure of societies and found the states of collective sentiment with which they were associated. He, then, argued that the association of this sentiment and the social structure was not an accident. In fact, the two social facts were functional or necessary for each other.

The sense in which Durkheim uses sentiment is as a social fact. Individuals in a collectivity may possess more or less of the elements of collective sentiment in their individual sentiments but the collective sentiment is greater than the aggregate of the individuals' sentiments. This is the basis of the sociological realism discussed earlier.

Durkheim was interested in explaining how solidarity was generated and maintained in society. This question is perhaps as basic as the nature of life for the biologist. The answers and the approaches to the answer may be even more difficult. The biologist is able to approach experimentally the apparent boundary between animate and inanimate objects and consider the different characteristics of each. The sociologist must attack the same problem without the benefit of experimental method and without the range of animate and inanimate. It would be similar for the biologist if the world consisted only of perpetually living things. The biologist would then be restricted to a comparative examination of the different forms of life in order to illuminate his curiosity about the nature of life. The sociologist is restricted to this approach.

Measuring Repression

The central feature of Durkheim's discussion of repressive sanctions is that they are severe. Although it is probably true that in every society members could achieve high levels of agreement on what is a more or less severe sanction, it appears to be difficult to develop a culture free definition of repression. Obviously, what is a severe sanction in one society may not be in another. Social ostracism might be very severe in one society and relatively mild in another. The loss of life in a society which has a strong belief system emphasizing life after death may not be as severe as in a culture which does not have such a belief system.

In spite of the operational problems, a promising source of data is the Human Relations Area Files. This provides more rigorously classified information on a wider variety of cultures than scholars in the late 1800's had access to; however, the problem of definition and classification of repression is not thereby solved. The first weakness in these data for this type of study is the unknown, uneven emphasis in the descriptive accounts of the various cultures. Another is the unknown extent of cultural diffusion that occurs in the various geographic areas. Even assuming that the accuracy of description problems were minimal or that they resulted in random error which would not bias, but only weaken generalizations, the problem of constructing a culture free definition of repression remains where the data are ethnographic.[24]

Measuring Differentiation

Durkheim, in his concern with the differences between less and more advanced societies, was describing social differentiation or complexity. This can conceivably be of at least two types: (1) Complexity can be measured as a property of social structure and attention can be directed at measures such as the number of different occupations, classes, institutions or other features of the structure. (2) Cultural complexity can be indexed in the variations of religious ideologies, the degree of ethnic or traditional pluralism, the variation in political ideology, or other features of the culture.

Durkheim, as well as most other sociologists, see these two levels of abstraction as connected. It would be expected, therefore, that structural complexity would be found in societies which were also characterized by cultural complexity. The concept of collective sentiment, the strength and homogeneity of which was the basis of cohesion in a simple society for Durkheim, seems to be a concept which fits in the cultural level of abstraction. Similarity of collective sentiment or homogeneity of culture was associated with a low degree of division of labour or structural complexity. Complexity, then, is measurable both inter- and intra- societally as the degree of homogeneity or heterogeneity in both social structure and culture.

However, some form of cross cultural analysis may be the most appropriate way of testing any macro-sociological evolutional theory, like Durkheim's. Even if the variables isolated as important in this model (repression and differentiation) are operationalized reasonably within a single society, it would seem likely that there would be insufficient range on the variable within one culture to test an evolutionary model.

Research Problem of this Section

In spite of his strong commitment to rigorous, empirical study, Durkheim could not offer more than illustrations of the arguments he was advancing on the evolution of society from a mechanical to an organically based solidarity. One of the tasks of this research is to apply a more rigorous methodology to Durkheim's central proposition on this evolution without sacrificing the high level of abstraction or the Durkheimian style of sociology.

The proposition we will test is "the less differentiated the social system the more repressive the sanctions". We will conceive of this relation as holding when the units being compared are not societies but population groups within a society. We will also conceive of repressive sanctions as being supported by repressive sentiment in these population groups.

One problem with which this research is confronted is that the range of variation which Durkheim had in mind was very large. He was comparing the laws of primitive and complex societies. The range on one variable, social differentiation or complexity, was very wide. Given its high level of abstraction, it would seem likely that the proposition would be difficult to confirm or disconfirm if the range of societal complexity was less than the maximum. In this research, a measure of complexity comprising measures of both cultural and social structural levels of abstraction is used for the independent variable. The opposite of complexity is simplicity or similarity. This study operationalizes the independent variable with degrees of similarity or homogeneity in a population. The measure includes measures of cultural and structural homogeneity.[25] The rationale for combining these measures was that, taken together, they would provide the most general basis for testing the proposition. The measures of homogeneity are then separated in the analysis and their independent effect is described.

Within modern industrial societies, it appears that the most repressive sanction is capital punishment. If this is true, then a comparison of populations on complexity which was also compared on sentiment for or against capital punishment would provide a reasonable test of the Durkheimian proposition. It would be expected that populations which were more homogeneous would be more supportive of capital punishment.

Research Setting and Operations

This study compares political constituencies in Canada which varied in complexity. The research is similar to Durkheim's suicide research in that a comparative method is employed and indicators of social conditions are used. The degree of complexity in the population of 265 political constituencies is compared at single points in time, 1961 and 1971[26] (which are the years of the Canadian Census). Complexity is measured by the amount of variation in the religious, ethnic and educational characteristics of the population of each constituency. Repressive sanctions are assumed to be supported by repressive sentiment in the population. Repressive sentiment is measured in the vote of the political representative of the constituency on a motion in Parliament to abolish capital punishment.[27]

Measures of Complexity in this Research

The technical operations used in constructing these measures are presented in Appendix I. As was previously mentioned (p. 154), complexity is measured on two levels, cultural and structural. It is operationalized as the degree of homogeneity of a population on three characteristics:

Culture: ethnicity: A political constituency is defined on ethnic homogeneity by the proportion of the population which identifies themselves as belonging to a single ethnic group.[28]

Culture: religion: A political constituency is defined on religious homogeneity by the proportion of the population which identifies themselves as belonging to a single religious faith.

Structure: education:[29] As an occupational system becomes more differentiated, it is usually accompanied by a greater variety of educational preparation. Thus, in any population, the variation of years of education completed indexes the variety of occupations. Since this variety can be taken as a property of the division of labour or the degree of structural differentiation, we treat the variation in education in a population as an indicator of structural complexity. Homogeneity of structure is indicated by the homogeneity of the population on education.

Measure of Repressive Sentiment in this Research

Sentiment is a complex phenomenon. A conceptual distinction must be retained between collective and individual sentiment. Individual sentiment can vary in specificity and clarity as well as in intensity and salience. Discussion of these matters is taken up in the chapter on public opinion.

Collective sentiment probably varies along the same dimensions of clarity and intensity. But collective sentiment is more than the sum of individual sentiments. It is a group phenomenon seen in group processes and outcomes. It can be represented in legitimated moral leaders, cultural artifacts and social patterns such as the institutionalized collective response to crime.

Thus, in the investigation of societies in which there is a mechanical basis of solidarity, Durkheim describes the sanctioning behavior of people in the society when some rule is violated. He was particularly attentive to sanctions which were codified in laws and punishments. Laws, punishments and the codification of these in the political and legislative institutions are an indicator of the collective sentiment. The behavior of one member of such a collectivity whose role it is to represent the sentiments of that collectivity in a legislative institution can be taken as an index of the collective sentiment and is in this research design.

Indicator of Repressive Sentiment in this Research

The index of repressive sentiment in this study is the behavior of a Member of Parliament, in his role as representative of a constituency population. It is, of course, true that the Member of Parliament is not in any sense the "average man" of his constituency.

Most Members of Parliament are considerably wealthier and better-educated than their constituents. It seems reasonable, however, to accept the notion that the successful candidate in a district will have the trust of a large number of his constituents, which can be interpreted as his possessing and representing their sentiment. It would also seem reasonable that he would act in accordance with their sentiments as he perceived them in his legislative behavior.

One study of the 25th Parliament (the present research is based on the 27th Parliament) indicates that 49 per cent of the Members of Parliament interviewed saw this representational role as the single most important aspect of their position and another 36 per cent saw it as an important part.[30] Only 15 per cent of the Members of Parliament saw themselves acting independently of their constituents. His accountability at the polls would as well seem to be a significant inducement. A separate analysis of representatives of the Member of Parliament is taken up in Chapter 3. There is, then, support for the *assumption* that Members will tend to vote in Parliament in accordance with the constituency sentiment as they see it.

If this assumption were not reasonable, only two other assumptions are possible. One would be that there is no relationship between constituency sentiment and the behavior of the Member of Parliament.[31] Another assumption would be that the Member of Parliament behaves in the opposite direction to constituency sentiment. In general, this is that non-punitive Members will tend to represent punitive constituencies and *vice versa*. In the case of this research, the assumption would be that constituencies which tend to repressive sentiment have Members of Parliament who tend to vote for abolition of capital punishment. That there should be such a pattern across all 265 constituencies in Canada seems to be unreasonable. This leaves the assumption of either a positive relation or no relation at all between the Members' of Parliament behavior and constituency sentiment. There is some evidence from the speeches of Members in the House of Commons that they were responding to constituency sentiment to retain the death penalty.

This section of the research *assumes* that there is a positive relation between the sentiment of the constituency and the behavior of the Member of Parliament. The Member of Parliament's behavior is, therefore, used as an index of sentiment (more or less repressive) of his constituency. The votes on capital punishment were free votes with party discipline suspended because of the moral nature of the question. Party control was supposed to be absent and the idea of a vote according to conscience was emphasized.[32]

The proposition derived from Durkheim's *Division of Labour* when operationalized becomes the following hypothesis: *The more homogeneous a political constituency, the more likely the Member of Parliament from that constituency will be to vote to retain capital punishment.*

Advantages of this Research Design

It is particularly strategic, then, to compare repressive sanctions within one society. If it is possible to compare population groups within one society on complexity and compare acceptability of repressive sanctions between the same population groups, it would seem that the definitional problems of repression, discussed on page 154 (measuring repression), are reduced or eliminated. This allows a more precise comparison of empirical cases than in available in ethnographic data.[33] To gain this increase in precision on repression required a decrease in the range on complexity. This design then allows a relatively precise test of Durkheim's proposition on a limited range of his independent variable.

Findings and Discussion of Homogeneity, Repressive Sentiment and the Constituency

This section will present evidence on the major hypothesis of this research which derives from the discussion of Durkheim in the foregoing. The hypothesis predicts to the relationship between homogeneity, on several variables in the population of political constituencies, and the vote to abolish capital punishment. The prediction is that, as the homogeneity of the population of a political constituency increases, the likelihood of the Member from that constituency to vote for retention of capital punishment will increase. This prediction is confirmed. (See Table 67.) Table 67 shows that seventy-four per cent of those representatives from the very homogeneous constituencies voted for the retention of capital punishment whereas fifty-six per cent of those from the very heterogeneous constituencies voted for the abolition of capital punishment. The percentages of Members voting for and against capital punishment relate to the relative homogeneity of the constituency in the predicted direction.

It is clear from Table 67 that the predicted relationship is strongest amongst the homogeneous constituencies compared to the heterogeneous ones. If it is argued, that in simpler social organizations repressive sanctions are neessary for the preservation of solidarity but not necessary in more complex social organizations, then, in a sense, repressive sanctions are "optional" in more complex systems. This would predict to the kind of pattern found in Table 67, with

Table 67:
Capital Punishment Vote (1966) and Homogeneity* of Constituency
(Percentages)

Vote on Capital Punishment	Homogeneity Level: Very Homogeneous		Homogeneous		Heterogeneous		Very Heterogeneous		Total	
No vote	3.1	(2)	3.1	(2)	5.6	(4)	3.1	(2)	3.8	(10)
Abolish	23.1	(15)	35.9	(23)	52.8	(38)	56.3	(36)	42.3	(112)
Retain	73.8	(48)	60.9	(39)	41.7	(30)	40.6	(26)	54.0	(143)
Total	24.5	(65)	24.2	(64)	27.2	(72)	24.2	(64)	100.0	(265)

* Homogeneity level is a composite index including ethnic, religious and educational homogeneity.

homogeneous areas showing stronger repressive sentiment and heterogenous areas showing a more even distribution of sentiment.

Homogeneity on Religion and Ethnicity and Repressive Sentiment

This section examines the relationship between vote on capital punishment and homogeneity variables taken one at a time. Table 68 shows that the proportion of Members of Parliament from religiously homogeneous areas who voted in favour of capital punishment was relatively high (67.6 per cent) and those from heterogeneous areas, relatively low (39.5 per cent). The same pattern emerges when homogeneity on ethnicity is used as the independent variable. (See Table 69.)

Table 68:
Vote on Capital Punishment (1966) by Homogeneity on Religion (Percentages)

Vote on Capital Punishment	Religious Homogeneity*					
	Homogeneous		Heterogeneous		Total	
No vote	2.2	(3)	5.4	(7)	3.8	(10)
Abolish	30.1	(41)	55.0	(71)	42.3	(112)
Retain	67.6	(92)	39.5	(51)	54.0	(143)
Total	51.3	(136)	48.7	(129)	100.0	(265)

* When over 70% of the population of a political constituency are classified in one religion on the census, that constituency is defined as homogeneous.

Since Tables 68 and 69 are very similar, it is important to establish whether or not measurements of homogeneity on ethnicity and religion, in fact, are selecting the same constituencies. The two measures are closely related. Two hundred and fourteen constituencies are rated the same on the two measures and fifty-one are rated differently. The selection of these constituencies out of the total population does not seem to substantially increase the association

Table 69:
Vote on Capital Punishment (1966) by Homogeneity on Ethnicity
(Percentages)

Vote on Capital Punishment	Ethnic Homogeneity*					
	Homogeneous		Heterogeneous		Total	
No vote	4.7	(6)	2.9	(4)	3.8	(10)
Abolish	29.1	(37)	54.3	(75)	42.3	(112)
Retain	66.1	(84)	42.8	(59)	54.0	(143)
Total	47.9	(127)	52.1	(138)	100.0	(265)

* When over 70% of the population of a political constituency are classified in one ethnic group, that constituency is defined as homogeneous.

between homogeneity and capital punishment vote. When all constituencies that are consistent on religion and ethnic homogeneity are compared to those which are not consistent, support for the hypothesis does not seem to increase significantly. (See Table 70.)

Table 70
Vote to Retain Capital Punishment (1966) by Homogeneity on Religion and Ethnicity Taken Separately and Together
(Percentages)

Homogeneity Level	Religion and Ethnicity*	Religion	Ethnicity
Homogeneous	70.8 (106)	67.6 (136)	66.1 (127)
Heterogeneous	38.9 (108)	39.5 (129)	42.8 (138)
Total	54.7 (214)	54.0 (265)	54.0 (265)

*Selected from total number of constituencies on the basis of the same score on both ethnic and religious homogeneity.

Homogeneity on Education and Repressive Sentiment

When homogeneity on education is examined separately in its relation to the capital punishment vote, there is only a slight relation between the two variables. Table 71 shows this tendency for the educationally homogeneous constituencies to have Members that vote for retention more than the educationally heterogeneous constituencies. However, the most apparent and surprising feature of the table is the lack of a strong relationship.[34] Homogeneity of education, thus, does not appear to be related to repressive sentiment. This apparent disconfirmation of the Durkheimian hypothesis presents an interesting theoretical possibility.

Table 71:
Vote on Capital Punishment (1966) by Homogeneity on Education (Percentages)

	Educational Homogeneity*					
Vote on Capital Punishment	Homogeneous		Heterogeneous		Total	
No vote	3.8	(5)	3.8	(5)	3.8	(10)
Abolish	38.6	(51)	45.9	(61)	42.3	(112)
Retain	57.6	(76)	50.4	(67)	54.0	(143)
Total	49.8	(132)	50.2	(133)	100.0	(265)

* Constituencies were ranked from high to low on the variance in years of education in the population. The bottom half were defined as honogeneous and the top half were heterogeneous.

Durkheim indicates that the existence of repressive sanctions are indicative of a strong and homogeneous culture which is the source of social solidarity. This strong and homogeneous culture exists because there is no other source of social solidarity. Collective sentiments which are strong and coercive are the basis of social order, where functional differentiation is low. Where functional differentiation is greater and as it becomes greater, culture becomes enfeebled and abstracted from social interaction, and other bases of solidarity, intrinsic to social structure, emerge. In connecting division of labour and repressive sanctions, Durkheim appears to treat collective sentiment or culture as a variable which depends upon the degree of structural differentiation. Sanctions are then treated as an indicator of this sentiment which characterizes the society as mechanical or organic.

It appears that Durkheim saw only two of the four logically possible relations between culture, structure and sanctions. The two he discussed were simple structure with constraining homogeneous culture and complex structure with abstract differentiated culture. The possibilities of a complex structure and a homogeneous culture, or a simple structure and a complex differentiated culture were not examined. Considering the range of variation in complexity, and the qualitative data with which Durkheim worked, these two logical possibilities would be remote empirical possibilities. When his proposition is examined against a more limited range of empirical variation in social complexity, as it is in this study, which is more rigorously measured, the empirical possibility of these two cases is enhanced.

If it is possible for societies to be structurally complex and culturally homogeneous and vice versa, then what should be predicted for the state of repressive sentiment in these societies? Would the proposition from Durkheim state that the variable of structural homogeneity is associated with repression?

If we accept variation in years of education in the population as an indicator of the degree of complexity in a social structure, then evidence from the present study supports the notion that cultural homogeneity is more strongly related to repression and structural homegeneity is less so. When educational homogeneity is controlled, as it is in Table 72, it is clear that cultural homogeneity is associated with repression more strongly than structural homogene-

Table 72:
Vote to Retain Capital Punishment (1966) and Religious Homogeneity by Educational Homogeneity (Percentages)

	Education					
Religion	Homogeneous		Heterogeneous		Total	
Homogeneous	70.4	(81)	63.6	(55)	67.6	(136)
Heterogeneous	37.3	(51)	41.0	(78)	39.5	(129)
Total	57.6	(132)	50.4	(133)	54.0	(265)

ity. Table 72 shows that the proportion of homogeneous constituencies whose Members vote to retain the death penalty increases slightly when the constituency is also homogeneous on education. This pattern is also present for ethnicity, and ethnicity and religion together.

These findings would seem to support the interpretation that, of the two other logical possibilities in the Durkheiman model in which culture and structure are independent, the collective reaction of repression depends on cultural rather than structural homogeneity.

This rather laborious and complex analysis of the 1966 capital punishment vote and its relation to various conceptions and operational definitions of homogeneity was necessary in the beginning of this research. There is no "common sense" reason to expect homogeneity of the constituency population to be related to the death penalty vote of Members of Parliament. However, the theoretical inspiration of Durkheim does allow and encourage this. It was, therefore, necessary to examine the various facets of homogeneity and their relation to repression.

Cultural homogeneity emerges as the most interesting and reliable aspect of homogeneity which relates to repression. Thus, a more simplified design was possible in the continued analysis of these 1966 data, the 1971 census and the 1973 capital punishment vote. Ethnic homogeneity[35] is used, hereafter, as the indicator of cultural homogeneity.

Cultural Homogeneity and Repression, 1966 and 1973

The next section of this chapter examines the relationship between cultural homogeneity and repression when other characteristics of the population in each constituency are taken into account.[36] Since structural homogeneity (measured by homogeneity of education) does not appear to substantially affect the relationship in 1966; only cultural homogeneity (ethnicity) is used in further analysis of that, and the 1973, vote.

Table 73 shows the relationship between homogeneity and capital punishment vote in 1973. This table is directly comparable to Table 69 for the 1966 vote. An overall reduction of 14 per cent in support for retention and an increase of 2 per cent in abolition votes occurs. Most of this change occurs in homogeneous constituencies. While the relationship between cultural homogeneity and repression is preserved in 1973, MP's from heterogeneous constituencies are more stable in their support for abolition than those from homogeneous constituencies who change more over time.[37]

Table 73:
Vote on Capital Punishment by Homogeneity-Heterogeneity on Ethnicity (1973)
(Percentages)

Vote on Capital Punishment	Ethnicity: Homogeneous		Heterogeneous		Total	
No vote	19.8	(23)	11.5	(17)	15.2	(39)
Abolish	33.6	(39)	53.4	(79)	44.7	(119)
Retain	46.6	(54)	35.1	(52)	40.2	(106)
Total	43.9	(116)	56.1	(148)	100.0	(264)

Religious Affiliation and Repression

Tables 74 and 75 show that there is a tendency for predominantly (over 70 per cent Roman Catholic constituencies to be more supportive of the retention of capital punishment than the predominantly Protestant constituencies in 1966. However, the differences between Catholic and Protestant constituencies is less than the differences between homogeneous and heterogeneous constituencies which also have over 70 per cent of one religious group.[38] It, therefore, appears that homogeneity is a more powerful predictor of repression than religion. It would be expected that the Roman Catholic population would be more favourable to retention since the Church's position was not to oppose capital punishment in 1966, whereas several Protestant Church organizations have opposed capital punishment in Canada. If homogeneity of religion is a variable with continuous predictive power on repression, it would also be expected that predominantly Roman Catholic constituencies (over 70 per cent) would tend to be more repressive since there is a larger proportion of these constituencies with very high proportions of Catholics.[39]

The basic relationship is changed in 1973. Homogeneous constituencies still tend to be more repressive than heterogeneous ones.[40] However, the effects of the specific religion has altered as can be seen in Tables 76 and 77. MP's from predominantly Protestant constituencies have become more retentionist and Roman Catholic constituencies less so. The official position of the Church on the death penalty had changed to support a moratorium on the death penalty in 1973.[41]

Table 74:
Vote to Retain Capital Punishment (1966) and Homogeneity*
by Proportion Roman Catholics
(Percentages)

Homogeneity Level	Percentage Roman Catholic 0-9		10-19		20-29		30-39		40-49		50-59	
Homogeneous	66.7	(3)	60.7	(28)	50.0	(14)	60.0	(5)	66.7	(3)	66.7	(3)
Heterogeneous	0.0	(0)	50.0	(32)	51.1	(47)	38.9	(18)	27.3	(11)	29.4	(17)
Total	66.7	(3)	55.0	(60)	50.8	(61)	43.5	(23)	35.7	(14)	35.0	(20)

Homogeneity Level	60-69		70-79		80-89		90-99		Total	
Homogeneous	0.0	(2)	66.7	(3)	71.4	(14)	75.0	(52)	66.1	(127)
Heterogeneous	14.3	(7)	50.0	(4)	50.2	(2)	0.0	(0)	42.8	(138)
Total	11.1	(9)	57.1	(7)	68.8	(16)	75.0	(52)	54.0	(265)

Homogeneous constituencies have 70% or over either English or French ethnic origin.

Table 75:
Vote to Retain Capital Punishment (1966) and Homogeneity by Proportion Protestants (Percentages)

Homogeneity Level	Percentage Protestant 0-9		10-19		20-29		30-39		40-49		50-59	
Homogeneous	75.5	(53)	66.7	(12)	66.7	(3)	0.0	(2)	33.3	(6)	100.0	(2)
Heterogeneous	0.0	(2)	50.0	(2)	50.0	(8)	30.0	(20)	23.8	(21)	46.2	(26)
Total	72.7	(55)	64.3	(14)	54.5	(11)	27.3	(22)	25.9	(27)	50.0	(28)

Homogeneity Level	60-69		70-79		80-89		90-99		Total	
Homogeneous	45.5	(11)	63.3	(30)	71.4	(7)	100.0	(1)	66.1	(127)
Heterogeneous	51.4	(37)	55.0	(20)	0.0	(0)	50.0	(2)	42.8	(138)
Total	50.0	(48)	60.0	(50)	71.4	(7)	66.7	(3)	54.0	(256)

Table 76:
Vote to Retain Capital Punishment (1973) and Homogeneity by proportion Roman Catholics
(Percentages)

Homogeneity Level	Percentage Roman Catholic 0-9		10-19		20-29		30-39		40-49		50-59	
Homogeneous	100.0	(1)	82.4	(17)	47.1	(17)	57.1	(7)	33.3	(6)	33.3	(3)
Heterogeneous	75.0	(4)	48.0	(25)	43.1	(51)	33.3	(21)	25.0	(16)	0.0	(13)
Total	80.0	(5)	61.9	(42)	44.1	(68)	39.3	(28)	27.3	(22)	6.2	(16)

Homogeneity Level	60-69		70-79		80-89		90-99		Total	
Homogeneous	0.0	(2)	0.0	(1)	21.4	(14)	43.8	(48)	46.6	(116)
Heterogeneous	14.3	(7)	12.5	(8)	100.0	(2)	0.0	(1)	35.1	(148)
Total	11.1	(9)	11.1	(9)	31.3	(16)	42.9	(49)	40.2	(264)

Table 77:
Vote to Retain Capital Punishment (1973) and Homogeneity by Proportion Protestants
(Percentages)

Homogeneity Level	Percentage Protestant 0-9		10-19		20-29		30-39		40-49		50-59	
Homogeneous	39.6	(53)	33.3	(9)	0.0	(1)	40.0	(5)	28.6	(7)	37.5	(8)
Heterogeneous	12.5	(8)	33.3	(6)	10.0	(10)	19.0	(21)	39.3	(28)	43.1	(51)
Total	36.1	(61)	33.3	(15)	9.1	(11)	23.1	(26)	37.1	(35)	42.4	(59)

Homogeneity Level	60-69		70-79		80-89		90-99		Total	
Homogeneous	64.0	(25)	87.5	(8)	0.0	(0)	0.0	(0)	46.6	(116)
Heterogeneous	41.2	(17)	25.0	(4)	100.0	(2)	100.0	(1)	35.1	(148)
Total	54.8	(42)	66.7	(12)	100.0	(2)	100.0	(1)	40.2	(264)

Ethnicity and Repression

Tables 78-81 show that ethnic background like religious affiliation makes a difference in repressive sentiment in 1966. As in the case of religion, we find that the differences between homogeneity level are greater than the differences between English and French ethnicity.

Tables 80 and 81 show this relation in 1973. Although there are no heterogeneous constituencies which have over 70 per cent of one ethnic group (by definition), MP's from homogeneous constituencies support capital punishment more than their counterparts from heterogeneous ridings. An interesting finding occurs when we see that there has been a substantial decline between 1966 and 1973 in the proportion of MP's from predominantly French constituencies to vote for the death penalty. The predominantly English constituencies remain relatively unchanged. Again in 1973, we find a greater difference (almost 20 per cent) in the support for the death penalty between levels of ethnic concentration (homogeneous and heterogeneous constituencies) than between the ethnic groups which are concentrated.

Education and Repression

It could be argued that education and repressive sentiment would be negatively related in any population. Education is thought to be related to liberal political ideology which would lead to abolitionist sentiment on the rational, instrumental grounds discussed earlier. The proportion of the population with various years of education in each constituency is presented in the next two tables. These tables show that, in general, constituencies with higher levels of education tend to be slightly less repressive than constituencies with lower levels of education. Within each level of education, the association between homogeneity and repression is retained.

Table 82 shows that for all but the highest and the lowest levels of education, there is very little difference in the proportions of Members of Parliament voting to retain the death penalty in 1966. The homogeneous constituencies consistently have a larger proportion of Members voting to retain capital punishment. In those twenty-seven constituencies in which sixty-five per cent or more of the population is relatively highly educated, there is a marked reduction in support for capital punishment and a reversal of the relationship between homogeneity and repression. It appears that only very high levels of education in a population do produce clear non-repressive sentiment in 1966.

Table 78:
Vote to Retain Capital Punishment (1966) and Homogeneity Level by Proportion English Ethnicity
(Percentages)

Homogeneity Level	Percentage English 0-9		10-19		20-29		30-39		40-49		50-59	
Homogeneous	75.6	(45)	68.8	(16)	75.0	(8)	0.0	(0)	0.0	(0)	0.0	(0)
Heterogeneous	0.0	(3)	33.3	(3)	50.0	(12)	50.0	(24)	41.2	(34)	48.5	(33)
total	70.8	(48)	63.2	(19)	60.0	(20)	50.0	(24)	41.2	(34)	48.5	(33)

Homogeneity Level	60-69		70-79		80-89		90-99		Total	
Homogeneous	0.0	(0)	60.0	(37)	64.7	(17)	16.7	(6)	66.1	(127)
Heterogeneous	33.3	(27)	0.0	(0)	0.0	(0)	0.0	(0)	42.8	(138)
Total	33.3	(27)	59.5	(37)	64.7	(17)	16.7	(0)	54.0	(265)

Table 79:
Vote to Retain Capital Punishment (1966) and Homogeneity Level by Proportion French Ethnicity (Percentages)

Homogeneity Level	Percentage French 0-9		10-19		20-29		30-39		40-49		50-59	
Homogeneous	52.3	(44)	66.7	(12)	100.0	(1)	0.0	(0)	100.0	(1)	0.0	(0)
Heterogeneous	48.3	(89)	38.9	(18)	12.5	(8)	40.0	(10)	12.5	(8)	66.7	(3)
Total	49.6	(133)	50.0	(30)	22.2	(9)	40.0	(10)	22.2	(9)	66.7	(3)

Homogeneity Level	60-69		70-79		80-89		90-99		Total	
Homogeneous	0.0	(0)	64.3	(14)	77.8	(18)	77.8	(36)	66.1	(127)
Heterogeneous	50.0	(2)	0.0	(0)	0.0	(0)	0.0	(0)	42.8	(138)
Total	33.3	(3)	64.3	(14)	77.8	(18)	77.8	(36)	54.0	(265)

Table 80:
Vote to Retain Capital Punishment (1973) and Homogeneity Level by Proportion English Ethnicity (Percentages)

Homogeneity Level	Percentage English 0-9		10-19		20-29		30-39		40-49		50-59	
Homogeneous	47.8	(46)	16.7	(12)	0.0	(4)	0.0	(0)	0.0	(0)	0.0	(0)
Heterogeneous	33.3	(6)	50.0	(2)	25.0	(16)	36.4	(22)	22.2	(36)	45.9	(17)
Total	46.2	(52)	21.4	(14)	20.0	(20)	36.4	(22)	22.2	(36)	45.9	(17)

Homogeneity Level	60-69		70-79		80-89		90-99		Total	
Homogeneous	0.0	(0)	59.3	(27)	57.9	(19)	37.5	(8)	46.6	(116)
Heterogeneous	41.4	(29)	0.0	(0)	0.0	(0)	0.0	(0)	35.1	(148)
Total	41.4	(29)	59.3	(27)	57.9	(19)	37.5	(0)	40.2	(264)

Table 81:
Vote to Retain Capital Punishment (1973) and Homogeneity Level by Proportion French Ethnicity (Percentages)

Homogeneity Level	Percentage French 0-9		10-19		20-29		30-39		40-49		50-59	
Homogeneous	56.0	(50)	100.0	(2)	0.0	(2)	0.0	(0)	0.0	(0)	0.0	(0)
Heterogeneous	40.6	(96)	23.5	(17)	33.3	(9)	14.3	(7)	14.3	(7)	33.3	(6)
Total	45.9	(146)	31.6	(19)	27.3	(11)	14.3	(7)	14.3	(7)	33.3	(6)

Homogeneity Level	60-69		70-79		80-89		90-99		Total	
Homogeneous	0.0	(0)	10.0	(10)	42.9	(21)	45.2	(31)	46.6	(116)
Heterogeneous	33.3	(6)	0.0	(0)	0.0	(0)	0.0	(0)	35.1	(148)
Total	33.3	(6)	10.0	(10)	42.9	(21)	45.2	(31)	40.2	(264)

Table 82:
Vote to Retain Capital Punishment (1966) and Homogeneity by Education Level of Population
(Percentages)

Homogeneity Level	Percentage with Some High School or University Education											
	0-24		25-29		30-34		35-39		40-44		45-49	
Homogenious	71.4	(14)	81.8	(11)	76.9	(13)	66.7	(18)	57.1	(21)	90.0	(10)
Heterogeneous	0.0	(0)	100.0	(2)	33.3	(9)	66.7	(12)	52.4	(21)	36.8	(19)
Total	71.4	(14)	84.6	(13)	59.1	(22)	66.7	(30)	54.8	(42)	55.2	(29)

Homogeneity Level	50-54		55-59		60-64		65 over		Total	
Homogenious	58.3	(12)	80.0	(10)	55.6	(9)	22.2	(9)	66.1	(127)
Heterogeneous	35.0	(20)	40.7	(27)	50.0	(10)	27.8	(18)	42.8	(138)
Total	43.8	(32)	51.4	(37)	52.6	(19)	25.9	(27)	54.0	(265)

Table 83
Vote to Retain Capital Punishment (1973) by Homogeneity Level and Education Level of Population
(Percentages)

Percentage with Some High School or University Education

Homogeneity Level	0-24		25-29		30-34		35-39		40-44		45-49	
Homogeneous	44.4	(18)	44.4	(18)	33.3	(18)	46.2	(26)	70.0	(20)	14.3	(7)
Heterogeneous	0.0	(1)	50.0	(8)	30.0	(20)	26.9	(26)	39.5	(43)	42.1	(19)
Total	42.1	(19)	46.2	(26)	31.6	(38)	36.5	(52)	49.2	(63)	34.6	(26)

Homogeneity Level	50-54		55-59		60-64		65 over		Total	
Homogenious	50.0	(4)	0.0	(0)	75.0	(4)	0.0	(1)	46.6	(116)
Heterogeneous	37.5	(16)	20.0	(5)	50.0	(6)	0.0	(4)	35.1	(148)
Total	40.0	(20)	20.0	(5)	60.0	(10)	0.0	(5)	40.2	(264)

Table 83 shows these patterns for 1973. Here, we find again substantial support for the independent effect of homogeneity on the Members' vote for capital punishment. The only important reversal in the pattern occurs in constituencies where between 45-54 per cent of the population have the education level specified in the table.

Rurality and Repression

When constituencies which are in or not in major metropolitan areas are compared, it appears that Members of Parliament who are not in metropolitan constituencies are generally more likely to vote to retain capital punishment. However, a large difference between Members from homogeneous and heterogeneous constituencies is preserved whether the constituency is in a metropolitan area or not in 1966 (see Table 84) and a reduced tendency to the same pattern occurs in 1973 (see Table 86).

**Table 84:
Vote to Retain Capital Punishment (1966)
by Homogeneity Level and Metropolitan Area
(Percentages)**

Homogeneity Level	Location in Metropolitan Area: No		Yes		Total	
Homogeneous	70.3	(101)	50.0	(26)	66.1	(127)
Heterogeneous	51.1	(92)	26.1	(46)	42.8	(138)
Total	61.1	(193)	34.7	(72)	54.0	(265)

* The major metropolitan areas used in this study had the largest population. In descending order of size they were—Montreal, Toronto, Vancouver, Winnipeg, Ottawa, Hamilton, Quebec, Edmonton and Calgary.

The decline in retentionist support from 1966 occurs with greatest force amongst those MP's representing rural, homogeneous ridings. Those representing urban, heterogeneous areas are clearly abolitionist in both periods but become slightly more retentionist in 1973. The difference in levels of support for hanging between rural and urban areas closes between 1966 and 1973, as it does for differ-

Table 86:
Vote to Retain Capital Punishment (1973)
by Homogeneity Level and Metropolitan Area
(Percentages)

Homogeneity Level	Location in Metropolitan Area*					
	No		Yes		Total	
Homogeneous	50.0	(94)	25.0	(20)	46.6	(116)
Heterogeneous	39.8	(88)	28.3	(60)	35.1	(148)
Total	45.1	(182)	27.5	(80)	40.2	(264)

* 2 constituencies could not be classified on location.

ences in cultural homogeneity. All groups are becoming more abolitionist.

It is surprising to find that Members of Parliament in the most urban areas tend to vote to abolish capital punishment even though crime rates and, hence, the objective danger of crime is more common in cities.[42] A rational theory of punishment as deterrence would predict that where crime rates are high the sentiment for punishment would be positive. Durkheim's theory emphasizes that the reaction to crime is not related to its objective danger to society. Comparing rural and urban areas (as are done in Tables 84-86) would seem to be an appropriate demonstration of the validity of the Durkheimian perspective on crime and punishment.

Table 85 shows this feature of the Canadian data again. In this table, the proportion of the population living on farms is used to measure rurality and this provides more increments on a rural/urban dimension. The general pattern of rural areas tending to more support of retention appears in this table. Again, however, with only one exception, homogeneous constituencies were more supportive, at all levels of rurality, than were heterogeneous constituencies in 1966. The data to produce a comparable table on per cent on farms were not available in 1973.

Criminality and Repression

One of the arguments in the House of Commons during both capital punishment debates was that prison guards and policemen were

Table 85:
Vote to Retain Capital Punishment (1966) by Homogeneity Level and Rurality
(Percentages)

Homogeneity Level	Percent living on Farm 0-4		5-9		10-14		15-19		20-24		25-29	
Homogeneous	41.0	(39)	72.2	(18)	83.3	(12)	75.0	(12)	66.7	(15)	81.8	(11)
Heterogeneous	28.6	(56)	19.0	(21)	63.6	(11)	33.3	(6)	75.0	(4)	44.4	(9)
Total	33.7	(95)	43.6	(39)	73.9	(23)	61.1	(18)	68.4	(19)	65.0	(20)

Homogeneity Level	30-34		35-39		40-44		45 over		Total	
Homogenious	75.0	(8)	83.3	(6)	100.0	(2)	100.0	(4)	66.1	(127)
Heterogeneous	66.7	(3)	75.0	(4)	66.7	(9)	80.0	(15)	42.8	(138)
Total	72.7	(11)	80.0	(10)	72.7	(11)	84.2	(19)	54.0	(265)

protected by capital punishment. This implied a rational "common sense" theory of punishment as deterrence. It would be expected then that in areas of high risk, such as areas close to prisons, that sentiment to retain would be positive. The evidence of MP's from the six constituencies which have federal penitentiaries in them is very much to the contrary in 1966. The one Member from a homogeneous constituency in which there is a federal penitentiary voted to retain the death penalty and the five Members from heterogeneous constituencies with penitentiaries voted to abolish.

There is a stereotype in Canada of native people as having high crime rates. It would be likely that the presence of a substantial proportion of Indians and Eskimos in a constituency would tend to increase repressive sentiment in the constituency. The evidence[43] is unclear on this (see footnote) but no confirmation of this is warranted.

Summary on Cultural Homogeneity and Repression

This section examined the proposition, which is derived from Durkheim, that homogeneity is associated with repressive sentiment. It was found that indicators of cultural homogeneity were clearly associated with an indicator of repression but that an indicator of structural homogeneity was not.

Cultural homogeneity was associated with repression under many conditions. It appears that the religious affiliation, ethnicity, level of education and rurality of a population do not seriously affect the fundamental relation between homogeneity and repressive sentiment. This important finding was sustained for the most part when these "test factors" were introduced and remained stable over two Canadian Parliaments.

Of course, many characteristics of the constituency, such as those examined in this section, seem to influence the MP's vote. Some influence it more than cultural homogeneity, and these are important discoveries. However, the intention of this portion of the research is to submit to empirical disconfirmation a hypothesis which is based on a uniquely important way of thinking about criminal punishment. By taking a Durkheimian perspective, we not only are alerted to the symbolic importance of punishment as opposed to its practical importance, but we can forecast the characteristics of populations which will support retribution and induce their MP's to vote for the death penalty in Canada.

Durkheim's view that the sentiment for punishment is independent of the danger of the offense to the society seems to be supported. Homogeneity predicted repression within categories of constituencies which could be seen as "endangered" by crime.

Constituency populations which are homogeneous in their culture tend to produce Members of Parliament who vote in favour of capital punishment, and those that are more mixed in cultural background tend to produce representatives who vote against it.

Any unequivocal conclusion is foolish when such a global assertion as Durkheim's idea on repressive law is being empirically examined. Strong evidence emerges over two parliamentary votes separated by six years, where 40 per cent of the individual Members are different, that the Durkheimian perspective on repression is important. Of the population variables which could be tested to show that homogeneity had a spurious relation to repression, none produced such a finding. We now turn to test an array of other variables which can show that homogeneity may be an artifact of some other relationship. Again, we employ as many test factors for which data is available and compare results at two time periods, 1966 and 1973.

Findings and Discussion of Repression, the Representative and the Constituency

In this research, the political behavior (vote on capital punishment) of the Member of Parliament is used as an indicator of the sentiment of the constituents he represents. In the beginning of Chapter 4, it was pointed out that the theoretical perspective being employed utilizes concepts at the level of the social aggregate and attempts to show their relationship. Therefore, the vote in Parliament of the representative of a constituency is treated as an indication of the state of the collective sentiment of that constituency.

Durkheim argued, when he was setting aside the opinions of philosophers as explanations of moral phenomena, that the moralist has a consciousness which is more representative of the moral reality than the average man.[44] The design of this research assumes that the Member of Parliament is a moral representative. For various reasons, including self-interest, the Member of Parliament can be expected to act in conformance with the sentiment of his constituents as he perceives it (see Chapter 3). In fact, when the population is culturally homogeneous, he may be more likely to be a moral delegate because he can be more confident that he knows what the collective sentiment is.[45]

The next section presents data which are used to examine the relationship between selected characteristics of the Member of Parliament and his constituency as they relate to homogeneity and repression.

Political Party, Homogeneity and Repression

Although the vote to abolish capital punishment was defined as a free vote in 1966, 1967 and 1973, and party discipline was suspended for this issue, there is evidence that party affiliation was important in the voting. Table 87 shows that none of the members of the New Democratic Party voted for retention and all of the Ralliement des Creditistes[46] members voted to retain capital punishment in the earlier debate. Within the two major parties, the Liberals, who were the government in 1966, tended to vote against capital punishment, and the Progressive Conservatives who were the official opposition were more strongly in favour of capital punishment.

Within these two parties, there were substantial differences between Members from homogeneous constituencies and those from heterogeneous constituencies in 1966 in the direction predicted by the Durkheimian hypothesis.

Table 87: Vote to Retain Capital Punishment (1966) by Homogeneity Level and Political Party* (Percentages)

Homogeneity Level	Political Party: LIB		PC		SC	
Homogeneous	52.1	(73)	86.0	(43)	0.0	(0)
Heterogeneous	24.6	(57)	74.5	(55)	80.0	(5)
Total	40.0	(130)	79.6	(98)	86.0	(5)

Homogeneity Level	NDP		RC		TOTAL	
Homogeneous	0.0	(1)	100.0	(9)	66.1	(127)
Heterogeneous	0.0	(20)	0.0	(0)	42.8	(138)
Total	0.0	(21)	100.0	(9)	54.0	(265)

Independents are not included.

Table 88:
Vote to Retain Capital Punishment (1973) and Homogeneity Level by Political Party*
(Percentages)

Homogeneity Level	Political Party									
	LIB		PC		SC		NDP		TOTAL	
Homogeneous	21.2	(52)	60.4	(48)	86.7	(15)	0.0	(0)	46.6	(116)
Heterogeneous	16.1	(56)	70.0	(60)	0.0	(0)	3.2	(31)	35.1	(148)
Total	18.5	(109)	65.7	(107)	86.7	(15)	3.2	(31)	40.2	(264)

In 1973, the difference between parties becomes very great (Table 88). The Progressive Conservatives continue their relatively high level of support for the death penalty but it is reduced from 1966. The Liberals become quite abolitionist in 1973. Support for the importance of homogeneity is seen again in 1973 with the exception of a reversal with the Conservatives.

Characteristics of Individual Members of Parliament and Repression

Religion: From statements made in the debate on capital punishment, it can be taken that Roman Catholic Members of Parliament would be more inclined to retention than Protestant Members, since their respective churches took compatible positions in 1966. Table 89 shows data which supports this generalization.

Table 89:
Vote to Retain Capital Punishment (1966)
by Homogeneity and Religion of M.P.
(Percentages)

	Religion					
Homogeneity Level	No Information		R. C.		Major Protestant	
Homogeneous	50.0	(8)	71.0	(69)	61.2	(49)
Heterogeneous	8.3	(12)	35.7	(28)	51.1	(88)
Total	25.0	(20)	60.8	(97)	54.7	(137)
Homogeneity Level	Jewish		Minor Protestant		Total	
Homogeneous	0.0	(0)	100.0	(1)	66.1	(127)
Heterogeneous	0.0	(5)	60.0	(5)	42.8	(138)
Total	0.0	(5)	66.7	(6)	54.0	(265)

Among Catholic Members of Parliament in homogeneous constituencies, a high proportion voted in favour of the death penalty. However, among Catholic Members of Parliament in heterogeneous constituencies, a relatively low (35.7 per cent) proportion supported capital punishment. The difference is not as great among Protestant Members of Parliament.

In 1973, the effect of homogeneity is still strong but a reversal of the support for the death penalty between Protestant and Catholic MP's has occurred. Protestant MP's are now more in favour of it overall than their Roman Catholic colleagues. The only large group which has grown more retentionist over time has been Protestant Members who are in homogeneous constituencies.

In both periods, those for whom there is no religion reported in their biographies are the least retentionist. As in public opinion (see Table 12) those who report no religion or unconventional religions tend to abolition (see Table 90).

Table 90:
Vote to Retain Capital Punishment (1973) by Homogeneity Level and Religion of M.P. (Percentages)

Homogeneity Level	Religion: No Information		R. C.		Major Protestant	
Homogeneous	40.0	(15)	37.7	(61)	65.8	(38)
Heterogeneous	25.8	(31)	27.3	(33)	43.1	(72)
Total	30.4	(46)	34.0	(94)	50.9	(110)

Homogeneity Level	Jewish		Minor Protestant		Total	
Homogeneous	0.0	(1)	0.0	(1)	46.6	(116)
Heterogeneous	0.0	(5)	57.1	(7)	35.1	(148)
Total	0.0	(6)	50.0	(8)	40.2	(264)

Age: Tables 91 and 92 show that age and repressive sentiment are related. Fewer of the younger Members of Parliament in both types of constituencies tend to vote for retention of capital punishment than do the older. With the exception of the oldest Members of Parliament in 1966, there is no reversal in this pattern. In 1973, there is an anomaly in the youngest MP's who violate the pattern of increasing retentionism with age.

Table 91:
Vote to Retain Capital Punishment (1966)
by Homogeneity and Age of M.P.
(Percentages)

Homogeneity Level	Age of M.P. No Information		18-27		28-37		38-47	
Homogeneous	50.0	(6)	0.0	(0)	52.6	(19)	62.5	(48)
Heterogeneous	33.3	(3)	0.0	(0)	21.4	(14)	37.2	(43)
Total	44.4	(9)	0.0	(0)	39.4	(33)	50.5	(91)

Homogeneity Level	48-57		58-67		68-77		Total	
Homogeneous	75.0	(44)	87.5	(8)	50.0	(2)	66.1	(127)
Heterogeneous	45.0	(40)	60.7	(28)	40.0	(10)	42.8	(138)
Total	60.7	(84)	66.7	(36)	41.7	(12)	54.0	(265)

Table 92:
Vote to Retain Capital Punishment (1973)
by Homogeneity and Age of M.P.
(Percentages)

Homogeneity Level	Age of M.P. No Information		18-27		28-37		38-47	
Homogeneous	33.3	(9)	0.0	(0)	33.3	(15)	45.2	(31)
Heterogeneous	42.9	(7)	50.0	(4)	30.4	(23)	32.6	(46)
Total	37.5	(16)	50.0	(4)	31.6	(38)	37.7	(77)

Homogeneity Level	48-57		58-67		68-77		Total	
Homogeneous	46.2	(39)	61.9	(21)	100.0	(1)	46.6	(116)
Heterogeneous	37.0	(46)	31.6	(19)	66.7	(3)	35.1	(148)
Total	41.2	(85)	47.5	(40)	75.0	(4)	40.2	(264)

In both years, the basic hypothesis holds when the age of the MP is used as a test factor. The differences between Members of Parliament in homogeneous, as opposed to those in heterogeneous constituencies, is consistent in the predicted direction.

Education: There is a consistent tendency for education level of the Member of Parliament to make a difference in his tendency to support capital punishment in 1966 and in 1973. Tables 93 and 94 show that those with the highest education (2 or more college degrees) vote for capital punishment less frequently than those with lower levels of education. The tendency is continuous but there is relatively little difference between Members of Parliament with one college degree and those with none in 1966. In 1973, there is a large difference in these groups.[47] Again, the differences between those Members of Parliament in homogeneous constituencies and those in heterogeneous ones is consistent in the predicted direction for both years.

In 1973, there is a substantial reduction in support for the death penalty among those with one university degree. There is a small reversal of the homogeneity pattern among those with low education.

Occupation: There were substantial differences in tendency to retain capital punishment among different occupational groupings of Members of Parliament. Of the larger groups, business men and farmers tended to be the most repressive. Lawyers, who composed the largest single occupational group in Parliament in 1966, were somewhat less repressive than the Members of Parliament as a whole. Table 95 shows that "Other Professionals" (doctors, teachers, etc.) were less repressive as were white collar workers.

These patterns of the relation of occupation to repression are remarkably consistent over the two periods. In every occupational group, the difference between Members of the same occupation was in the predicted direction for those in homogeneous and heterogeneous constituencies in 1966. In 1973, the only reversals in the pattern of homogeneity of constituency predicting a repressive vote was in the smaller occupations, like farmers (12) and skilled blue collar (5) (see Table 96). All the large groups conform to the pattern over both years. A particular reduction in repressive sentiment betwen 1966 and 1973 is to be noted amongst business men who represent homogeneous constituencies.

Summary of Individual MP's and Repression

In this section, repression and homogeneity were examined against various characteristics of individual Members of Parliament. Many

Table 93
Vote to Retain Capital Punishment (1966)
by Homogeneity Level and Education of M.P.
(Percentages)

Homogeneity Level	Education of M.P. No Information		Two or More Degrees		One Degree		No Degree		Total	
Homogeneous	60.0	(5)	54.2	(48)	73.7	(19)	74.5	(55)	66.1	(127)
Heterogeneous	25.0	(4)	25.9	(54)	56.0	(25)	54.5	(55)	42.8	(138)
Total	44.4	(9)	39.2	(102)	63.6	(44)	64.5	(110)	54.0	(265)

Table 94
Vote to Retain Capital Punishment (1973) by Homogeneity Level and Education of M.P.
(Percentages)

Homogeneity Level	Education of M.P.									
	No Information		Two or More Degrees		One Degree		No Degree		Total	
Homogeneous	50.8	(65)	42.4	(33)	37.5	(16)	50.0	(2)	46.6	(116)
Heterogeneous	43.8	(48)	17.3	(52)	39.5	(43)	100.0	(5)	35.1	(148)
Total	47.8	(113)	27.1	(85)	39.0	(59)	85.7	(7)	40.2	(264)

Table 95
Vote to Retain Capital Punishment (1966) by Homogeneity Level and Occupation of M.P.
(Percentages)

Homogeneity Level	Occupation of M.P.: No Information		Lawyer		Other Profession		Clergy		Business		White Collar	
Homogeneous	66.7	(6)	57.6	(33)	52.0	(25)	0.0	(0)	83.3	(42)	45.5	(11)
Heterogeneous	57.1	(7)	30.6	(36)	27.6	(29)	33.3	(3)	57.7	(26)	25.0	(8)
Total	61.5	(13)	43.5	(69)	38.9	(54)	33.3	(3)	73.5	(68)	36.8	(19)

Homogeneity Level	Skilled Blue Collar		Farmer		Unskilled Blue Collar		Retired		Total	
Homogeneous	100.0	(1)	83.3	(6)	50.0	(2)	100.0	(1)	66.1	(127)
Heterogeneous	0.0	(3)	80.0	(20)	20.0	(5)	100.0	(1)	42.8	(138)
Total	25.0	(4)	80.0	(26)	28.6	(7)	100.0	(2)	54.0	(265)

Table 96
Vote to Retain Capital Punishment (1973) by Homogeneity Level and Occupation of M.P.
(Percentages)

Homogeneity Level	Occupation of M.P.											
	No Information		Lawyer		Other Profession		Clergy		Business		White Collar	
Homogeneous	41.7	(12)	37.5	(24)	45.0	(20)	0.0	(0)	52.2	(46)	33.3	(3)
Heterogeneous	28.6	(14)	27.9	(43)	25.6	(34)	25.0	(4)	53.1	(32)	20.0	(5)
Total	34.6	(26)	31.3	(67)	32.3	(59)	25.0	(4)	52.6	(78)	25.0	(8)

Homogeneity Level	Skilled Blue Collar		Farmer		Unskilled Blue Collar		Retired		Total	
Homogeneous	66.7	(3)	57.1	(7)	0.0	(1)	0.0	(0)	46.6	(116)
Heterogeneous	100.0	(2)	62.5	(8)	0.0	(1)	0.0	(0)	35.1	(148)
Total	80.0	(5)	60.0	(15)	0.0	(2)	0.0	(0)	40.2	(264)

of the characteristics did seem to exert an effect on the tendency of Members of Parliament to vote to abolish or retain capital punishment. These effects were always differentiated by the homogeneity level of the Members of Parliament constituency, in the direction predicted by the central hypothesis. The results were quite stable over the two periods under study, 1966 and 1973. The credibility of the relation between homogeneity and repression is thereby enhanced.

For the individual MP, a cluster of attributes, such as 'no religion', high education, liberal political ideology, youth and professional occupation, seems to encourage an abolitionist stance. These attributes imply a cosmopolitan, non-authoritarian, pragmatic outlook. When they are combined with constituency characteristics, such as a mixture of several religions and ethnic groups, a high level of education in the population and location in one of the major metropolitan areas, the tendency for an abolitionist vote is quite strong.

There are two related points to be emphasized from the preceding analysis. Homogeneity of culture is generally and consistently related to variations in repressive sentiment in the Canadian Parliament. Thus, Durkheim's orientation to repressive law finds contemporary empirical support.

The second point is that support for the death penalty is associated with a cluster of individual and collective characteristics including cultural homogeneity which imply an "expressive" orientation to law. Religious concentration in the population and commitment to "conservative" political ideology in both MP and constituency are examples. Similarly, the abolitionist parliamentarian is characterized by personal attributes and constituency characteristics including cultural heterogeneity which bear up under their interpretation as producing an "instrumental" approach to law.

So the analysis of public opinion, individual MP voting and their convictions encourage the view that some social and individual forces encourage an instrumental orientation to law and other forces encourage an expressive view. For the issue of death penalty legislation, these two orientations lead to contradictory public policy positions.[48] Those with an instrumental orientation reject hanging in Canada because it does not survive their utilitarian criteria. Those with an expressive orientation encourage the availability of the death penalty since it meets their view that law should express the strongest evaluation on human life.

Some Implications, Interpretations and Speculations

Let us take seriously the macro-social, evolutionary view of law and society which stimulated some of this empirical research. We rely here on the Canadian Parliament as only a "positive instance" for this global view.

The feeling that one gets from reading Durkheim on repression is that he holds an optimistic view on the evolution of society away from primitive barbaric sanctions. He sees that increasing complexity establishes a different basis of social order, interdependence, which reduces the reliance for social order on common sentiment, supported by frequent bloodletting. Even a casual reading of the Human Relations Area Files promotes the optimism. Modern societies appear in the normal course of events to eschew the kinds of repression that are described in the ethnographies of simple socieites.

But what of Auschwitz? How can it be that in modern industrial Germany in 1940 that unprecedented repression can occur? And what of other instances of repression that frequently occur in other modern complex societies? Must we rely on ad hoc explanations of these events as if they were aberrations or can they be interpreted with a Durkheimian perspective? One of the findings in the preceding research points to a possible interpretation. If the foregoing research findings on Canada are evidence for a generalization, then it might be that the independence of culture and social structure in the evolution of society are important.

One would expect that, in general, the complexity of culture and social structure would vary together through societal evolution. Sociological theory and findings support this view. This, however, may be due to a western bias because of our familiarity with the North American history of modernization. This modernization has been accompanied by massive infusions of migrant populations which have led to the present cultural pluralism of North America. So the North American case of modernization may have an exaggerated pattern of cultural differentiation due to migration. This may be the case also where nation states are arbitrarily drawn around contiguous but dissimilar indigenuous ethnic groups. Strange and often hostile bedfellows are found in the past colonial societies of Africa, for example. So there are at least two types of societies in which the differentiation in social structure and in culture are not aligned. Because of either migration or indigenous variety, a relatively simple society may contain a variety of cultures.

On the other hand, induced modernization through such things as the importation or imposition of advanced technology, may produce a relatively complex social structure, in a short time, without generating varieties of occupational or regional culture.

The varieties of possible relations are depicted below. The interesting point is that either of the two error cells, where the degree of differentiation in culture and structure is not articulated, could produce repressive law. Where the culture is undifferentiated, the tendency for moral indignation and repression occurs independent of the *potential* for organic solidarity in the differentiated structure.

Figure 1 The Evolution of Culture and Social Structure.

Structural Differentiation	Cultural Differentiation: HIGH	Cultural Differentiation: LOW
HIGH	Modern Society Organic Solidarity Restitutive Law	Imposed or induced Modernization Mechanical Solidarity Repressive Law
LOW	Simple Society Ethnically Plural Imposed Mechanical Solidarity Repression	Primitive Society Mechanical Solidarity Repressive Law

Where the structure is undifferentiated, there is no source of solidarity and order other than in the imposition or inducement of a homogeneous culture. This is an interesting case since the culture can be historically based; the ferreting out of a real or imagined culture which predates current distinctions, or ideologically based; the selection or creation of a nationalist ideology which renders current cultural distinctions irrelevant. The presence of at least a homogeneous political culture prevents the extremity of repression, terrorism and a police state, and solves the problem of order at least temporarily. The other error cell is where a homogeneous culture, with its repressive reaction to deviance, is contained by a complex social structure, with its potential for organic solidarity. It seems that through time the homogeneous culture and its repressive law should whither away because of its functional irrelevance. Since structural differentiation tends to be autonomous, especially in modern bureaucracies, the theoretical problem in this error cell becomes one of the *rate* of change. Organic solidarity can exist only when the rate of structural change is below some level;[49] then, it follows that if the rate of modernization is above that level, either social order will diminish or mechanical solidarity will emerge. It appears in the cases of rapidly modernizing nations that both disorder and repression occur. It would be of interest to examine this model comparatively, with a view to establishing what *rate* of structural change is possible without either repression or disorder. This would seem to be an important feature of social change and would be of great interest to those social scientists whose applied interest is in the area of developing nations.

These wide ranging guesses and speculations at least revolve around one theme. The evolutionary path from simple to modern societies is not always a straight and continuous process in which there is a balance between culture and social structure. In both cases where there is imbalance, where officials and people in these societies may be striving for modernity, harmony and humane law, there are forces which pull and push towards the order and repression of mechanical solidarity.

The non-repressive, automatic regulation of a society with an organic basis of solidarity may be quite fragile. It is hard to attain and retain. According to these speculations, both error cases where culture and structure mismatch tend to devolve towards a mechanical basis of solidarity, a homogeneous culture, and repressive law.

Ascription, Gemeinschaft and Repression: A Suggestion

It will be recalled that educational homogeneity was less associated with the vote to retain the death penalty than ethnic and religious homogeneity. This is a very suggestive finding. Education is an achieved characteristic, whereas ethnicity and religion are ascribed.[50]

The social relevance of ascriptive properties of people have been found to be characteristic of *gemeinschaft* forms of social organization. That is, their sex, name, place of birth, etc. are the most important determinants of their rights and obligations. On the other hand, it has been argued that achieved characteristics are the most important characteristics in *geselleschaft* forms. That is, sex, name, place of birth, etc. are less important determinants than education, occupation, power, etc.

It may follow then that with increasing gemeinschaft the relevance of achieved characteristics decreases. Since in this study the measure of structural differentiation was *also* an achieved characteristic, then a measure of its dispersion-concentration in a population would be irrelevant to the state of repression. On the other hand, the concentration of an ascribed characteristic, such as religion, would characterize a gemeinschaft system which would also be characterized by greater repression. In short, this highly speculative suggestion is that it is the degree of gemeinschaft in a collectivity that predicts repression. If this could be established, it would lead to a convergence between Durkheim, Tonnies and Parsons.

Research Suggestion on Punitiveness

One of the major problems with Durkeimian theory is that it offends the common sense, at least the common sense of those in individually oriented cultures like ours. We are used to thinking, both in everyday life and in our social science, of the individual as the unit of analysis or at least part of the equation. There are persuasive epistemological arguments that Durkheim was excessive in his insistence on the separation of the psychological level of causality from the sociological. Homans, for example, implies that the two levels are complimentary rather than mutually exclusive.[51]

What then are the mechanisms by which some social variable such as homogeneity impinges and constrains the behavior of a Member of Parliament to vote for executing people or not? How do we fill up this correlation? We are not just interested in causes, we are interested in explanations. Unfortunately, no evidence in this research could be marshalled to directly establish a causal claim from the causes of constituency sentiment to the MP's vote. It would be a contribution if psychological propositions connecting the two social facts of homogeneity and repression could be established. It is clear for this research that if the vote to retain the death penalty is considered at the psychological level to be punitive, then culturally homogeneous constituencies tend to either elect more punitive political representatives or induce more punitive behavior in them after they are elected. Vidmar's research[52] begins this convergence by correlating ethocentrism with authoritarianism. Further research on the voting records of political representatives both in Canada and elsewhere might uncover patterns of punitive votes on various issues from certain types of representatives.

It would be interesting to discover by what processes voters came to recognize the more punitive from the less or came to influence this kind of tendency in their representative. It was shown in this research that individual characteristics made some difference in an MP's vote (for example, lawyers tended to be more abolitionist than business men) but whether voters know and attend to these individual differences like occupation and religion as indicators of more punitive candidates remains to be discovered.

In general, the connection between the characteristics of a constituency is of interest to the political scientist. The homogeneity property of the constituency which has been found to affect the outcome of the vote under consideration in Canada is typically not used by political scientists.

Summary: Where Do Repressive Laws Come From?

Canada has been poised on the edge of fully abolishing capital punishment for a decade. This has been interpreted in this book as a result of the equivalence of two sets of social forces in Canadian society. Those with an expressive orientation to law tend to support the death penalty and those with an instrumental orientation tend to oppose it.[53] Such a situation provides an opportunity to describe and analyze the characteristics and correlates of these two orientations to law.

In this research we have found that behind the tendency for an elected representative to support a repressive law lies a culturally homogeneous population. As Durkheim proposed, there inheres in culturally uniform groups a tendency to view deviance as a moral violation rather than as a practical problem. Revulsion at the act dictates a repressive response whether it is practically effective at reducing deviance or not. Law for culturally homogeneous populations is primarily an expression of evaluation. As societies evolve they typically become more diverse. Cultural diversity appears to weaken moral revulsion as a social response to deviance and a more practical or instrumental approach to law replaces the expressive one.

There are other correlates of these views of law in people and in groups. For MPs we found that conservative political ideologies created, attracted or reinforced an expressive stance on criminal punishment. Similarly those who were more religious, had relatively low levels of formal education, were engaged in business or farming occupations, were older, and were born in the constituency they represented tended to support the death penalty. Evidence also indicates that those who affiliated with more liberal political parties, were unaffiliated with organized religion, were younger, were more highly educated, with professional occupations and were more geographically mobile tended to vote against the death penalty. In addition to cultural homogeneity some characteristics of the population of the political constituency seemed to influence the MP to vote to retain the death penalty. These were a rural location of the constituency, often in Quebec or Alberta, where the people had relatively low levels of education and where the Social Credit party received support. These constituencies also seemed to be less politically competitive.

Analysis of public opinion polls corroborates these trends. People who had low levels of formal education, who were religious, especially Roman Catholic, and who were French, tended to support the death penalty more than others. Those from rural areas supported it more than urban Canadians. The only interesting disparity between the conclusions derived from polls as opposed to the analysis of parliamentary data is on the role of politics in the death penalty question. For the public, sentiment on the death penalty is virtually unrelated to political preference. There is only a slight tendency for supporters of conservative parties to favour retention more than others. In parliament on the other hand, party affiliation is strongly associated with preference for abolition or retention.

The evidence on the question of how closely the MPs represent their constituents is not clear. In general the commons appears to be leading the people towards abolition. This is particularly true for Liberal MPs from Quebec. However, the elections of 1968 and 1974 indicate that abolitionist MPs were not turned out by a retaliating electorate. Liberals gained seats in both of these elections.

Canada's decade of death penalty debate is shown to be a standoff between the view of law as a useful tool and the view that it is a vehicle to express important values. The best evidence on this period of Canadian socio-legal history is that secular, cosmopolitan influences favour a practical approach to the law, and hence abolition, of the death penalty.

The Future of the Death Penalty in Canada

Between 1967 and 1973 the Liberal MPs increased their support for partial abolition. If this trend holds then a Liberal majority government could abolish the death penalty, when the present legislation terminates in 1978. Even with a free vote the abolition leaning liberals, combining with the staunchly abolitionist NDP and the small core of abolitionist PCs could muster a majority against the death penalty. This would depend, of course, on whether influentials within the Liberal party could hold a large majority of back bench MPs to a full abolition bill, in a free vote situation. It may be that the large Liberal vote in 1973 depended in part on the compromise nature of the partial abolition bill.

A full abolition bill could pass in parliament almost in spite of public opinion. Although public opinion was in favour of retention in 1973, only a handful of Liberals voted to retain it. The election of 1974 showed that the death penalty is not an election issue. Most MPs reported that they felt an honest vote on a matter of conscience will not jeopardize them at the polls. Their theory that elections turn on more immediate "bread and butter" issues seems to be born out.

Although the content of public opinion varies with circumstances its intensity is also important. Public opinion on the death penalty doesn't seem to be very intense, and may be getting weaker through time. Only a small proportion on each side of the issue feel strongly about it. Parliament therefore has a lot of freedom on this issue. Although it would be unlikely, since the leadership is abolitionist, a Conservative majority government in 1978 could probably reinstate hanging. The Canadian public would probably accept some restrained use of it. By the same token they would tolerate its abolition under ordinary circumstances. There are two caveats in this judgment. A dramatic, heinous, rational crime such as political terrorism may intensify public support for the death penalty to a point where full abolition would be foreclosed as a practical political possibility. On the other side a convincing disclosure of the execution of an innocent person would probably ensure abolition in parliament.

A larger curiosity concerns the evolution of law, and its alleged movement away from punishment for its own sake. In this analysis of the limited case of the death penalty in Canada we can see some components of this larger interest. One reason for the decline in the moral intensity of public opinion on the death penalty may be the increasing urbanity, education, mobility and diversity of the Canadian public. Everyone is becoming more like those who were traditionally abolitionists. An increasingly cosmopolitan outlook reduces the reliance on moral intuition for law, as it is replaced by more dispassionate rational calculation. Certainty on complex questions, such as the form criminal punishment should take, is reduced. Such decisions may be delegated to experts.

This process will also occur in legislative bodies. In addition it appears that legislative questions, such as inflation control, become more complicated as society becomes more complex. Moral certitude on simple truths becomes increasingly rare as a serious element of the legislative process although retaining its rhetorical significance. Rational calculation and the use of technical expertise becomes more evident in the legislative process.

All these aspects of social and legislative evolution point in the direction of a less punitive response to law violation, which will emanate from legislatures and be accepted by the public.

Footnotes

[1] Durkheim may be the most analyzed of all the founders of sociology. In a recent study, there are over 500 books and essays on his work. See Steven Lukes' *Emile Durkheim: His Life and Work*, (Harper and Row, 1973).

[2] Bronislaw Malinowski; *Crime and Custom in Savage Society* (New York, 1926).

[3] Alfred R. Lindesmith, "Punishment," *International Encyclopedia of the Social Sciences*, Vol. 13 (New York, 1968), p. 217.

[4] Svend Ranulf, *Moral Indignation and Middle Class Psychology* (Schocken, 1938).

[5] Sutherland and Cressey, *Principles of Criminology*, (Philadelphia, 1960), p. 300.

[6] Lindesmith, *op. cit.*, p. 221.

[7] George Homans, *The Human Group*, (New York: Harcourt, Brace and World, 1950); Edwin Hollander, "Conformity Status and Idiosyncratic Credit," *Psychological Review*, 65, 117-27; Rodalfo Alvarez, "Informal Reactions to Deviance in Simulated Work Organizations: A Laboratory Experiment, "*ASR*, 33 (December), 895-912.

[8] E. A. Ross, *Social Control*, (London, 1910), p. 412.

[9] Herbert Packer, *The Limits of the Criminal Sanction* (Stanford University Press, 1968).

[10] The ongoing debate on the extent of "value freedom" in social science does not concern us here.

[11] G. H. Mead, "The Psychology of Punitive Justice," *The American Journal of Sociology*, March, 1918, 585-592.

[12] E. Durkheim, *The Rules of Sociological Method* (London, 1938), p. 66.

[13] E. Durkheim, "Deux Lois de L'evolution Penale," *L'Année Sociologique*, IV, 1899, 65-95.

[14] *Ibid.*, p. 65. "L'intensité de la peine est d'autant plus grande que les sociétiés appartiennent à un type moins élevé et que le pouvoir central a un caractère plus absolu."

[15] *Ibid.*, p. 78. "Les peines privatives de la liberté et de la liberté seule, pour des periodes de temps variables selon la gravite des crimes, tendent de plus en plus à devenir le type normal de la répression."

[16] Emile Durkheim, *The Division of Labour in Society* (Glencoe, 1964), p. 89.

[17] The focus of this section is not on law as such but it should be noted that the field of comparative law has a rich tradition. There has always been extensive attention paid in the writings of philosophers to the nature of law and society but it was not until the end of the nineteenth century that the sociology of law became a recognized discipline. Perhaps the most important contribution to this recognition was the attention of anthropologists. The nature of law in primitive people became a focus for prominent anthropologists such as Malinowski and Radcliffe-Brown, and vigorous debates in the field on the presence, definition and function of law in primitve societies ensued. An excellent review of the treatment of law in anthropology can be found in Max Gluckman, *Politics, Law and Ritual in Tribal Society* (Aldine, 1965). See also Max Gluckman, *The*

Judicial Process among the Barotse of Northern Rhodesia (The Free Press, 1955) for an excellent illustration of a theoretically important ethnographic analysis of law.

The contribution of other social scientists to the sociology of law can be found in N. S. Timasheff, "Growth and Scope of Sociology of Law," *Modern Sociological Theory*, H. Becker and A. Boskoff, eds. (New York, 1957), p. 424. See also his earlier work, N. S. Timasheff, *The Sociology of Law* (Cambridge: Harvard University Committee on Research in the Social Sciences, 1939), for a comprehensive and scholarly treatment of the field, to that date.

18 E. Durkheim, *op. cit.*, p. 110.

19 Pitrim A. Sorokin, *Contemporary Sociological Theories*, New York, 1964, p. 466.

20 E. Durkheim, *The Division of Labor in Society*, p. 64.

21 *Ibid.*, p. 69.

22 Bronislaw Malinowski, *Crime and Custom in Savage Society*, New York, 1926, p. 56.

23 Richard D. Schwartz and James C. Miller, "Legal Evolution and Societal Complexity," *American Journal of Sociology*, LXX, Sept., 1964, 159-169.

24 These general comments on the HRAF are based on remarks of G. P. Murdock at an Anthropology Colloquium, University of Hawaii, November 1968.

25 The mechanics of this construction are presented in Appendix I.

26 The procedures for measuring complexity vary between the two time periods. The more elaborate procedures used in the first phase of the empirical study were replaced by simplified measures in the second phase.

27 See Appendix I for more detailed information and discussion of the methods used in constructing these measures.

28 There are conceptual problems in interpreting self-reports of ethnicity. We use Canadian census reports for this measure.

29 Education was the only variable aggregated by political constituency in these census reports.

30 A. Kornberg, *Canadian Legislative Behavior* (New York, 1967), p. 108.

31 Available biographical data were collected on each Member of Parliament. These were analyzed in conjunction with the central hypothesis and illuminate the relationship between individual characteristics, constituency characteristics and the vote on capital punishment.

32 For a detailed description of the parliamentary procedures and history of this vote, see Chapter 3 on legislative behavior and the introduction.

33 It should be stressed here that the cases being compared are social aggregates. The theory of repression being tested involves the comparison of two aggregate properties, homogeneity and repression. Homogeneity is clearly an aggregate property (individuals cannot be homogeneous) and the vote of the Member of Parliament is being used as an index of constituency sentiment which is conceived in Durkheimian terms as a property of an aggregate. Since properties of social aggregates are under investigation in this research and not properties of individuals, then the possibility

of the "ecological fallacy" is absent. The "ecological fallacy" is a danger only when inferences about individual characteristics are being made from aggregated data. See Herbert Menzel, "Comment on Robinson's 'Ecological Correlations and the Behavior of Individuals" *American Sociological Review*, XV, 1950, p. 674.

[34] Although there is some relationship in the expected direction for educational homogeneity, it is relatively weak in comparison to the association of cultural homogeneity and repression. Additional and more direct measures of structural differentiation, such as occupation, would allow more confidence in this interpretation than the relatively indirect indicator, education. Years of education was the only measure available to index structural complexity.

[35] This was operationally defined as the number of constituencies which had over 70 per cent of the same ethnic group. All others were heterogeneous.

[36] The data tables in the following section are more elaborate and detailed than necessary to support the interpretation in the text. The risk of obscuring what is emphasized in the text is consciously taken to expose the detailed variation which allows criticism and further work by students of these topics.

[37] See Chapter 3 for data on electoral history which shows proportion of MP's who were elected in 1972 and who were also present in the 1966 Parliament.

[38] Vote to Retain Capital Punishment in 1966 by religious concentration and homogeneity. (Data is taken from tables 74 and 75.)

	Over 70% Roman Catholic	Over 70% Protestant	Total
Homogeneous	73.9	65.8	66.1
Heterogeneous	50.0	54.5	42.8

[39] There are 51 or 20.3% of all constituencies which have over 90% of the population Roman Catholic compared to 3 or 1.2% which are over 90% Protestant in 1966. In 1973, after substantial redistribution of seats in 1968, we find 49 or 18.6% of all constituencies having over 90% Roman Catholic but only 1 or 4% Protestant.

[40] Vote to retain Capital Punishment in 1973 by religious concentration and homogeneity. (data taken from tables 76 and 77.)

	Over 70% Protestant	Over 70% Roman Catholic	Total
Homogeneous	875	38.1	46.6
Heterogeneous	57.1	27.3	35.1

41 The Canadian Catholic Conference. Letter to MP's, January 26, 1973.

42 The rural crime rate in Canada appears to be substantially lower than the urban rate. In 1962, 18.7 per cent of the convictions for indictable offenses occurred amongst people of rural residence. In 1961 30.4 per cent of the population was classified as having rural residence. These were computed from *Canada Year Book 1966*, Dominion Bureau of Statistics, pp. 189, 422.

43 Vote to Retain Capital Punishment and Homogeneity Level by Proportion of the Population Indian and Eskimo (1966) Percentages

Homogeneity Level	Percentage of Population Indian & Eskimo					
	-1		1-3		4-6	
Homogeneous	68.7		93.3		66.6	
Heterogeneous	37.2		47.1		75.0	
Total	52.6	(183)	61.2	(49)	73.3	(15)

Homogeneity Level	7-8		9+		Total
Homogeneous	0.0		0.0		66.1 (127)
Heterogeneous	16.7		63.6		42.8 (138)
Total	16.7	(6)	58.3	(12)	54.0 (265)

44 Emile Durkheim, *Sociology and Philosophy* translated by D. F. Pocock (Glencoe, 1973), p. 40.

45 Malcolm Jewell, *op. cit.*, p. 482.

46 The Quebec wing of the Social Credit Party. By 1973 the only Social Credit members in the Parliament of Canada came from Quebec.

47 Coding differences in 1966 and 1973 tend to increase the number of the 'no information' group in 1973 and deplete the number with no degree. If they are combined in 1973, the overall retention proportion is 50.0%.

48 These two orientations to law do not always lead to a contrary position on a particular law. If, for example, there was an empirically demonstrable deterrent effect to the death penalty, we might find the instrumental and the expressive motivations to law satisfied by the legal application of the death penalty.

49 The simplest interpretation of organic solidarity is that because of the division of labour in the economy individuals and groups in a society are dependent on each other. This dependence induces cooperation or "reciprocal sacrifice" as Durkheim puts it. Although in his analysis the emphasis is placed on the laws governing these reciprocal sacrifices, it would

seem that there must be some recognition of dependency for cooperation, even in the most general way, to occur. Now since individual contributions to others and to the whole is dependent on the function performed in the division of labour, it should follow that if this differentiation is *changing* then non-recognition of the function by others is more likely. A proposition at this point would be (a) the faster the rate of structural differentiation, the higher the likelihood of non-recognition of dependency. Thus, as new occupations emerge generated by the thrust of technology and laws lag in codifying the reciprocal responsibilities between occupants of these emerging functions, disorder becomes more likely because of the non-recognition of dependency. (b) The greater the non-recognition of dependency, the greater the reduction of organic solidarity. (c) The greater the reduction of organic solidarity, the greater the mechanical solidarity. Here we assume that mechanical and organic bases of solidarity are exhaustive of the bases of solidarity in society. (d) The greater the mechanical solidarity, the greater the repression. If all these speculations are true, then we could conclude that the faster the rate of structural differentiation, the greater the repression. If the non-recognition of dependency is crucial, then the above may also be a theory of repression in mass society (post-organic may be a useful term for it), where the complexity and impersonality of existence leads to non-recognition of self/other functions.

50 The "Pattern Variables" which include "ascription-achievement" as one are outlined in Talcott Parsons, *The Social System* (Glencoe, 1951), p. 67. A simple view of the pattern variables is that they are an attempt to make more specific conceptually the orientations to action of actors in roles. The most interesting aspect of this formulation by Parsons for this research is the consonance of these variables with one of the most important themes in social science. That is, the systematic differences between primitive and modern, folk and urban, gemeinschaft and geselleschaft (F. Tonnies) forms of social organization. In addition Sir Henry Maine has argued that law evolves from status to contract. The first emphasizes rights and obligations, determined by ascribed characteristics of the person, as the law. The second emphasizes voluntarily agreed upon rights and obligations.

51 George C. Homans, "Contemporary Theory in Sociology," *Handbook of Modern Sociology* (ed. by Robert E. L. Faris), Chicago, 1964, p. 970.

52 Neil Vidmar, *op. cit.*

53 In this summary, as in the main body of this research, it is well to note that the instrumental/expressive distinction is used to interpret the overall socio-legal situation in Canadian society, as it relates to the death penalty. As with all general distinctions, many particular cases contradict it. There are undoubtably some who support the death penalty only because they believe, in spite of the weight of evidence, that it is a practical deterrent. There are abolitionists who are simply outraged morally at the state taking a life. They would hold to this view even if a deterrent effect were proved.

However most abolitionists and retentionists in the Canadian case fit the instrumental/expressive distinction. But people don't fall easily into these categories. Evidence from the parliamentary debates and from interviews with MPs indicate that they are often torn between these two orientations within themselves. So the distinction represents sometimes contradictory tendencies within both society and people.

Appendix I: Methods and Procedures

Index Construction: Homogeneity

This research is, in part, based on data collected in the 1961 and 1971 census of Canada. Some of the information collected in the census was compiled separately from the regular census report, and was based on the political constituency rather than the census tract. In these data, the number of people in various social categories was presented. The categories were age[1], sex[1], marital status[1], ethnicity, religion, education, language, birthplace and farm residence[1].

These raw numbers were converted to percentages and frequency distributions for Canada were computed. These distributions were then divided into subcategories (usually into nine equal interval classes). These were then coded and punched on IBM cards, one for each constituency. One criterion at this point in the research was to preserve the greatest possible variation on the largest number of variables for all the political constituencies in Canada which was consistent with reducing these data for analysis. Some information was lost through the collapsing of categories. This reduction occurred for religion, age, ethnicity, marital status and language. Some of these data were then used to construct indices of more theoretically relevant and analytically useful concepts.

Religion: Each constituency was given a homogeneity-heterogeneity score on religion. Although the religion variable as first coded had three categories (Roman Catholic, Jewish and Protestant), only two (Roman Catholic and Protestant) were considered to be large enough to be useful in obtaining the homogeneity score. A constituency was considered homogeneous if 70 percent or more of the population were all either Protestant or Catholic. If neither of the categories contained 70 percent or more, then the constituency was considered to be heterogeneous. Seventy percent of one religion was selected because it was the largest proportion which divided all constituencies into roughly equal proportions.[2] Approximately one-half of the constituencies are homogeneous, and the others are heterogeneous. The breakdown within the homogeneous group between Roman Catholic and Protestant was also about equal. The last consideration is most important in selecting 70 percent as the basis for a definition of religious homogeneity. Having roughly equal numbers of cases in each of categories makes the measurement of religious homogeneity independent of any one religion. In 1971 census material, there appears to be a shift in the concentration of Major Protestant groups. However, the 70 percent division was retained for comparability.

Ethnicity: Each constituency was given a homogeneity-heterogeneity score on ethnicity. The ethnicity variable as first coded had six categories: British; French; German; Netherlands and Scandinavian; Italian; Polish; Russian and Ukranian; and Indian and Eskimo but only two types (British and French) were large enough to be useful for the homogeneity analysis. The rationale is similar to the one discussed above for religion. A constituency was defined as homogeneous when more than 70 percent of the population was either British or French. Approximately one-half (125 or 48 percent in 1961, and 116 or 44 percent in 1971) of the constituencies were homogeneous on ethnicity and one-half (138 or 52 percent in 1961, and 147 or 56 percent in 1971) were heterogeneous. Again, the homogeneous group had about the same number of cases in each of the two categories.

Education: Each constituency was also given a homogeneity-heterogeneity score on education. Education was coded with percentages of the population distributed on various years of education, and standard deviations were used as the measure of variation. Percentages were used as raw scores and the categories, years of education, were unequal. Relative homogeneity on education was determined by rank ordering each constituency on the magnitude of the standard deviation.[3]

The standard deviation at the midpoint of the ranking was used to divide the constituencies into homogeneous (low variation on education) and heterogeneous (high variation on education) categories. One hundred and thirty-two (50 percent) constituencies were defined as homogeneous and 131 (50 percent) were heterogeneous.[4]

Homogeneity Summary Score: A composite score was created to summarize the three indices of homogeneity. This composite score which was called the Homogeneity Summary Score was created simply by the addition of the three homogeneity scores of religion, ethnicity, and education. Homogeneity was given the value 1 and heterogeneity the value 2. For each constituency, on each of three variables, four possible summary scores could be obtained.[5]

Table 1 shows the distribution of constituencies which results from this summary. These four levels of homogeneity are the operational classification of complexity, the independent variable in the basic proposition. This operation was performed for the 1961 census data only.

Table 1:
Distribution of Political Constituencies by Pattern of Homogeneity-Heterogeneity* On Religion, Ethnicity and Education, 1966

Pattern	Variables			
	Religion	Ethnicity	Education	(N)
A	1	1	1	62
B	1	1	2	40
C	1	2	1	16
D	2	1	1	6
E	2	2	1	41
F	2	1	2	12
G	1	2	2	14
H	2	2	2	60
Total Constituencies**				251

* Homogeneity is indicated by 1. Heterogeneity is indicated by 2.

** Only those constituencies whose representatives voted on the motion are included. There are 263 constituencies in Canada. Note: Constituencies are classified into four levels of homogeneity: Pattern A is hereafter called "Very homogeneous," Patterns B, C, D are hereafter called "homogeneous;" Patterns E, F, G are hereafter called "heterogeneous;" Pattern H is hereafter called "very heterogeneous."

Source of Data for Members of Parliament of Canada

The Canadian Parliamentary Guide is published annually in Canada.[6] It contains information on the government of Canada, the Members of Parliament (MP) and the Members of the legislatures of the various provinces. The following information was selected for use in this study from the 1967 and 1973 Parliamentary Guide for Members of the Federal House of Commons in 1966 and 1973 respectively. The history of election of the MP in his constituency, his political popularity and the political participation in his constituency were computed. The MP's age, religion, birthplace, ethnicity, generation, occupation, education and political party were recorded from the Guide.

Coding Information from The Canadian Parliamentary Guide

Member's Electoral History: This index was constructed by coding the electoral history of the MP in the last four general elections in 1966 and the last five in 1973. It produced six categories of political career patterns. These ranged from those who had been elected for the first time in the last general election (1965 and 1972, respectively) to those who had been consecutively elected in more than four elections. There were a few Members (8 percent) who did not have a consecutive election history.

Popularity: This is a simple measure of the popularity of the MP constructed by dividing his vote by the total vote cast. The larger the percentage, the more popular the MP. Dividing by total vote cast controls the effect of the size of the voting population of the constituency which varies considerably.

Characteristics of Members of Parliament: The variables of age, birthplace, generation, religion, occupation, education and political party were obtained from the biography of the MP, found in *The Canadian Parliamentary Guide*. Age, religion and political party were directly coded from the Guide. Birthplace was obtained by finding the birthplace of the MP from his biography and then finding whether it was located within his constituency. This was accomplished by referring to the *Census of Canada Population, Electoral Districts* (92-530, 1961, 1971) which lists the towns and villages within each constituency. Birthplace was then coded on whether the MP was born in his constituency, in Canada, or elsewhere. In 1973, this code was altered to produce a distinction between those born in the constituency they now represent, those born in the same province but not in their constituency and those born elsewhere. Occupation is described for most of the MP's in the Guide. These were coded into nine categories approximating a prestige ranking. Education was coded on the number of university degrees (Bachelor, Masters, Doctorate) that were listed with two additional residual categories of no information and no degree. Generation was coded into 4 categories: no information, foreign born, second generation, and third or more.

Parliamentary Records: The analysis of speeches of Members of Parliament was made from the transcript of their speeches and their vote on the bills to abolish capital punishment were obtained from "Hansard"[7] for the appropriate periods.

Public Opinion Polls

Original data from the relevant Public Opinion Polls[8] was analyzed to examine one set of indicators about public opinion on the death penalty, its distribution and determinants in the Canadian population.

Other Sources of Public Opinion

National newspaper articles in the periods surrounding the debates of 1966-67 and 1973 were collected. In addition, several Members of Parliament allowed access to their files of letters from constituents and organizations.

Information on the Parliamentary and Party Activity

Interviews with members of the Solicitor General's staff and Members of Parliament were conducted which focussed on the location and dynamics of influence and opinion in Parliament.

Footnotes

[1] Available in 1961 only.

[2] There were 263 political constituencies in Canada. All but two elect one Member each. Halifax, Nova Scotia and Queens, Prince Edward Island each elect two Members. In 1968, substantial changes in constituency boundaries occurred and there was a reduction to 264 seats.

[3] The original information was coded into the percentage of the population, five years or older, who were not in school, who had the following years of education: 0, elementary 1-4, elementary 5+, high school 1 and 2, high school 3 and 4, high school 5, university 1-4, university graduates. These were given values 1-8 and the standard deviation was calculated. The range on the standard deviation was 1.0 - 1.87. The median was 1.40.

[4] As this variable did not show any important relation to the vote on capital punishment, it was not computed for 1971.

[5] If a constituency was very homogeneous, its total score would be 3 (a score of 1 on each of the three variables). If a constituency had two variables which were gomogeneous and one variable which was heterogeneous, its total score would be 4 (a score of 2, 1 for each of the two homogeneous variables and a score of 2 on the one heterogeneous variable). The same, of course, applies to the score construction of the heterogeneous constituencies. This yielded the four possible summary scores which could be obtained: 3 (very homogeneous)
4 (homogeneous)
5 (heterogeneous)
6 (very heterogeneous).

[6] *The Canadian Parliamentary Guide*, Pierre Normandin, ed. (Ottawa P.O. Box 513, Canada, 1967, 1973).

[7] *House of Commons Debates: Official Report* (Ottawa: Queen's Printer and Controller of Stationary).

[8] Canadian Institute of Public Opinion Polls #310 (1965), #317 (1966), #344 (1970), #350 (1971). Original data decks from Carleton University, Department of Sociology and Anthropology, Data Archives.